The Lively Kindergarten

The Lively Kindergarten

Emergent Curriculum in Action

Elizabeth Jones, Kathleen Evans, and Kay Stritzel Rencken
with Carolyn Stringer and Marsha Williams

National Association for the Education of Young Children
Washington, D.C.

National Association for the Education of Young Children
1509 16th Street, NW
Washington, DC 20036-1426
202-232-8777 or 800-424-2460
www.naeyc.org

Through its publications program the National Association for the Education of Young Children (NAEYC) provides a forum for discussion of major issues and ideas in the early childhood field, with the hope of provoking thought and promoting professional growth. The views expressed or implied are not necessarily those of the Association. NAEYC thanks the authors, who donated much time and effort to develop this book for the profession.

Library of Congress Control Number: 2001092217
ISBN 0-935989-99-4
NAEYC #112

Publications editor: Carol Copple
Associate editor: Millie Riley
Illustrations and editorial assistance: Natalie Klein
Book design and production: Malini Dominey

Printed in the United States of America

Children's art: Provided by the authors

Photographs: © by Nancy P. Alexander, 53; Kathleen Evans, 62, 69; Jean-Claude Lejeune, 7, 22, 48, 155; Marilyn Nolt, 38; Elaine M. Ward, 41; Francis Wardle, 47

Permissions acknowledgments: The following publishers and authors have generously given permission to use quotations from copyrighted works.
p. 3, from D. Hawkins, "Messing about in Science," *The Informed Vision: Essays on Learning and Human Nature,* © 1974 by Agathon Press; p. 8, from S.B. Sarason, *The Creation of Settings and the Future Societies,* © 1972 by the author; pp. 73, 87, 114, from A. Dyson, *Social Worlds of Children: Learning to Write in an Urban Primary School,* Teachers College Press, © 1993 by Teachers College, Columbia University; p. 76, from C. Ballenger, *Teaching Other People's Children,* Teachers College Press, © 1999 by Teachers College, Columbia University; p. 79, from H. Cuffaro, *Experimenting with the World,* Teachers College Press, © 1995 by Teachers College, Columbia University; p. 83, from L. Malaguzzi in L. Gandini, "Educational and Caring Spaces," *The Hundred Languages of Children: The Reggio Emilia Approach—Advanced Reflections.,* 2d ed., © 1998 by Ablex Publishing Corp.; p. 92, from "So Long," *Rhyme Me a Riddle, Sing Me a Song,* © 1989 by Houghton Mifflin; p. 98, from M.C. Bateson, *Peripheral Visions: Learning along the Way,* © 1994 by HarperCollins; p.111, from K. Moore, "Extending Experience: John Dewey—Intercommunication and Conversation in the Early Childhood Classroom," master's thesis, Pacific Oaks College, © 1998 by the author; pp. 130, 135, from L. Malaguzzi, "History, Ideas, and Basic Philosophy," and pp. 136, 137, from C. Rinaldi, "Emergent Curriculum and Social Constructivism," *The Hundred Languages of Children: The Reggio Emilia Approach to Early Childhood Education,* © 1993 by Ablex Publishing Corp.; p.152, from L. Birdsall, "The 'Factory School' Should Be Retired," *Los Angeles Times,* © 1998 by Los Angeles Times.

All books need editors—midwives even. Some books, like some babies, require a longer labor than others. This one has had a particularly lengthy birthing, and we are grateful to those who have brought us both fresh perspectives and hands-on help. Our special thanks go to Carol Anne Wien, author of *Developmentally Appropriate Practice in "Real Life,"* and to NAEYC editorial staff: Carol Copple, Millie Riley, and Natalie Klein.

Developmentally appropriate and culturally relevant teaching based on constructivist principles asks children to move more than to sit still, to talk more than to listen, to ask questions more than to give answers. It asks them to bring their own interests, language, and culture to school and contribute these to the emergence of curriculum unique to their classroom group. It asks them to become responsible members of a genuine classroom community in which the teacher is not the only authority, although she is indeed the adult in charge.

Such teaching is difficult to implement in our public schools because it demands innovative thinking by teachers and by children. Innovative thinking threatens both familiar system constraints on behavior and public perceptions of what school is supposed to be like. Also each generation's memory of its own schooling is reinforced by political appeals for back-to-basics instruction, standardized testing, drills and worksheets, and reading materials guaranteed to offend nobody. Textbook and test publishers' self-interests provide further barriers to the individualization of teaching. In a standardized curriculum, there is little room for the interests and experiences of children or of teachers. Emergent curriculum, in contrast, isn't fixed; it is co-constructed among children and teacher.

The idea of *emergent curriculum* keeps company with many good approaches in early care and education—*responsive curriculum, negotiated curriculum, Reggio Emilia, project approach, developmentally appropriate practice, constructivist teaching, progressive education*—and also with the latest findings in brain research. These concepts reflect efforts to acknowledge complexity—the complexity of learning, of the individuals who do the learning, and of the community of the classroom and the wider world. All concepts share the vision of John Dewey, evident in the titles of his books *Experience and Education* (1938) and *Democracy and Education* (1916) and in his insistence that a democracy is enriched by the differences among its members.

Simple, fixed plans for learning—prescribed curriculum—fail to do justice to the talents and experiences of children gathered in any classroom or to all the possible learnings in the world. Children learn most effectively when they are interested; all the energy of their intrinsic motivation can be tapped to see them through. Teachers teach most effectively when they are interested—in the subject matter as well as in the children.

Children need thinking teachers—skilled observers of child behavior, responsive to the strengths of each child, and able to create a democratic classroom community in which all members contribute and all are respected. Learning cannot be standardized. It happens in nonlinear paths, diverging in unexpected ways as new connections are made. No lesson plan offers a prescription for successful curriculum. Each new idea is a starting point, a doorway into the lively, endlessly complex world of children learning.

This book is about planning and letting go. It's about risk taking—working to create developmentally appropriate curriculum for 5-year-olds within the constraints of American public schools and within prevailing demands for accountability based on standardized measures that ignore diversity.

Following an overview of emergent teaching, this book plunges into the stories of four kindergarten teachers. After any event, human beings tell stories in an effort to understand what happened. We can't analyze things until we've experienced them. Oral storytelling is one step away from the event, because memory is selective and there is an audience to consider. Written storytelling is another step away. In writing a book one keeps tidying up the reality for public consumption. But it is by remembering, talking, and writing that thoughtful teachers reshape classroom happenings. They may even make beautifully orchestrated emergent curriculum look easy. It isn't.

Each story is unique, and thus limited in its applicability to future events. To predict the future we need to invent theories. Inventive thinking takes place in dialogue, especially dialogue with peers. This is as true for adults as it is for children. As thinking teachers, we are able through our writing to come together to try to convert our stories—our practice—into collective theories or generalizations about how things work.

In this book there are "Learning From . . ." reflections between the stories, in which we ask each other questions about what happened and connect each other's stories with our own. And following the stories we take turns at pulling some of the strands together, creating patterns, and building our collective theories. A "Perspective" links each of these segments to the next.

We also share some of our frustrations, acknowledging the external constraints we face as teachers and sharing strategies for survival under pressure. These constraints arise both from any school's need to control the behavior of children in groups and from society's investment in the future of its children. In a diverse society there are different views of desirable classroom behavior, and on a broader scale there are conflicting visions of desirable outcomes for children's learning. As advocates for teacher professionalism, we work to articulate our own visions underlying why we teach as we do. We are activist teachers, supporting children toward becoming critical thinkers, curious rather than fearful of differences, and able to take responsibility for envisioning a more just and peaceful world— in the classroom and throughout their lives.

PART I

Facing the Challenges

Introducing Elizabeth Jones

Elizabeth (Betty) Jones has been at Pacific Oaks College in Pasadena, California, for many years. She has taught preschool and primary classes in its Children's School and a wide variety of college classes in its human development and teacher education programs.

Pacific Oaks was founded as a community education center at the end of World War II by a group of families "concerned that our lives show forth our belief in the way of love" and hoping to contribute to building a more peaceful world that "all begins with little children." Its programs have emerged over the years in the context of its dedication to principles of social justice, respect for diversity, and valuing the uniqueness of each person.

In this setting, Betty has grown as teacher and learner. Her first NAEYC publication was *What Is Music for Young Children?* (1958/1969). Each of her more recent books has continued her effort to understand educational issues by writing about them: *Teaching Adults: An Active-Learning Approach* (1986), *Growing Teachers: Partnerships in Staff Development* (1993), *Emergent Curriculum* (with John Nimmo, 1994), and *The Play's the Thing: Teachers' Roles in Children's Play* (with Gretchen Reynolds, 1992) and *Master Players: Learning from Children at Play* (with Gretchen Reynolds, 1997). Her first NAEYC journal article appeared in 1960 in the *Journal of Nursery Education* (later to become *Young Children*).

The other teacher/writers in this volume all were Betty's graduate students at some point in their careers. Kathleen Evans and Kay Stritzel Rencken are also teaching colleagues in the Pacific Oaks distance learning program. The teacher dialogues in this book, like those in *Emergent Curriculum* and *Teaching Adults*, "could have happened this way," especially as we have added e-mail to our phone and face-to-face communication resources.

All of us, experienced teachers though we are, rely on reflection and dialogue with peers to carry on the continual theory building basic in the life of any growing teacher.

Emergent Teaching

We are profoundly ignorant about the subtleties of learning, but one principle ought to be asserted dogmatically: That there must be provided some continuity in the content, direction, and style of learning. Good schools begin with what children have in fact mastered, probe next to see what in fact they are learning, continue with what in fact sustains their involvement.

—David Hawkins

Emergent curriculum, I am convinced, is the most sensible approach to teaching young children. The dynamics in any group of children and adults who meet together daily over time cannot be predicted in advance except in broad outline.

Preselected, presequenced lesson plans cannot possibly offer a good fit in guiding the interactions of one classroom's unique group of people. Such lesson plans reflect only one of the three important agendas feeding into any classroom, namely the school system's agenda. This agenda—which reflects community expectations, practical constraints, and educational theory—stems from legitimate concerns about control of children's behavior and attainment of curriculum objectives. But the teacher and the children have agendas—personal priorities—as well.

The teacher's agenda is not static; it is dynamic, based in part on her or his evolving goals for the children, individually and collectively. All good teachers have goals for children's learning—both content goals and process goals. This agenda also reflects the teacher's personal values, survival concerns, educational theory, and habit. It may or may not closely match the school's agenda.

Children's agendas are idiosyncratic. And the larger the class, the more different agendas come into it. Children's agendas also derive from personal values and expectations, survival concerns, and habit.

Paying attention to children

The first lessons many children learn in school are that school is where you don't get to do what you want to do, that the things that interest you may not interest your teacher, and that teachers want you to learn the things *they* know. Some children know those things—teacher things—before they come to school. Some children do learn them at school. Other children don't, and their failure in the classroom spills over into the lives of their families and communities. They seek ways—often socially dangerous ones—to compensate for their inability to make it in the educational system.

Ours is an increasingly diverse society. But in highly teacher-directed and standardized instruction, diversity of learners is a problem (and winners and losers are a foregone conclusion). In this setting traditional curriculum is created by the teacher or outside experts before children arrive in the classroom. Scope and sequence are logically determined. The curriculum may or may not relate directly to children's lives outside of school; in part that depends on who the children are and where they come from.

In contrast, with democratic, constructivist approaches, diversity is an asset (and everyone can win). Diversity enriches what children can learn from each other. It increases the challenges of learning to live together—experiences of disequilibrium and conflict maintenance as well as conflict resolution. Through disequilibrium, as Jean Piaget (1973) maintains, significant learning happens; through diversity, as John Dewey ([1916]1966) maintains, the democratic community is enriched.

A child-centered, developmental curriculum takes seriously the challenge to educate every child, building on the competence and interests he or she brings to school. A recent national report charges that a "convergence of advancing knowledge and changing circumstances calls for a fundamental reexamination of the nation's responses to the needs of young children" (Shonkoff & Phillips 2000).

In Dewey's vision, the strength of democracy is in its respect for diversity. The ideal democratic community is one in which everyone's talents and concerns are valued and included. Vivian Paley writes that "the whole point of school is to find a common core of references without blurring our own special profiles" (1997, viii).

Few of America's schools are democratic in this inclusive way. They teach respect for preestablished order, not respect for diversity of interests, strengths, intelligences, learning styles, culture, class, and gender. And the expectations most teachers face are, first, to control the group and, second, to cover the curriculum. Preoccupation with covering the curriculum, however, leaves no time to pay attention to each child. Without engagement of every child in genuine learning, the community is deprived of part of its talent. Close adherence to a standardized curriculum is certain to leave many children unengaged and unable to connect.

Teachers as creators of curriculum

From an emergent perspective, the curriculum is not fixed but potential. This potential is contained in the space and materials; the teacher's knowledge, ideas, and values; the children's interests and concerns; the challenges of living together in a classroom; and the community's expectations (knowledge and skills judged important for children to acquire) (see "Sources of Emergent Curriculum," p. 23). Relationship building, living together as a classroom community, is of immediate interest to all members and the beginning of curriculum in any class.

In emergent curriculum the *particulars* of curriculum come from the children and teacher as they learn and work together. For instance, one class may get interested in studying pond life while another group becomes fascinated with a forest's regrowth after fire. The topics are different, but both groups learn about the diversity of living things and their interdependence, two *big ideas* in science. Teachers need to know and keep in mind such foundational concepts and knowledge as they plan and develop emergent curriculum (see "Guidelines for Curriculum Content" opposite). In language, mathematics, science, social studies, and the arts, teachers need to know how important concepts and skills build on other concepts and skills.

Children can learn key skills of literacy, numeracy, and social problem solving through shared exploration of virtually any topic—houses, sand, fishing, playwriting,

Guidelines for Curriculum Content

1. The curriculum has an articulated description of its theoretical base that is consistent with prevailing professional opinion and research on how children learn.

2. Curriculum content is designed to achieve long-range goals for children in all domains—social, emotional, cognitive, and physical—and to prepare children to function as fully contributing members of a democratic society.

3. Curriculum addresses the development of knowledge and understanding, processes and skills, dispositions and attitudes.

4. Curriculum addresses a broad range of content that is relevant, engaging, and meaningful to children.

5. Curriculum goals are realistic and attainable for most children in the designated age range for which they are designed.

6. Curriculum content reflects and is generated by the needs and interests of individual children within the group. Curriculum incorporates a wide variety of learning experiences, materials and equipment, and instructional strategies to accommodate a broad range of children's individual differences in prior experience, maturation rates, styles of learning, needs, and interests.

7. Curriculum respects and supports individual, cultural, and linguistic diversity. Curriculum supports and encourages positive relationships with children's families.

8. Curriculum builds upon what children already know and are able to do (activating prior knowledge) to consolidate their learning and to foster their acquisition of new concepts and skills.

9. Curriculum provides conceptual frameworks for children so that their mental constructions based on prior knowledge and experience become more complex over time.

10. Curriculum allows for focus on a particular topic or content while allowing for integration across traditional subject-matter divisions by planning around themes and/or learning experiences that provide opportunities for rich conceptual development.

11. Curriculum content has intellectual integrity; content meets the recognized standards of the relevant subject-matter disciplines.

12. Curriculum content is worth knowing; curriculum respects children's intelligence and does not waste their time.

13. Curriculum engages children actively, not passively, in the learning process. Children have opportunities to make meaningful choices.

14. Curriculum values children's constructive errors and does not prematurely limit exploration and experimentation for the sake of ensuring "right" answers.

15. Curriculum emphasizes the development of children's thinking, reasoning, decisionmaking, and problem-solving abilities.

16. Curriculum emphasizes the value of social interaction to learning in all domains and provides opportunities to learn from peers.

17. Curriculum is supportive of children's physiological needs for activity, sensory stimulation, fresh air, rest, hygiene, and nourishment/elimination.

18. Curriculum protects children's psychological safety, that is, children feel happy, relaxed, and comfortable rather than disengaged, frightened, worried, or stressed.

19. Curriculum strengthens children's sense of competence and enjoyment of learning by providing experiences for children to succeed from their point of view.

20. Curriculum is flexible so that teachers can adapt to individual children or groups.

Source: Reprinted, by permission, from S. Bredekamp and T. Rosegrant, eds., *Reaching Potentials: Transforming Early Childhood Curriculum and Assessment, Volume 2* (Washington, DC: NAEYC, 1995), 16.

dinosaurs, names, and many, many more. Children learn best when they are interested. Teachers need to ask themselves, "What interests these children at this time?" "What potential interests might hook them during our time together?" "What will be memorable and useful to them once our time together as a classroom community ends?"

Teachers too are people with interests of their own that are worth sharing with children. By including in the group's experiences some things they themselves like, teachers model knowledge and enthusiasm. Even adults keep on learning and stay interested in teaching.

Values that adults hold for children's learning in the school and community, family and culture, help to determine curriculum content. Researchers study the knowledge and skills that are critical for later learning and within the group of children at a given point in development. This knowledge base should guide teachers in an emergent curriculum approach, as in any other.

Lesson plans written before the fact are often required of teachers by supervisors who wish to ensure that careful thought is given to the activities provided for children. Any thoughtful curriculum is planned, both to be responsive to where children are developmentally and to take them in the direction of agreed upon goals. But when curriculum is tightly preplanned and directed toward behavioral objectives, it is typically linear and open to only one path to learning.

Some standardized curricula are advertised as "teacher-proof." With completely scripted lessons, all a teacher has to do is to read the teacher's manual that goes with the textbook, teach the lesson provided, and ward off interruptions from children who don't get it.

The teacher who respects diversity, recognizes individual differences, and pays attention to children is continually creating curriculum tailored to her group of children at the particular point in time. She is necessarily a constructivist in theory, convinced that each member of the classroom community, including herself, must build continuing understanding out of action and interaction. Learning is more than memorizing what one is told.

Putting theory into practice

Developmentally appropriate practice is less common in kindergarten than it is in preschool programs. Kindergarten and primary teachers face many constraints and pressures that teachers of younger children are not yet experiencing in the same intensity (although preschool appears to be next in line for "pushdown" curriculum). Now that the kindergarten year is a regular fixture in elementary school, many people expect it to mirror the images they have of their years in school; for example, that the teacher talks and the children listen. Very often emergent curriculum and other child-oriented practices, not fitting this top-down image, are suspect.

Environments for young children's active learning have a long history in the work of John Dewey, Jean Piaget, Lev Vygotsky, and

---

For learning to be truly engaging and meaningful, the learner must own it. For that to happen, the topics must emerge from the community of learners. No way can the people in Princeton or Austin, wherever basal texts and programs come from, know what Iu Mien children in Oakland, California, have on their minds. In fact, unless the teacher herself makes an effort to observe, talk with, and reflect on the children in her care, she cannot know what is meaningful and engaging to the children.

—Kathleen Evans

many others. Dewey's progressive education emphasized an education for democracy, in which through collaboration each learner's strengths contribute to the classroom community (Cuffaro1995). Piaget's *construction of knowledge* theory requires action with things and interaction in which one child's understandings can be tested within the disequilibrium created by new experiences and peers' divergent understandings (Labinowicz 1980; Peterson & Felton-Collins 1986; Kamii 2000). Vygotsky wrote of teaching as *scaffolding* the child's construction of knowledge through timely interventions that challenge the child to move on to another level of understanding (Berk & Winsler 1995).

These theories have had some impact on school practices, especially in kindergarten and primary grades. And kindergarten has its own tradition as preparation for school in a "children's garden" distinct from school. However, the emphasis in the last few decades on the significance of the early years for later learning parallels a greater pushdown of academic schooling into the kindergarten rather than an influence of developmental thinking on the primary grades.

NAEYC's developmentally appropriate practice guidelines (Bredekamp & Copple 1997) are relevant for the whole age range from birth to age 8. But in the real world of public education, even in kindergarten, these principles are likely to be evident only in carefully designed alternative programs (such as the Tucson primary magnet school described in Part 2, number1) that genuinely support constructivist classrooms. The public's unappeasable anxiety that all the children be "above average" (as National Public Radio's Garrison Keillor characterizes them) creates constant pressure on teachers from adults who have all been to school and believe they know what teaching looks like. When teachers are teaching, as these adults *know* from personal experience, they are

powerful authority figures; they do the talking, while children listen. They teach prescribed topics from prescribed textbooks. This image is imprinted in the minds of adults everywhere in the world. When teachers introduce changes in classroom practice, these changes will always be suspect unless they work instant miracles.

Enlivening learning for all

Teachers teach most effectively when they are interested in the subject matter as well as in the children. Emergent curriculum will reflect the teacher's preferences as well as the children's, and together they may discover new interests along the way. For example, I always teach natural history if I'm working with children; I love animals (even reptiles and bugs) and plants and am full of detailed knowledge about their identities and their lives. I don't expect every child to share my enthusiasm, but I think it's important for adults to model the sort of enthusiasms out of which serious inquiry and expertise—and commitment to disciplined practice—develop.

I don't feel obligated to care that much about all topics of study. If some children are really hooked on the solar system—which has always been too far away to spark my interest—I will, as a responsible teacher, help them find resources and acknowledge their work. But I'm not likely to pursue a class project on the topic because my interest would remain superficial. In-depth curriculum emerges in the intersections between teachers' interests, kids' interests, and school-community values. (There are a great many teachers teaching topics from the book, being good functionaries instead of passionate learners themselves. They model "not loving school.")

It is no accident that for many teachers schooling becomes more and more of a routine task. Seymour Sarason, who has "spent thousands of hours in American schools," says he quickly sensed that

> [T]he longer the person had been a teacher the less excited, or alive, or stimulated he seemed to be about his role. It was not that [teachers] were uninterested . . . But simply that being a teacher was on the boring side. Generally speaking, these teachers were not as helpful to children as they might have been or . . . as the teachers themselves would have liked to have been. It took me a long time to realize that what would be inexplicable would be if things turned out otherwise, because schools are not created to foster the intellectual and professional growth of teachers. (1972, 123)

The need to grow teachers

A school created to grow thinking teachers would be full of dialogue about children and their learning and about curriculum. Yet only a few schools provide opportunities for dialogue among teachers (Sarason 1996). In some, ideas are hoarded rather than shared. In many, curriculum is prescribed, and staff meetings are consumed with routine tasks. Lunchroom conversations only occasionally deal with children, except for complaints about the bad kids.

Teachers often have to find congenial peers for themselves by becoming active in professional associations and study groups, connecting with interested parents, and leading workshops for other teachers. Carolyn Stringer (see Part 2, number 3) discovered the early childhood programs of Reggio Emilia, Italy, and peers who also were interested in reading about this approach and observing it in action. But she had no one in her school with whom to reflect on her day-to-day efforts to reinvent herself as a constructivist teacher. Thinking in isolation, it is difficult to see the discrepancies between one's theory and one's practice.

Trying new curriculum strategies, a teacher may experience some moments of what the teacher next door perceives critically as *loss of control*. Such moments become learning opportunities for engaged and democratic problem solving by children and teacher. But day to day, the fact remains that actively learning children are often lively and noisy—characteristics routinely suppressed in many classrooms. To resist the prevailing definition of control is risky; any teacher who does stands out in the crowd. But such resistance is important for the growth of both children and teachers.

When it comes right down to it, all teaching is risky; it has a high probability of not working as it was intended. Teaching and learning are complex processes that follow different paths for every learner. Schooling brings a group of learners together, restricts their movement in space and time, and presents them with a common curriculum.

Educating for Democracy

Pluralistic democracy is a desirable ideal. America's founding fathers voiced this concept and more or less set it up, although their idea of pluralism was effectively limited to male Europeans. Although to every new manifestation of diversity, reactions, some vicious, have been expressed along the way, immigration has been and continues to be more open in North America than in many older nations.

Diversity creates conflict. In a democracy, respectful conflict is desirable; it enriches thought and broadens possibility. Critical thinking is one hallmark of a good citizen. It is the outcome of disequilibrium, the surprise that one's way is not the only way and the only investment of effort in reconciling different perspectives.

Community—mutual caring and collaborative action—is essential to human living.

Civilization is not easily accomplished. It requires a long process of education of the young, shaping dispositions to care and learn as well as practicing all the skills—physical, intellectual, and social—that a complex society demands. Civilizing goes on continuously; it is never finished, but it is easily lost.

Democratic behaviors and critical thinking are well learned only through practice. Educational systems, then, must create democratic learning communities where thinking is encouraged and communication is active.

The human child, fortunately, is an enthusiastic learner.

So what is education for?

All educational theories have an implied values base. Education is *for* something—we educate toward social goals. In traditional, homogeneous societies, the purpose of education is to socialize the young to the way things are. The way things are is a given, not to be critiqued. Faith, obedience, and patriotism are primary virtues; the goal is handing on the tradition unchanged. To sustain this goal anywhere in the modern world today has numerous drawbacks, among them inflexibility in the face of inevitable change and antagonism toward those whose ways are not like our own.

A diverse, rapidly changing society with an open and egalitarian democratic ideal must educate by welcoming critical thinking about the way things are. Questions are important, and the most telling questions—in Margaret Mead's (1970) words, "the questions that we would never think to ask"—are likely to be asked by those with the least power—children and adolescents, immigrant families, the poor. From their perspectives, the system isn't fair. Making education fair and effective for all is a challenge that arises for every democratic classroom, a microcosm of the dilemmas of larger society. It is an essential part of emergent curriculum.

The simplest reason to do emergent curriculum is that it works. When learners generate curriculum, their participation and engagement are ensured. When children take the lead in developing what is worth knowing, they want to come to school because school makes sense. They find their concerns and their own experiences represented there. And the teacher doesn't have to work hard at maintaining control, because she's not working *against* something. She is working *with* learner interest, a curriculum that is stronger than anything invented in any textbook.

Yet doing emergent curriculum is not easy, especially in the world of public schools. It reflects a teacher's choice to challenge her own professional growth, to pay genuine attention to each child, to do what she believes each child needs, and to invent strategies for accomplishing all this within the constraints of the system. To proceed with confidence requires a solid sense of oneself, lack of anxiety about being the authority in the classroom, and in-depth understanding of the social-emotional developmental levels of the children one is teaching. It also requires being committed to continued learning about what one is teaching, how children acquire knowledge and skills, and the big ideas central to various knowledge domains. All are necessary.

Why bother to work so hard? Because effective teaching becomes a vocation, a calling, what we are committed to doing in the world in order to share our talents for the good. The excitement of lifelong learning is a wonderful motivator.

PERSPECTIVE

Teacher and author Cynthia Ballenger (1999) says, "[T]he telling of a good story is an excellent way to create a sense of the individuals and of the particularities of the situation. The process of teaching is always a story of individuals and relationships." The four kindergarten teachers who tell their stories next are committed to a view of children as capable and curious and to the goal of effective education for all children. Their working theory is a more complex one than the seemingly straightforward approach so common in schooling—telling children what you want them to know and then checking to see if they have learned it. The beliefs of these teachers challenge them to create and re-create curriculum that is responsive to every child—a daunting task worthy of their professionalism and continuously stimulating to their intelligence. Sometimes the process is exhausting, and surviving is an issue. In these classrooms teachers as well as children keep on growing.

Meeting the teacher/writers

In complex tasks like teaching, beginnings are the hardest; there are far too many variables to keep track of (see "Stages of Teacher Development" on the facing page). Our four teachers— Kay Stritzel Rencken, Marsha Williams, Carolyn Stringer, and Kathleen Evans—are all experienced and well past the survival stage. They have been in the classroom long enough to have

Stages of Teacher Development

Survival

During the first year of teaching "the teacher's main concern is whether or not she can *survive.* This preoccupation . . . may be expressed in terms like these: 'Can I get through the day in one piece? Without losing a child? . . . Can I really do this kind of work day after day?'"

Consolidation

"By the end of the first year the teacher usually has come to see herself as capable of surviving immediate crises. She is now ready to consolidate the overall gains made during the first stage and to differentiate specific tasks and skills to be mastered next [such as] focus on individual problem children and problem situations."

Renewal

"During the third or fourth year . . . The teacher begins to tire of doing the same old thing. She starts to ask more questions about new developments in the field . . . If it is true that the teacher's own interest or commitment to the projects and activities she provides for children contributes to their educational value, then her need for renewal and refreshment should be taken seriously."

Maturity

The mature teacher "has come to terms with herself as a teacher and has reached a comfortable level of confidence in her own competence. She now has enough perspective to begin to ask deeper and more abstract questions, such as: 'What are my historical and philosophical roots? What is the nature of growth and learning? How are educational decisions made? Can schools change societies?'"

Source: Excerpted, by permission of the publisher, from L.C. Katz, *Talks with Teachers of Young Children: A Collection* (Norwood, NJ: Ablex, 1995), 205–08.

mastered basic group management strategies and have become secure in their relationships with children and parents. But the developmental progression Lilian Katz (1995) describes—*consolidation* to *renewal* to *maturity* as a teacher—generates periodic searches for new challenges and the *disequilibrium* Jean Piaget (1973) describes as sparking learning. Each teacher is also a risk taker, setting for herself new goals as old ones are reached and reflecting continuously on the events of the classroom and the world beyond the classroom.

These stories catch the tellers at different points in their careers. **Kay** is experiencing the best fit between herself and her setting. For nearly two decades she has taught at a primary magnet alternative school, constructivist in its philosophy. Here she has established a strong collegial relationship with the principal and has found support both for teaching (in a class of 20 children with two adults who are full-time) and for thinking about teaching. The new challenge in the year of her story is the school's move to temporary quarters, less spacious than those to which she'd been accustomed. It's a change that makes the frequent walking field trips a desirable escape as well as an opportunity to investigate a new neighborhood.

Kay, Marsha, and Kathleen all have come into kindergarten from preschool teaching; they are already practiced in provisioning for play and taking children's interests seriously. **Marsha** worked for her local school district for several years as a child care and preschool teacher before moving into a kindergarten position at the same school in the year she completed her credential. The children, parents, and place are all familiar to her the year of her story. However, she faces unexpected challenges. Her father experiences a serious illness, and starting to teach kindergarten brings with it new pressures from her principal, who now perceives her as a real teacher.

Carolyn taught second grade before she moved to kindergarten. Seven years later at the time of this story, she has reached a career turning point and is challenging herself to create a curriculum that builds strongly on children's play. She seeks to "invent a new way of being a teacher." A dancer, torn between ballet and teaching, she is inspired by her learning about the preschools of Reggio Emilia in Italy and the aesthetic vision that permeates their curriculum. The intentional reshaping of her teaching is part of her effort to decide whether to remain in the profession. Carolyn's story reveals the risks she takes, the uncertainties she struggles with as she tries to let go of a traditional elementary teaching approach, and the professional isolation she experiences at her school site. She finds that these conditions and pressures undermine her ability to sustain an emergent curriculum drawn from the real interests of 5-year-olds.

Kathleen, after long experience as a preschool teacher and a director working primarily with affluent families, chose for herself nearly 10 years ago the challenge of teaching in inner-city public schools. She brought to this daunting task her strong commitment to social justice, learning to work effectively with children often shortchanged by their families' poverty and experiences of racial oppression. Early in this period she responded enthusiastically to the opportunity in her school district to be trained as a Reading Recovery teacher. The training enables her to work individually with children for half a day and, at the time of her story, to teach kindergarten in the afternoon. Kathleen's next self-chosen challenge, which she first undertook several years before the year of her story, is teaching a class of mostly refugee children from a tribal culture in Southeast Asia—the Iu Mien people, who have no written language of their own, and whose spoken language and culture were altogether unfamiliar to her.

All four teachers are European American women, ranging in age from their thirties to their fifties. Only Marsha is currently rearing children; Kay is a grandmother; Kathleen's children are also grown. In these characteristics they are typical of American public school teachers today, even though the children served by today's schools, especially on the West Coast where these teachers work, represent many colors, cultures, and languages.

Each teacher's story illustrates the cyclical process of planning, paying attention (What are the children interested in? What do they know?), and letting go of a perfectionist vision of teacher-determined curriculum in order to co-create with children an emergent curriculum no one teacher could have foreseen.

—BJ

PART II

Teachers' Stories

Introducing Kay Stritzel Rencken

Kay is a 30-year veteran teacher. She has taught at Borton Primary Magnet School since 1978, the first two years in a Title I PACE (Parent and Child Education) classroom of 4-year-olds and since then in the school's full-day kindergarten. An inner-city school and one of three primary magnets in the Tucson Unified School District, Borton became a magnet school in 1979 after the district lost a class action suit to end segregation in some of its schools. It provides a unique setting for primary school-age children of both majority and minority populations.

Many features at Borton are unusual among Tucson public schools, including full-day kindergartens, before- and after-school programs, a physical education teacher, a fine arts teacher, transportation to and from school for all children, full-time instructional assistants in all classrooms, clerical and support staff, a full-time librarian, and certified bilingual teachers. Borton consistently has a very high response rate and performance rating from parents in a district-wide survey. As a primary program (K–2), no state or district tests are given, although a trial kindergarten learning assessment has been introduced.

Kay resists being typed as a teacher, but she provides an eclectic, child-centered, emergent, progressive, and developmentally appropriate program that is always changing. In Kay's story, Charlene Centers is the instructional assistant who worked with Kay in the full-day kindergarten for 16 years before retiring. Kay's new assistant, who is bilingual, has worked at Borton many years. Their collaboration creates a setting that meets young children's social, emotional, physical, and cognitive needs.

Additional adults assist in the room each year. Typically, a few parents come regularly for varied amounts of time. The University of Arizona's Whole Language Block Program meets at Borton, and its students work in various classrooms. The university also assigns student teachers. All this help—together with the resources of time, space, and materials—makes it easier to go walking around the neighborhood, discover the tomato-colored house, and turn this experience into curriculum.

The Tomato-Colored House

In the year our school, Borton Primary Magnet School, was being rebuilt, we moved into a temporary facility in a nearby city park. Borton-in-the-park was just south of downtown Tucson, with a church, a bank, stores, and many houses in a concentrated area.

In contrast, our school's permanent site is in an industrial part of Tucson, and there children and teachers have taken walks to interesting places nearby—the United Parcel Service Depot, the moving company, the bread bakery, the bagel bakery, the meat plant, and so on. Field trips are a wonderful way to see what is going on around us. We used to have buses for trips too, but their availability has been curtailed in recent years due to budget cuts.

There were, of course, disadvantages to our school's move. We found ourselves in a portable classroom about two-thirds the size of our usual room and lacking the amenities (running water, covered walkways, and a playground) we had come to take for granted. On the other hand, our temporary site did provide us with a new neighborhood to explore—one full of houses. As I drove around the new area, I was excited to see the variety in house styles—and a lot of color, which the children would later notice too. Nevertheless, this idea of neighborhood exploration was shelved for the first few months of our time at the new site.

The kindergarten environment

The beginning months of kindergarten are a time for establishing children's trust in the regularities of the schedule and the space. Children learn to count on the fact that every day there'll be time to play outdoors, build with blocks, paint, rest, and meet together in small and large groups.

In the prepared environment of my classroom and the outdoors, there is so much to do once the kids learn the routines (which doesn't take very long) that they're very adept at directing their own learning. They have two hours of choice time each morning—an hour outside, an hour inside. I find that this readies them for more directed tasks in the afternoon of our full-day kindergarten.

(In our temporary location in the park, it was because there wasn't enough to do outdoors that field trips became a larger part of our week.)

One end of our room is for dramatic play—a house area that becomes restaurant, store, or whatever is needed for supporting elaborated language and ideas. The other end is for construction activities/dramatic play, with blocks and accessories. I allow space at both ends of the room for expanding the boundaries as needed.

Through this hands-on activity experiencing the living-together values of sociability, community, gaining one's voice, and antibias, the children learn to trust one another. All of this takes time—time well spent.

Planning our neighborhood walks

It was March when I decided to start taking the whole class on regular walking trips. The walks came about out of my frustration with our outdoor time, which was not as productive of complex play as it had been at our regular school site. The park playground had very little shade, was poorly equipped, and had no tricycle paths. We needed to do something more stimulating. I had only vague plans—developing a theme of recycling and cleanup, perhaps, or making a neighborhood map in order to learn mapping skills and to enrich the block play. For the moment I had forgotten about the interesting variety in neighborhood houses.

My full-day kindergarten has 20 children, with two adults—myself and an assistant, Charlene. I often have student teachers from the University of Arizona as well. During the time of this project, two students from the teacher education program's Whole Language Block (headed by Ken and Yetta Goodman) were assigned to our classroom one day a week. I decided to schedule walking trips on the days the students were with us.

When I arranged our trips with the principal, I was surprised at first that we were instructed to take one of the school's two-way radios with us. I was not worried about anything happening to us in this neighborhood, because I felt as safe here as in our school's old familiar neighborhood. But our principal, secretary, and security guard all felt strongly about our safety. I realized it was a sensible idea in case a child was sick or hurt or should an adult fall. And the kids loved the thought of having a radio with us. It made our walk feel very adventurous.

Off we went, talking and chatting. Each adult had five children in tow, so there was a lot of opportunity for adult-child conversation. We had a loose idea of where we would go—straight down Meyer Street and then back. With mapping in mind, I brought along the camera so I could record the houses and put pictures of them around the room or in a book.

At one house—the one we came to call the Tomato-Colored House—we were invited in by construction workers who were busy there. Here was a great chance, I thought, to see the inside of this house! Trooping through it, the children noticed all sorts of things—

    fireplaces
    skylights
    an almost enclosed porch
    the back room
    holes for toilets and for water
    and more

Debriefing: Representing the experience

When we returned to the classroom, all of us sat on the floor in a circle and talked about the differences in the houses. (I sit on the floor too; everyone can see me, and I facilitate the conversation.) The children didn't need much help or direction; our walk was near the end of the year, and they had become quite skilled at talking without interrupting or having me call on them. The conversation flowed for a long time—20 to 25 minutes. Kindergarten children, I have found, have a short attention span for teacher-led activities but a much longer one when they are excited about a topic. This is a time to put aside the planning book and go with the children's interest.

I noticed that the children were especially excited about the unusually bright colors of the houses. When I mentioned I was glad I had taken pictures so we could look at them, one child complained that it would take too long to get the pictures developed; the rest moaned in agreement. Another child suggested that we each draw a house we had seen. Agreed! We all set about drawing a house, using markers on 8½-by-11-inch white paper.

The children worked long and hard. Some of them drew a second house after finishing the first. I dated the drawings and put the children's names at the top. The children then went outside for lunch, and I put their drawings up on the chalkboard. After lunch we looked at them and discussed them. It had not been my intent to study the houses of the neighborhood, but this was clearly the children's interest. All their drawings were of houses! After school I went to the library and checked out a lot of books on houses for the children to look at and *read*.

Replay: Returning to the scene

The next week on our walk, I wanted to take the children to a yellow house on 17th Street. I had noticed this house on my drive around the neighborhood, and its gables and colors intrigued me. The house was mostly yellow, but its three apartments each had a door of a different color. All sorts of colors were used on the window frames, and there were bright-colored porch swings and fences. It was wild!

So off we went. Again, the children talked all the way. As we passed some of the houses on Meyer Street, they remembered which each one of them had drawn. When we got to the yellow house, they were amazed and had many different comments.

"It looks like a kid's house."
"It has so many colors."
"What is that color, Kay?"
"This would be a fun house to live in!"

"Remember that book you read where the kids painted the house?"

Most of the children were familiar with apartment houses; quite a few lived in them. Many of the neighborhood children lived in the same big apartment house. But the yellow house had only three apartments, and it looked very different. All the way back to school and even after our return, we all talked more about what makes an apartment house.

During choosing time many of the children got right to work drawing the yellow house. I dated their drawings and put them on the classroom walls. Other children were busily building houses with the blocks. Some of these buildings resembled the ones they had seen; other creations came straight from their imaginations. Georgia and Kate and Carl and Jorge spent a great deal of time in the blocks trying to add those design elements they had seen in the houses. The house with many colors had a slanting roof with gables (How do you build that?). Eventually the four building artisans agreed to put triangular blocks together on top of their flat roof—not a full, slanted roof but at least a recognizable representation of gables.

Deepening the discussion

As I moved around the room during choosing time, I listened in on a lively discussion about painting the blocks so that the constructions would look like the buildings we had seen in the neighborhood.

What colors should they use to paint the blocks, and how many blocks of each kind would they need? the children contemplated. They engaged the class lawyer—our classroom's most argumentatively skilled child—in a discussion that went on for two days. I had the feeling that the *case* was going to be presented on Friday. But it never was, even though I asked in one of our Friday circles if there was anything the children wanted to talk about from the week's activities. Since there wasn't, I let it drop.

I guess I had missed something, or the children lost interest, or they figured out that painting the blocks was something I wouldn't agree to no matter what. But I wished in our temporary move to the portable classroom in the park that I hadn't packed away our smaller set of unit blocks in many colors.

The house photos came back from the developer, and I displayed them on a board. The discussions were lively, and the children asked many questions:

"Should we put the photos with the drawings?"
"Could we make graphs?"
"Could we make more drawings?"
"Could I take down a drawing to do a 'better' one?"
"When can we go walking again?"

Going walking again: New discoveries

It was a Monday, and some of the children had figured out that we walked on Wednesdays. I suggested that we only had to wait two days. But where should we walk? Some of the children wanted to return to Meyer Street; some wanted to go to the yellow house; some wanted to explore.

How could we do all this? I wondered. This class was into problem posing and problem solving in a *big* way. One child thought it was silly to have only three choices; since we had four adults, we needed four choices. Another child said that the two university students could be in one group because that would be safer anyway. I put a sign-up sheet on the door, and the children made their choices, distributing themselves quite evenly.

We have a set of Masonite boards that we use as writing boards when we are outside or sitting on the carpet. Some of the children wanted to take these along so they could sketch. Others thought the boards would be a bother, adding that there was no place to sit and sketch anyway. We gave the children the option: Take a sketch board if you want. Someone suggested that the adults take paper and pen so that they could write what the children said when we were out there, and this was easy enough to do.

Children who had noticed all the debris around the area where we walked suggested bringing bags to pick up the garbage. (We do that regularly at our school.) We didn't follow up on this idea because enthusiasm was high for exploring, not for working. Some of the children thought we could pick up trash on another day. (This could have been an excellent time for a small group to go off on a tangent and work on another project.) So the class continued to work on our houses. And we did pick up a lot of debris on our playground but not outside the fences.

Wednesday came, and it was hot! Our water bottles were filled and each one was put into a plastic bag to make a sleeve. We hooked them onto pants where possible. Some children carried the plastic bags like a backpack. We took only one radio with us, though some of the children thought we should have three. But the office didn't want to tie up all the available radios with us.

We all set out down Meyer Street. I had the group that had chosen to go exploring, since I felt more comfortable with this idea than did the other adults, who wanted a little more definition. We began to zig and zag and in our exploring wound up again at the tomato-colored house. We examined the roofline of the house from three angles, talking about

> the pitch of the roof,
>
> how many triangles we saw,
>
> pipes coming out of the roof,
>
> skylights, and
>
> windows.

I was ready to move on, when the construction crew arrived. The foreman recognized us and asked if we wanted to walk through the house again. "Of course!" we said. (I shudder to think of the liability if anything had happened, but in we went.)

The children saw lots of changes inside; bathroom equipment had been installed and so had the kitchen sink. I noticed other changes too subtle for the children to discern, including molding, wiring, and switches, but they were fascinated by the plumbing. I took some pictures, and then we left so the crew could get to work.

Right outside the house we almost ran into the *bicycle cops* who regularly patrol the downtown area. This encounter was well worth it! We found out that one of the cops had just visited our school with the SWAT team, *and* that he was Jim Murray, the son of Nancy, one of our favorite extended day teachers. Jim told the children that before he became a cop he used to work at Borton, playing soccer and other outdoor games with the kids. Now we had tons to talk about on the way back!

Charlene's group had been off to revisit the yellow house, because most of the children wanted to redo their drawings of this very complex structure. They had jotted down a lot of notes so they "could get it right this time." After having Charlene note the colors, the number of windows, and so on, the group set off down the street. They passed a house we had previously viewed from the front, and they talked about how it looked from the side. And then the woman who lives there came out to feed her animals, and the children discovered that chickens, cats and kittens, rabbits, and a pig were all hidden in that backyard (they had heard the chickens, but all the rest were a surprise). The woman welcomed the children, and they flocked in to help feed the animals. Charlene reported that they were so well behaved even in such exciting circumstances that she just couldn't stop telling them how wonderful they were—high praise indeed!

The group that went off to see the *already seen* houses on Meyer Street came back with lots of details for their drawings. They didn't have any new grand adventures, but they were excited to hear the tales told by the others.

More complex representations: Integrating skill learning

I have long been interested in block play and its contribution to children's learning (Stritzel 1989). The Caroline Pratt unit blocks are often seen primarily as a useful way to learn math concepts—and of course they are—but the artistic expression in building by the young child is often overlooked. Building what they had seen on their walks offered the children in our class another means for expressing themselves. In my observations, boys seem to re-create what they have seen more accurately by building, while girls seem to draw more accurately. I like to offer both activities so the children can stretch their abilities.

The discovery of a backyard "farm" on this latest walking trip really enriched the children's block play. They had been using toy animals to create farms all year long, and many dramatic "playscapes" were enacted around the farm. This was largely fantasy play, however, since none of the children had been to a farm and I couldn't arrange a trip to one. The children read books about farming and built their own farms for toy animals. Good guys and bad guys inhabited the farm, and other scenes from TV entered into their play. But the visit

to the backyard farm added some reality to the children's play. They made cages and put in their animals. And because there weren't enough chickens or cats in our set of toy animals, the children made do with some of the pattern blocks, carefully choosing blocks so that all the chickens were one color and shape and all the kittens were another.

Our repeated trips also brought about many changes in the children's drawings of the houses. We kept adding house pictures to the walls. Not only did each trip enrich the drawings, but children also helped each other remember house details or improve their skills at drawing. (Given the opportunity, children naturally provide scaffolding for each other's thinking.) The classroom was abuzz with talk of the buildings—children comparing the photos with their drawings, comparing drawings, and comparing the real houses with the pictures. There were many comments about the drawings getting better, and children noticed elements of some children's drawings that were really interesting. We devised a *good* list, which included something good said about everyone's drawing. This wasn't contrived by the adults; the children were seeing good points in each and every child's rendering of a house.

Critiquing as learning

I have always believed that children's work on a drawing or painting is guided by an inner voice and requires no adult intervention. A teacher can comment on a child's work but not grade it, lest the creativity be stifled. In the past I have been reluctant to ask children to "do it over," fearing they would understand this request to mean that the drawing was not good enough. But I began to rethink this idea as I offered suggestions during the children's guided

Sources of Emergent Curriculum

Children's interests. Children whose own interests are acknowledged and supported don't need to be motivated to learn; their own excitement will keep them learning. Different children have different interests; how many of them can be built into the emerging curriculum?

Teachers' interests. Teachers are people with interests of their own, which are worth sharing with children. By doing some things *they* like, they can model knowledge and enthusiasm—even adults keep learning—and stay interested in teaching.

Developmental tasks. At each developmental stage, there are tasks to be mastered: crawling, walking, talking, pouring, cutting, skipping—the list goes on and on. Appropriate curriculum provides many opportunities for children to choose activities providing spontaneous skill practice. Similarly, appropriate curriculum is responsive to the social-emotional issues that characteristically surface powerfully at different stages: autonomy, power, strength, and friendship among them.

Things in the physical environment. Children's experience of place is unique to the place they are in. The man-made things in their physical environment are typically standardized and predictable; thus unit blocks facilitate orderly building. The natural things are nonstandardized and unpredictable—each plant and animal is different—and reflect the local climate and terrain. Children need experience with both.

People in the social environment. Children are interested in all sorts of people, who they are and what they do. Parents and cooks, big brothers and librarians, custodians and bus drivers, and neighbors are right there to learn about and relate to.

Curriculum resource materials. Teachers need not reinvent the wheel. Libraries, exhibits at conferences, school resource centers are full of curriculum ideas ready to use. Use them and *adapt them* to your own setting, your teaching style, and your children's interests.

Serendipity: Unexpected events. When the unexpected happens in the classroom, the community, the natural world, teachers have choices. They can try to ignore it, or join in briefly, or invent ways of incorporating it into their plans, short- or long-term. It's important to become skilled in on-the-spot decisionmaking.

Living together: Conflict resolution, caregiving, and routines. Cooperation, expression of feelings, conflict resolution, and all the daily tasks of living together are potential curriculum for young children. Physical care, self-help skills, eating and resting and washing and dressing are the everyday life experiences that nurture the growth of young children. Caregiving and the resolution of interpersonal issues are not interruptions to the curriculum; they are basic curriculum.

Values held in the school and community, family, and culture. It is important to be accountable to others' expectations and to evaluate programs in that framework. It is not necessary to teach directly from expectations; learning activities should be developmentally appropriate and adapted to the situation. It is important to define the curriculum planning process clearly so that you know when you are actively engaged in it.

Source: Reprinted, by permission of the publisher, from E. Jones & J. Nimmo, *Emergent Curriculum* (Washington, DC: NAEYC, 1994), 127.

work/play. In this instance critiquing the drawings came from the children; they looked at their drawings and talked about what they had missed. We spent a lot of time discussing these drawings in small and large groups. It was hard for some children to grasp the idea that the efforts were different, not *best* or *bad.* Their impulse was to throw some drawings away, but I intervened and asked the children if we could keep them all and if they would number each drawing.

I thought it would be a good idea to do some story writing and make a book. The children wanted no part of it, saying "We do that all the time!" But some of the writers made captions for their pictures, either on the computer or by hand, and they attached these to the wall. The pictures stayed up for the rest of the year, with children adding to them as the spirit called. Each time we had visitors—frequent at Borton, and even more so at the end of the year—children engaged them in a discussion of what we had done.

Extending children's interests

We teachers talked about extending the children's interest with a planned unit on Houses. We checked out more books from the library, some showing different kinds of houses and some with architectural drawings. I put out a rubber stamp set that included images of pillars, arches, domes, and so on. Children read the books and used the stamps, but their main interest was in their drawings. They did make some large paintings of the houses during this time, but mostly they worked on revising their crayon

and marker drawings. Drawings got tacked up one on top of the other, some three or four pages deep. Our walks happened in March and April, and the school year ended in the middle of May. We didn't go on any more walks after May 1, as the weather was getting hotter and the university students were no longer with us. However, when we were outdoors, the children would stand on the picnic table to spot the houses on Meyer Street. We shared a set of binoculars, and some children brought binoculars from home for all to use. They could see the roof of the yellow house from the playground.

The children who came to school in cars persuaded their parents to drive down the streets to see the houses, and parents got into the conversation. We also began creating a map of our walks, beginning with blocks. One afternoon I put tape down on the rug to create the streets. This inspired children to build the houses we had seen and to discuss where to locate them accurately, not just where some kids wanted to put them. Many of the children were now 6 years old, and they wanted things *right.* Others just wanted to build within the new frames.

Persisting in their view, the *right* crew asked us to help them make a map on paper. Each child drew her or his own map first on a small sheet of paper. The children put in the streets and the houses, referring to the pictures for placement. They discussed the numbers on the houses. "What did these mean?" they wondered. I thought maybe some of the readers or *math-ers* (children adept at working with numbers) in the crowd would figure out the numbering scheme; they could have but weren't yet interested in the system, only in putting numbers on the buildings. After some refining of their small sketches, children began to use the big sheets of manila painting paper to create large maps.

The children took days to do all of this. They kept coming back to it! On many days we skipped our formal committee time (in which children are assigned to task groups), and children grouped themselves to work on their sketches, their maps, or their block buildings. Those with skills in building, writing, or drawing helped others who were less skilled; this was a very cooperative group, eager to *get going* on the various aspects of this project. Some children read books, did pattern blocks, or worked on the computer instead. But everyone was busy.

Finally, with the year ending, we took down the pictures. Most of the children bound their 8½-by-11-inch drawings between two pieces of colored construction paper. They put their names on their books and very carefully carried them home. I didn't find any of these blowing around on the playground as I do so many papers! These were treasures to be taken care of.

Why all this happened

This emergent curriculum was stimulated first by the school's move to a new neighborhood, a too-small classroom space, and a too-barren and hot outdoor space; next by my looking around to see what aspects

of the environment might be of interest to children and adults alike; and then by my ongoing interest in the project approach, stimulated by the ideas of Lilian Katz and Sylvia Chard (1989) in their book *Engaging Children's Minds,* and my reading about the Reggio Emilia approach (Edwards, Gandini, & Forman 1993). (See "Sources of Emergent Curriculum, p. 23.)

What did our house project have to do with Reggio? The children were working on a project over a long period of time and at their own pace. Most of their work was self-initiated. I did not say "Do it over" about any child's drawing at any time; the children took the initiative in appraising their own work and returning to it. They never tore up an old drawing as if it were *bad;* they just kept adding to it.

The main ingredient was time. I was more than willing to revise the schedule to make room for their project work. I found myself letting go of some notions I had about

> the schedule,
> what this group needed,
> what a particular child needed,
>   the appropriateness—for fives—
>   of repeating work, and
> flexibility.

Unlike the teachers in the Reggio Emilia district in Italy, we carried out this project without an art teacher or a room set up for art. We were doing it in our own small room and making it work. And I was not in charge of the documentation—the children were. Viewing displays from Reggio Emilia, I often had had the feeling that the documentation was being done for someone else. In our classroom we were documenting for ourselves, documenting what worked for us. Ours was not an aesthetically organized display of the children's work on houses; it was a functional display, largely controlled by the children, and it was always *in process*. We used every bit of space inside the classroom and outside. The walls were filled with drawings, paintings, sketches, and maps.

I could have changed the children's focus, but I chose not to. I took pictures, and I acted as scribe for what was going on. Maybe as my documentation techniques improve, future displays will become more teacher directed. I don't know.

I did employ an oral story technique. I told the stories, "Our Walks," many times, never the same way twice. The children listened and asked for stories again. Once I told the tales as a bedtime story when they were all in their places for rest time, and that was delightful. But at other times there were many opportunities for talking about what everyone had seen and done.

We were making the project up as we went along. This was emergent curriculum with a Reggio twist. We adults had many discussions about intervening: Should we, Shouldn't we? When? One of the university students wanted to introduce the idea of homelessness into the discussion of houses. She had a class project to do, so she gathered some children and took them walking to the south of the park, where they saw homeless people. Nearby is a major eatery for the homeless, so children had plenty to observe. Our

student was interested, and she wanted the kids to be interested. They were—and also polite—to the point when their interest died and they went back to their houses.

Next year, however, this student aide will be the student teacher in our class, so she and I talked for a long time about what we could do with the homelessness theme. We decided it is worth pursuing because it's important to her. This year the excitement for me came from letting go of the planned unit and going instead where the children led us. Next year we will blend it all.

Thinking about this experience

Throughout the weeks when we went walking, I kept thinking about Caroline Pratt and the City and Country School in New York so many years ago, her walking all around Greenwich Village with her children, and then coming back to the classroom to re-create with blocks what they had seen (Pratt 1948). Our children did this too, and more. Our neighborhood hadn't the tremendous variety of New York City, but it had a lot for us. Now that we have moved back to our permanent school site, I am thinking of new possibilities for walks in this neighborhood. Our Meyer Street neighborhood and the tomato-colored house were special, but there is still more to be discovered.

Erik Erikson's (1950) early stages of life-cycle development help order our thinking about a child's growth in kindergarten. It is necessary for children to establish trust, behave autonomously, take initiative in self-directed activity, and move toward industry—that is, competent work in response to the expectations of school. Kindergarten curriculum that tries to begin with industry, often in the form of assigned worksheets, builds on no foundation of identity and understanding. Many children simply don't get it, and many never recover from their confusion, remaining bewildered all through school.

Curriculum emerges by need and choice

Emergent curriculum topics don't necessarily originate with the children. In Kay Stritzel Rencken's class the study of houses emerged out of practical circumstances—the school's temporary move to a new neighborhood full of houses and the children's restlessness in this location's inadequate outdoor play space.

Kay explains, "By spring, I wanted out of there. The children weren't exhibiting the sort of outdoor play behavior I value. They weren't focused in their play; they just ran around and around. I expected some of that every Monday morning as children reoriented themselves to school space and with each other, but not all week!"

Clearly, the children wanted out too. So out they went, on weekly walks around the neighborhood. Kay had checked out the neighborhood's possibilities months earlier, before school began in the fall. But she had learned, as all child-centered teachers must, to wait for the children, giving them all the time they needed (while in the process of separating from home) to orient themselves to the place, to the people big and little, and to the materials and what could be done with them. Learning to live together as Kay's children did in this new place, is basic curriculum for 5-year-olds at school (Jones & Nimmo 1994).

The goal of emergent curriculum is to support all children in their construction of genuine understanding. If this is to happen, children must buy into the possibilities of any curriculum topic and make some part of it their own. That can happen only if there are many activity choices, many different hooks to catch the widely varying interests and skills of the children in a class.

If the children in Kay's class had not risen to the bait or not shown enthusiasm about houses, there would have been no house project. Kay would have let it go and cast about for other possibilities. She liked the idea of looking at houses, but she wasn't wedded to it. There were many more ideas in her head, in the neighborhood, in the children's heads, in books, and in the unexpected events that happen from day to day.

Kay's confidence enables her to plan—but also to let go when ideas fail to fly. As it turns out, she didn't need to let go of houses as a topic for study. The children buy into it eagerly. She offers them a great many hooks, of course—exploring, drawing, colors, storytelling, a backyard farm, toilet holes, block building. And the room fills with children's drawings and buildings. They generously critique each other's work, noticing what is included and what was left out, recognizing that everyone sees things differently. They listen to each other and take turns. Kay describes these 5- and 6-year-olds as capable of half an hour's whole-group discussion about houses without once raising their hands to be called on. She makes it all sound easy.

Kindergarten curriculum that tries to begin with industry builds on no foundation of identity and understanding.

It isn't that easy. And Kay is a veteran teacher in a school full of resources and support. Her skills and knowledge make her decisionmaking intuitive to the point that she is hard pressed to analyze how it's done. But in Kay's words here's a glimpse:

> In this all-day program the children have two hours of choice time every morning—an hour outdoors, an hour indoors. This may give the impression that everything is free and open and easy, but it's not! We adhere to a clear schedule, not in clock time but in sequence, so that children can count on the fact that every day there'll be time to play outdoors, build with blocks, paint, rest, and meet together in small and large groups.
>
> We do a lot of direct work as well, toward the living-together values of sociability, community, and gaining one's voice, and issues of bias. We talk and share and demonstrate care, love, and respect for one another in song, books, and talk throughout the day, in order to develop a sense of trust. Children can anticipate ample opportunities for pursuing their own interests in many active ways, without premature interruption. Generous scheduling helps them become generous with each other.

Marsha Williams, whose story follows, shares Kay's goal for developing a program responsive to every child. She begins the year with the hope of carrying out an inquiry-based science curriculum using preselected monthly themes. For various logistical and personal reasons, this plan peters out during the fall. Feeling discouraged, she simply operates on cruise control, a survival strategy available to experienced teachers. So if it's

January, what do we start talking about in a traditional curriculum? Valentine's Day, of course. Marsha has holiday boxes stored; she can pull out party and craft resources, even props for a play. She is open to the children's ideas.

As a longtime preschool teacher, Marsha has learned to pay real attention to children's ideas and needs and to provide choices among activities. But this is her first year in kindergarten, and she has never had a Michael before—not this Michael, who is reading at fifth-grade level and gives promise of being bored in kindergarten. In meeting this challenge, one day she hands him a book of children's tales from Shakespeare. Why Shakespeare? It was just there.

The project that emerges, much to her surprise, comes out of the book and out of two children's heads. Why Romeo and Juliet? "It's all about love," says 5-year-old Elizabeth. "And Valentine's Day is about love."

—BJ

Introducing Marsha Williams

Marsha began her teaching career in 1982 as a child care provider in the public schools of Bellevue, Washington, a growing city of 100,000 just across the lake from Seattle. Working with 3- to 10-year-olds from 6:30 A.M. to noon each day sparked her interest in learning more about meaningful programming for children.

Marsha went back to school and completed an early childhood program in the community college. The district hired her as a preschool teacher. Four years later, having completed her bachelor's degree and teaching credential, she became a kindergarten teacher in the same school. Her story is about her first year in kindergarten.

Bellevue is a progressive district, providing ample resources and inservice opportunities for its teachers and allowing a wide range of teaching styles. Teachers are encouraged to take an active role at the district level, and Marsha is a part of the early childhood task force. Teachers are given time to engage in reflective dialogue and problem solving with colleagues.

The school in Marsha's story is located in a predominantly middle- to upper-middle-class residential neighborhood. Fifty percent of the children are bused in from less-affluent neighborhoods. Approximately 75% of the children are European American, with Asian Americans the next largest group in the school, which enrolls 350 children. Early childhood programs in Marsha's school include district-supported child care and a parent-supported preschool.

Marsha's class is an all-day (six hours) program called KEEP (kindergarten extended experience program), in which funding for half the day is provided by parent tuition. It enrolls 24 children. Marsha has the assistance of an aide for three hours each day and has actively recruited parent volunteers.

2

It's All about Love: Romeo and Juliet

The year I was going to write my thesis, I had a fine plan for introducing a hands-on science curriculum in my kindergarten classroom to develop critical thinking in 5-year-olds. I was looking forward to applying an approach new to me and to documenting children's thinking processes. Science seemed the right place to begin.

Before Shakespeare: The plan that didn't work

I began in October with a unit on magnets, which I designed to follow the play/debrief/replay process advocated by Selma Wasserman for teaching elementary science (1990). Children would (1) experiment with the magnets at the discovery table; (2) participate in a teacher-directed lesson; (3) explore the room with magnets, make observations, and then debrief in small-group time; and (4) return the magnets to the discovery table ready for replay. In replay, children would have more opportunities to examine the materials, again with the focus on thinking, and perhaps the materials would draw them deeper into more substantive inquiries. I planned to use a tape recorder and camcorder to document the

dialogue, then replay the tapes for myself to gain insights into how children think. On the day I first put out the magnets, I scheduled an hour for the experience. A class parent arrived to help. We set up the tape recorder. It was exciting.

Later that week I brought home the tape to transcribe. I turned on the tape recorder and waited. And waited. There was nothing to transcribe; something had not gone according to plan. Perhaps my batteries were low. Trying again the next day, I used the alternating current adapter. But again, when I played the tape at home, there was nothing.

Several weeks later I mentioned my woes to a teacher friend. She responded sympathetically, shaking her head and saying with great wisdom, "Yes, those magnets will do it to tapes every time." It had never occurred to me that the magnets were strong enough to erase the recording. I told myself there would be more opportunities for recording.

But time slipped away. It was mid-November before I realized I had not yet implemented my plans for the next science topic, sink-and-float. I felt off balance for a number of personal/professional reasons. My father was critically ill. My principal, who had allowed me autonomy as a preschool teacher, was putting new demands on me now that I was teaching kindergarten. I felt worn out, unsure if I would make it to June. Would I myself sink or float?

I tried putting these issues aside and set up the room. Unlike the magnets, the sink-or-float materials didn't interfere with recording equipment, but I was unable to cope with transcribing the tapes. I decided I would have to rely on anecdotal records and the camcorder, but how could I do this with all the interruptions that happen in a room with twenty-five 5-year-olds?

A play begins

During December and January I continued asking debriefing questions of the children, but I had given up on my thesis work. I made no attempt to record children's replies or the wonderful conversations they had. Interestingly, though, debriefing was no longer a separate event; it was becoming an integrated part of our explorations, and not only in science.

In the last week of January, I asked the children what they would like to do for Valentine's Day—a party, or what? Chester thought we should have a party with valen-tines and food. Tyler thought we should create a puppet show, which sounded manageable. Ben suggested we do a play, and I thought about "Mother Goose," which would be appropriate for their age. I had visions of making cute, little pig noses out of small, paper souffle cups, as I'd done a few years before when my preschoolers acted out "The Three Little Pigs" story. My mind was racing ahead, thinking of materials and props I already had and possible places to find more.

Hands were still up in the air, waving for attention. Everyone had an idea. We had been sitting in our circle for a long time, and I was pleased that most of the children were still engaged. I also realized I was pushing my luck, so I said, "One more and then we'll stop for a while." I called on Elizabeth. A serious child, with long dark hair and bangs that came to the top of her large expressive brown eyes, Elizabeth cocked her head to the side and spoke shyly, "We could do 'Romeo and Juliet.'"

I was surprised, shocked, in fact! How did this child connect "Romeo and Juliet" with Valentine's Day? Is this an example of higher-order thinking? "Why Romeo and Juliet?" I asked her.

"Valentine's Day is about love, and Romeo and Juliet are about love," said Elizabeth.

Elizabeth had made this connection based on her prior knowledge of Valentine's Day and her new knowledge of the story of Romeo and Juliet. During quiet reading time, Michael, a classmate reading at a fifth-grade level, had been sharing with Elizabeth a book of Shakespearean tales I had given him at the suggestion of a colleague. I had wondered aloud, "What am I going to do about Michael? He shows off his smarts in front of the other

---

Serious Players in the Classroom

Selma Wasserman describes the focus of and the value in the play/debrief/replay learning sequence:

play—hands-on exploration of materials

debrief—discussion that the teacher facilitates, paraphrasing the children's ideas and encouraging analysis by asking open-ended questions

replay—further exploration with the same or additional materials

Under these conditions [children] learn habits of thinking, and they become more self-initiating, responsible, creative, and inventive.

Source: Reprinted, by permission of the publisher, from S. Wassermann, *Serious Players in the Primary Classroom*, p. 25 (New York: Teachers College Press). © 2000 by Teachers College, Columbia University. All rights reserved.

kids." My friend responded, "See if he can read this." Michael could. He and Elizabeth respected each other's abilities and had become friends.

"Romeo and Juliet!" How could we ever do this? I was thinking. The children all started looking at each other, talking and giggling. Michael thought this was the best idea he had ever heard. His large eyes grew larger, his mouth flew open, and he waved his arms. He knew exactly who he wanted to be—Romeo's best friend. Hesitantly, I told them okay, that we'd give it a try. I looked at the clock; circle time had gone on for 40 minutes and amazingly the children were still eagerly involved.

Later that evening I began to think about how I could explain to the children there was no way we could do "Romeo and Juliet" by February 14. "Let's just have a great party!" I would say, I thought. But the next morning when I shared my thoughts with the children, they favored having the party *and* doing the play. So I proposed that we do the play at a later date, and they agreed.

Whew! But that's what happens when you involve children in classroom decisions. Some day, some place in another world and time, I would like to meet up with John Dewey and have a good chat about running a democratic classroom.

Casting the play

I began reading to the class a simplified version of "Romeo and Juliet" from *Favorite Tales from Shakespeare* (Miles 1976). Occasionally Michael read a paragraph or two as well. As we read, I took a large sheet of chart paper and drew a circle in the middle, in which I wrote the word *characters*. Then, on several rays going out from the circle, I wrote *Romeo, Juliet, Mercutio, Benvolio, Juliet's nurse* (meaning *Nanny* to the kids), *Mr. and Mrs. Capulet, Paris, Tybalt, the Prince, the guards, Friar* (meaning *preacher* to the kids),

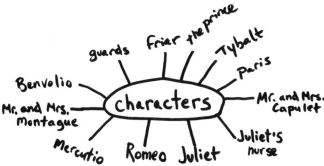

and *Mr. and Mrs. Montague*—all the characters in the story.

Next we began to talk about the characters. "What kind of person does Tybalt sound like?" I asked. Michael and Chester both said he was a good fighter. Ben reminded us that Romeo killed Tybalt. "What do you think about Romeo?" I asked. "Does he sound like a nice guy? Is he someone your parents would let you play with? What do you think about him sneaking into a party to meet Juliet? Would you ever sneak into a party?"

All the girls answered no to sneaking into a party; they thought it was wrong. Jill, the leader of that discussion, has a strong sense of right and wrong. Michael thought it would be great fun. Then Chester, Ben, Ian, and several other boys began to boast how they would break in and eat all the food and have sword fights. I couldn't help laughing with them in their enthusiasm.

As we continued with the story, we took time to talk about more of the characters. I explained that Juliet's nurse was like a nanny or a baby-sitter. We talked about Tybalt. The children thought he sounded like someone who had a bad temper, and no one wanted to play with him. The children could relate to Paris, a cousin to Juliet, for many had cousins themselves.

Each day I asked the children what had happened in the story the day before. We recapped, using chart paper to write the main points, and then I went on with the story until they got antsy. Often they listened for a long time and protested when I closed the book. They were clearly caught up in the drama, talking about it, responding eagerly to my questions and beginning to ask their own.

They were asking thinking questions; we were debriefing, I noticed happily. "What if you wanted to play with someone and your parents told you no, how would you convince them to let you play with that person?" I asked. The more confident children were the ones doing most of the talking. "I'd just play with them," said Lisa. I asked again, "But Lisa, if your parents said no, what would you do?" "I'd just play with them," she replied. Eventually Lisa and Michael were able to explain how they would tell their parents about the good points of the person in question: "He's an okay kid, and you should be nice to people." At this, other children nodded their heads in agreement.

After two weeks we had finished the reading and were ready to work on the play. First, children would sign up for parts. Out came the chart paper, and again we listed the characters in the play and talked about each. I began by letting the children sign up for the parts of their choice. And did they ever! Although only Ben and Chester signed up to play Romeo, eight boys and one girl signed up for the guards. Michael signed up for Tybalt but also for several other roles. Eight girls signed up for Juliet.

At this point I reintroduced the children to the story's many different characters. There was Nurse/ Nanny/Baby-sitter (whom Juliet loved), the Friar, and the moms and dads of Juliet and Romeo. Still, there were not enough acting parts for everyone, so I began talking about all the support people who make a play

possible. We talked about wardrobe and lighting people, stagehands, ushers, set designers. Soon we had more than enough roles to go around.

I had to ask some children to switch roles, and they graciously did. Chester said, "Sure, I'll be the prince. Can I wear a crown?" Amy, always poised, agreed to play Tybalt. Lisa thought she might enjoy being the preacher who gives Juliet the fake poison and then gets to "do that marriage thing" for Romeo and Juliet. There were negotiations and decisions about who would play which roles. Beverly—who originally wanted to play either Juliet or a guard—agreed to hand out programs. Andy switched roles as well, changing from his first-choice role as a guard over to Romeo's friend Benvolio.

Beginning with props

We began talking about sets and props for our play. "What do you think Juliet's house looked like?" I asked. First, I saw a lot of shrugged shoulders, and then Michael shouted out, "A castle." I asked him why he thought it was a castle, and he said that it was long ago, "That's why." "Well then," I continued, "what do you think her castle looked like?" "Just a castle," the children all told me. "Do you think it looked like Cinderella's castle?" I queried. More shrugged shoulders.

I wasn't sure what to do. On the one hand, I could see possibilities for getting into a big study of housing: different types of structures, how they are built, and kinds of houses people live in in different cultures or different historical times. We could tally and graph how many of us live in houses, apartments, and condos. We could investigate the materials that houses are made of and the skills of the people who build houses (Katz & Chard 1989). But what about getting on with the play?

The kids didn't seem that interested in the houses angle, and I didn't want to risk losing their enthusiasm for "Romeo and Juliet." Still, I decided to take it just one step further. That evening I went to the library and checked out the *Castle* video narrated by David Macaulay (his book *Castle* [1982] is in our block area). The children were entranced.

Messing about

After we watched the video, things I was uncertain about started falling into place. However, I still wasn't confident that all this activity would actually come together as a play. But that was okay with me. So far we were having great fun with "Romeo and Juliet"—just "messing about," as David Hawkins phrases it (1974b).

I brought out chart paper once again and wrote at the top, Things We Need. I asked the children what they thought we needed for the play. What could we use for the castle? For the costumes? We decided we needed boxes to make castle walls, materials for costumes, paints, and also food. I was not sure why we needed the food—perhaps because Romeo and Juliet met at a party and there is always food at a party. So a newsletter went home with the children and alerted parents to our needs and asked for help in making costumes.

Before long, Sarah came in one morning and said that her dad would give us boxes from the furniture store. Lisa's mom also donated boxes, square ones in which windows had been packed, with a cutout center in the shape of a hexagon. The shape fascinated the children. "Is there anything in our room shaped the same way?" I asked. A chorus of voices sounded, "Yes, the yellow hexagon shape in our pattern blocks."

One parent offered to help the children make ladies' cone hats with long flowing veils. The children learned how to fold and cut large poster board into a triangle shape and staple it to make a cone. As they manipulated the materials, they saw each hat take shape from the beginning as a rectangle to a triangle to a cone. A lot of conversation followed, some of it on the need for costumes and the types of materials to use. I had no idea where this play was going, but the messing about was a fun experience. Even I had a cone hat.

The day that Nathaniel's dad—a weekly classroom volunteer—worked with us, he took over the table where, at the request of several boys, making paper hats was available as a choice-time activity. A few girls wandered over to try too. When several hats were finished, Nathaniel's father asked the children, "What kind of characters wore hats like these?" "Robin Hood!" they all answered and instantly transformed themselves into this hero outlaw and his merry men. A few went for their cardboard swords, but I intervened.

When the large boxes arrived from the furniture store, we talked about painting them to look like a castle. "What color paint do we need?" I asked. "Gray," was the reply. If we only have black and white, how can we make gray? "We can mix black and white together," said Jill. "Okay, how can we make our work look like bricks?" I asked. Children brought out the castle book from the block area, and all gave a closer look to the design of the bricks. I found three two-inch, sponge paint brushes and put three very high-energy kids to work right away painting boxes.

Beyond messing

We were really on our way now. We talked about the play: I asked, "What do words mean? Could you use different words and mean the same thing?" We talked about love, hate, and getting mad at people and

What Is Love?

Mrs. W: Tell me about love.

Elizabeth: Valentine's Day is about love.

Mrs. W: Yes, but what is love?

Nathaniel: Yuck, it's that kissy stuff.

Michael: You know, it's kissing and when people get married.

Anna: I love ice cream.

Michael: Yeah, but are you gonna marry it? Ooooh, you're gonna marry ice cream.

Chester: That's dumb. No one can marry ice cream.

Lisa: You don't have to marry someone to love them.

Mrs. W: Can you say some more?

Lisa: I love my mom and dad, but they are already married. And I love my grandma.

What Is Hate?

Mrs. W: My question to you is, When is it okay to hate?

Michael: When somebody lies. I offer no comment. I just want to listen.

Tyler: I hate when my brother gets into my stuff.

Ian: I'm not sure it's okay to hate.

Ashley (our beauty queen): I hate it when I get dirty.

Ben: What if someone is mean to you?, You might hate them.

Mrs. W: Would you hate them forever or maybe not if they said they were sorry?

Ben: If they say they're sorry, then I won't hate them.

Children's feelings are usually strong, and they are learning to find their voices in this classroom. I can feel good about that: a classroom where children can talk and be taken seriously by grownups in the room. *Love, hate, sorry*—words used every day here. "Ooooh, I love your dress, your hairbow, your drawing." One day there's a fuss; by the afternoon the children have made up. And the next day is a brand new day just waiting for all the new love, hate, and sorry.

---

forgiving. Our curriculum, as defined by Elizabeth, was "about love" and related passions. These feelings are part of children's real-life experience.

I never considered providing the children with a script; their actions and words would be their own, improvised from their understanding of the play. Only at the beginning would we have a narrative introduction to be read by those children who were self-taught readers.

We talked about whether the same props could do double duty for both the castle party scene and the church and how we would make this work. Nathaniel thought that we could use the window boxes with the hexagon shapes to make the castle look like a church.

Nathaniel had been to France earlier in the year. He kept a journal during his visit, and

in it he had drawn several of the rose windows he'd seen in cathedrals. Now he knew just what he needed—colored cellophane paper. "You know, Mrs. Williams, the see-through paper." When I located some, he quickly began tearing long strips and taping them together with large pieces of tape. It was his own interpretation of the work of masters, and after the play it hung for many months in his living room window for all to see.

We talked about music for our play. I mentioned the overture, the song that is played before an operatic play. Elizabeth suggested that we have sweet music, and someone else asked the question, "What is sweet music?" "You know, romantic music," said Elizabeth. By the time our conversation had ended, I had all these ideas written down on chart paper.

We decided to have soft opening music while people came into the room and found a place to sit. We had a wild range of different suggestions for theme music to be played through the performance: Turtle music (I think this was for the Ninja Turtles), rock 'n roll for our party, rap by M.C. Hammer, and New Kids on the Block, The Judds, Madonna, Dolly Parton, Michael Jackson (a love song of his, but no one knew the name), Elvis, and TV's Bart (from The Simpsons). Michael told me he wanted the music from *Rocky* played for his character, Mercutio, who was a terrific sword fighter. Because Tybalt was described as "a pain," someone suggested that we play the theme from *Jaws* when Tybalt enters onstage. *Jaws* meant danger lurking about, something waiting to happen, and that was hot-headed Tybalt.

The usual three R's and more

Somewhere along the line the children had taken their "messing about" during choice time and turned it into a first-rate curriculum. Through playing a classic drama, they were learning not only about love and hate, feelings of great importance in a 5-year-old's life, but also about the three R's. We read together, sharing reading and writing (drawings of the characters in the play, with dictated stories). Arithmetic took the form of our measuring space in the room, deciding where the four stone-wall boxes would fit best. Measuring (estimation) skills were also used in making cone hats and garments. Children learned new vocabulary such as *overture, stage left, stage right, upstage, cone.* Their learning of familiar

shapes such as squares, rectangles, and hexagons was reinforced. The tasks asked of the children were not taken out of context; they had personal meaning.

The children learned more about the use of writing by observing me taking notes (I always had chart paper out). They understood very quickly that it was okay to write down a word's sounds as heard, then later check its spelling and rewrite the word. (I did this all the time.) They investigated related topics during choice time (learning about new ideas), and used communication skills to talk about their work. They learned about working cooperatively.

I observed the children's growth in cognitive skills as they made connections between previous knowledge and new learning; they made inferences. What had started as a choice-time activity now extended into the writing, math, and reading portions of the day. The curriculum became truly integrated.

Finishing touches

Time drew closer for our play's performance. The children had practiced enough, and the set and props were ready. I wanted to capture the moment, before anyone grew weary of playing Romeo and Juliet. There were one or two little details to finish—such as programs. Programs from real plays, I hoped, would help get the idea across to the children. Already we had written down our thoughts about programs and what should be in them.

During morning choice time, several children drew pictures for our program covers. We chose two drawings. At morning recess I typed up our thoughts for the inside script of the program. We were done, and it was time to perform.

Opening night/day

The big day arrived. The children and I set up our painted castle boxes. Two were window boxes, one the stained-glass window to represent the abbey church, and the other Juliet's bedroom window, which we dressed up with cone hats. From an overhead beam in the classroom, we hung a tan shower curtain. Our luck held—the bottom of the curtain came right to the top of the boxes, providing us with a backstage. We had a stage and backdrop all in one.

Behind the backdrop we kept our costumes and a small table to hold props (swords, turbans, cone hats, crown, and flowers). We had a record player and our chosen music. As wardrobe lady, Sarah would hang up costumes and make sure things were picked up off the floor. It was Nathaniel's job to stand by the door and flick the lights to warn people that it was starting time. (Ahhh, permission to play with the lights—what power!)

To our dress rehearsal we invited the morning kindergartners from next door, the

preschoolers, and our third-grade reading buddies. We stayed backstage trying our best to remain quiet—a challenge—while our readers Michael, Ben, Chester, and Elizabeth read the opening lines from Michael's book, each taking a sentence or two:

> This story takes place in Italy in a town called Verona . . . . It is about two young lovers whose families were refusing to let them see each other . . . . The prince made a law that there would be no more fighting in the streets . . . . The opening scene begins with a party where the two young lovers meet.

I started the party music, and our performers stepped out on the stage. They stayed bunched together, and I realized that we had not talked about stage positions nor had I put chalk marks on the carpet. I whispered to them to spread themselves out. Our first performance took 45 minutes; we would have to trim that!

It was time for lunch and then for our afternoon matinee, the one to which the parents would come. We had shoved our desks against one wall to create audience space and borrowed chairs for parents. With parents and another class that we invited to attend, it was a full house—close to 50 people. Needless to say we were nervous, and a few of us got whiny. But it was time again to get ready; the show must go on. Once again I had a pep talk with the children about expected behavior. "Our parents are going to be here. Let's do a really good job so everyone can be proud," I said. The talk resembled a sports huddle, ending with a cheer. "Who the best?" "We are!"

Nathaniel was poised by the lights, waiting for his signal. Beverly, who had decided a costume was needed to do her job of handing out programs, danced around in a pink ballet costume, complete with tutu and matching slippers. Grandparents as well as parents came. The performers were excited to see their families. I was overwhelmed!

I put on our rock-and-roll party music, and the actors went on stage to the strains of "A-keep away from-a runaround Sue." The audience laughed and clapped. The children, not quite sure what the laughter was about, took it for themselves and really got into the party scene. The play went on, without any major hitches. It was a roaring success.

After the play

After each production there was an audience question-and-answer time for the actors. I opened the discussion by introducing the actors, and then we took questions from the floor. Some of the older children asked how Chester, Ben, Michael, and Elizabeth had memorized their parts. The four said no, that they didn't memorize, that they were really reading their script. (The three or four sentences by these four were the only scripted pieces in the play. All other dialogue was improvised.) Other guests asked about our special stained-glass windows. Lisa told how we got the boxes, and Nathaniel explained the stained-glass effect.

And there were more questions. How long had we been rehearsing and practicing the script? What were the materials for costumes? Who made them? (Nathaniel's mom helped sew up some straight seams.) How did Romeo die? How did Juliet die?

My goodness, I thought, weren't they watching? They were; they just didn't have the experience with the play that we did. Not only did we perform it, but also we studied it.

There were questions about our cone hats. Why didn't we wear them? Ashley did a nice job explaining how some things don't work out as you think they will. "Since the hats kept falling off," she said, "we decided to use them for decorations." Then there were questions about the castle: What was it made of? What was the curtain? My answer, "A shower curtain!" got gales of laughter.

A questioner asked if we were going to do another play. The children's answers were wonderful; they included, "Yes," "No," "You

never know," "You never know with this group," "You never know until you do it!"

There was yet another question about memorizing the parts: Who helped the children, and did they have a lot to memorize? Ben answered this one. He said, "We talked a lot about what words mean and how you can use more than one word to mean the same thing. So sometimes we used different words, but they all meant the same thing. We never had a script to memorize." On that closing note I knew the kids and I had made it. We hadn't just followed a safe course. We were risk takers, and it paid off.

Valuing risk taking as a goal for the children, I worked on it throughout the year. For instance, when I didn't know the answer to one of their questions—and this did happen—I responded, "I'm not sure. How do you think we could find the answer to that question?" The children saw that it's okay not to have all the answers, and we would go on from there.

In a safe learning environment in which children are respected and treated with dignity, we all can take risks in learning. Together we'll ask such questions as, "What do you think?" "Why do you think so? What's another way?" "What if . . . ?" "What questions do you have?" Together we begin the journey of becoming lifelong learners.

One door closes, another opens

In this challenging year, which began with my thesis idea in shambles, another project evolved. This one was designed by the children and grew, with my support as their teacher, to culminate in a final presentation. When teachers and children are models and co-players together, it's called *emergent curriculum*.

Elizabeth Jones and John Nimmo (1994) caution us that curriculum does not simply emerge from the children. It comes from teachers too! We are the ones who must have a vision of where we and the children can go together with their interests and ideas. We are the stage directors. Curriculum is our responsibility, not the children's.

Originally I had thought of debriefing as a systematic teacher-controlled procedure—as in "Now we're going to debrief." But as this theatrical project emerged, we spontaneously asked ourselves questions, supporting each other as we reflected on our classroom experiences with "Romeo and Juliet." The children were using the higher-order thinking skills I had originally hoped to promote. Although "Romeo and Juliet" was not a focus I would have planned for kindergartners, the children's intense interest in this project of their choice galvanized their thinking, creating, and inventing. They explained, debated, negotiated, and took responsibility for their decisions.

Debriefing became as natural as coming into our classroom each morning and hanging up our jackets. Replay followed just as naturally. Of children engaged in this process, Wassermann writes, "They grow in their capacity to understand the concepts or important ideas within the curriculum. Concepts are learned and understood via the primary route of practical experience, the only way in which learners at any age actually learn to understand" (1990, 25).

Our classroom hooked up with the outside world. My experiment in debriefing had not failed! My thesis focus reconnected, this time with the real work of children, that of making connections between the world outside and their own thinking.

I asked children to think beyond the first thing that came to mind. "What if . . . ?" "What do you think would happen if . . . ?" These became our questions of the day. What-do-you-think questions require anticipation, speculation, hypothesizing, and risk taking.

My asking the children, "Why do you think so?" required them to use reasoning based on experience or knowledge in order to justify a response or a point of view. What-if questions require an application of knowl-

edge to novel situations and an imagination or the imaginative use of learned information. When I asked children about the questions they had, their own interests and purposes gave the basis for their inquiry.

I expected responses from the children to my questions. I allowed a child to pass once, but then I would come back to her or him. Although this demand created some stress at times for our younger fives, the practice soon became routine.

This project worked easily into our regular schedule because it was important. We played with it daily, until its culmination in the "Romeo and Juliet" performance. Then it became the wonderful thing that had happened in our classroom, to be talked about for the remaining three months of the school year.

At the end of each project, according to Lilian Katz and Sylvia Chard (1989), time must be given for reflection so as to acknowledge the understanding of a topic. Our reflection came as a presentation of our production to the school and our parents. We had made it personal by using our own words. After the event we continued to play with the props. The children used the boxes to make homes and beds for dolls and for scooting each other around the room.

As a closing activity I arranged a visit to our local Village Theater. We were the only class scheduled, which made it a perfect visit for 25 children and 4 adults. The theater staff allowed the children to explore the stage, the orchestra pit, and the prop area behind the stage. Each child was able to handle some of the items the actors were using in their play. Had I thought to ask if we could bring a few of our own props with us, we could have done a scene from "Romeo and Juliet" on the real stage!

Elizabeth asked if the actors got to take their costumes home after the play (a big issue in our classroom, and we had voted yes since there was no reason to keep them at school). Our guide explained to the children that the theater rented many of the costumes and had to send them back to the store at the end of the play. The visit gave us an opportunity to compare our own acting experience with that of professional actors and to celebrate our own theatrical accomplishment with a picnic in the park afterward.

How we changed

In this classroom experience children's thinking changed when Michael shared his reading with Elizabeth, Ben, and Chester. What is *thinking*? The children's language changed, and they became interested in this new thing of "Romeo and Juliet." Small transformations of our old way of thinking occurred, and through a gradual evolution we were able to think and use more adaptive language, better fitted to the children's immediate environment. Our thinking became a continuous process.

The use of *we* is authentic; I learned with the children. Just as they became actively engaged in their learning, so I became actively engaged in mine. The children were curious about Romeo and Juliet's world; I was curious about the children's learning. During the process we became alert, confident in our abilities to figure things out and take initiative in saying what we honestly thought. We came up with

interesting ideas, problems, and questions. To put things into relationships challenged our thinking.

My confidence as a teacher was renewed as I realized my strength in letting the children pursue their own learning. I provided all kinds of materials and media (books, videos, and field trips) so they could make rediscoveries of knowledge. I gave them information and asked lots of questions. And I served as a resource to their collaborative creation of the production.

My classroom remained a safe place to grow, to activate the process of learning. Through this experience I found my niche in being a responsible teacher, helping children make connections to the world outside the classroom. With my children that year, we wove a very rich tapestry.

Creating a play and presenting it to an audience is a challenge for children of any age and especially for their teacher. Had Marsha Williams an investment in its success as a polished production, she would have had a stressful spring. But her life outside the classroom was already stressful; for her own survival she had essentially let go of being the perfect teacher and had committed herself to a view of how young children learn by being playful—messing about.

Who owns the project—Children or teacher?

Marsha's prior long-term experience was in preschool, where children's open-ended exploration of materials and ideas has been much more generally accepted than it has been in elementary schools. Some of her kindergarten parents had had children in her preschool class; relationships and trust were already established. She taught in a six-hour program, with an assistant for three hours in the morning. Marsha's extended day, consistent help, ongoing parent relationships, and competence as a teacher of young children were all factors enabling her to take risks, even in her first year on an elementary school faculty.

Marsha's discouragement as she finds herself unable to follow through on her carefully planned science curriculum gradually turns to delight as she follows the children's serendipitous interest in Romeo and Juliet. Shakespeare's story of passion and violence is not on any lesson plan for kindergartners! When a play is suggested, Marsha thinks of Mother Goose and little pig noses. But here is Michael, a precocious child with needs unlikely to be met in the usual kindergarten classroom. Later, Marsha believes that it is the play that kept the year from being boring for him, giving him a challenge worth doing, while also meeting the full range of children's needs by offering many choices at each step of the way.

The play also brings to the classroom aspects of a larger world. Passion and violence are not altogether outside 5-year-olds' experience. Mother Goose is not the only source of stories that may help them make sense of the complicated world they are growing up in.

When Marsha asks the children what sort of music they should have for their play, their suggestions go far beyond songs usually thought of as suitable for the young—Madonna, Dolly Parton,

Michael Jackson, and Elvis are among their requests. Taking their requests seriously, Marsha helps them create a version of a classic drama in which the courtiers enter to the refrain, "A-keep away from-a runaround Sue," and the actors learn, really learn, that you can use different words to say the same thing.

Like Kay, Marsha defines the children's work as their own rather than for show. For a long time she doesn't believe that a play can actually be produced. Like many early childhood educators, she is accustomed to valuing process more than product.

Often bemused, Marsha acts as gofer, the adult go-between in finding the tools and materials the children need. When the cone hats won't stay on, Marsha and the children brainstorm other possibilities and decide to decorate the castle with the hats. Thus a project that could have become quite inappropriate for 5-year-olds ("What do you mean, you're doing *Romeo and Juliet?*") remains the children's idea, within their control.

Carolyn Stringer, whose story comes next, is elementary school-trained and has seven years teaching experience in second grade and kindergarten. She is at a point of change in her thinking and is trying to become a genuinely child-centered teacher, building curriculum on children's play interests. She describes the challenge as "being true to an aesthetic vision of teaching"—a vision she is in the process of constructing for herself.

Inspired by reading about the Reggio Emilia approach and projects, she hopes to become the sort of teacher in whose classroom such wonderful things can happen. The high point of her year is an unexpected opportunity to visit Reggio programs in Italy, and she takes it, even though the sand project she describes in her story has just begun.

Returning to school, Carolyn is full of creative energy but has neither the flexible time nor the many supports enjoyed by teaching staff in Reggio Emilia, where long-term projects engage only a small group of children intensely. Carolyn is responsible for two dozen children in a short half-day program. She falls back on a familiar structure—committees of children logically organized to get a task done—which she has not seen in the Reggio program.

Without previous experience with emergent curriculum and under the pressure of time constraints, Carolyn's vision falters. Writing in her journal throughout the year, she repeatedly catches herself "reverting to values of imposing knowledge on children." She describes, "While they saw a hamster playroom, I saw an opportunity for a lesson on measurement. Instead of tossing the ball back, I would steal it."

—BJ

Introducing Carolyn Stringer

When Carolyn wrote her story, she was teaching kindergarten at Willamette Primary School in West Linn, Oregon. The original school, built in 1896 as the mill town was being born, sits on a steep hill overlooking the Willamette River. What began as a thriving town of blue-collar workers is now part of a rapidly growing suburb of Portland, and enrollment at the school is approaching 500.

An influx of baby boomers in the 1980s and 1990s raised the status and income of West Linn, but Old Town Willamette, with its turn-of-the-century storefronts and Queen Anne-style houses, still maintains a village-style quaintness. The ethnic character of the town has not changed much from that in the days when mill jobs were held exclusively by European Americans.

Carolyn taught in three different schools in the district where she has lived, moving into kindergarten after five years teaching in second grade. Her story takes place in her third year of teaching kindergarten, following a year's leave for graduate study. She teaches a morning class with children who are present for two and three-quarters hours. There are three kindergarten classes in the school this year; the other two, a morning and an afternoon, are taught by one full-time teacher.

With a class of 25, Carolyn has assistance daily from parent helpers, each of whom comes once a week or biweekly and supports children's work in small groups; fifth-grade helpers for about an hour during the spring; and a grandmotherly woman assigned to a child with Down syndrome but who helps with other children. The limitations imposed by time, numbers of students, and Carolyn's experience-based perceptions of what teachers are supposed to do generates a yearlong struggle as she works to invent for herself a new way of being a teacher—creating emergent curriculum.

Waiting for Curriculum to Happen— Then Building a Sandbox

After seven years of teaching, I felt dried up.

I had taken classes on the latest ideas, such as holistic, child-centered teaching. I had learned how to be a smooth technician—with every moment in my classroom accounted for, cramming lessons into micro-minutes to make the most use of time, and running on a rigid schedule, which I told myself was really flexible. I racked my brain to create an impressive *child-centered curriculum.*

At the end of my seventh year, I felt spent and was bored with my own efficiency. My compulsive schedule making left no room for children's initiative. Something—the joy of the spontaneous moment—was missing. My focus on performance was killing my love of teaching.

I decided to take a year's leave of absence to pursue a master's degree and reassess this job of educating children. During that year, I discovered my true quest: to restore the voice of the artist in myself. I found inspiration in reading about the progressive preschool education practices in Reggio Emilia, Italy. Here, as I understood it, the arts support a consistent vision of young children as competent and promote teaching as a response to that competence (Edwards, Gandini, & Forman 1993).

Graduate work was my first experience in an educational institution empowering the learner. The challenges came from my own questions and passions and the freedom to move ever forward. As a student, I accomplished what I had desired as a teacher. As I trusted my own voice and my own demands, my educational pursuit became a canvas of unexpectedness, like the experience of a child at the easel. A young child doesn't try to control the destiny of her painting, unless she is painting to please someone else. This is the same critical choice we make as teachers: teach authentically or teach to please another power?

When I returned to teaching a year later, I felt like a first-year teacher, carrying new knowledge but with no known way of implementing it. I had no structure for what I wanted. I knew the terms, such as *emergent curriculum* and *project-based learning,* but I was unsure how to apply them myself. I had only an unwavering vision of supporting children to construct their own learning, which sustained me through a year of unrelenting self-examination.

Setting up a kindergarten classroom

In the first days of preparing my classroom, every decision seemed vital. Instinct battled with logic. I questioned every idea, doubting it but going ahead anyway. I experimented with room setup. I painted, scrubbed, and labeled. I pondered over furniture arrangements. I also wrote in my journal.

> I know that my own ability to work and play hard is often dictated by a pleasing environment . . . . This is the first time in eight years of teaching that I have had the luxury of leisurely and selectively setting up a classroom. I am enjoying the process.
>
> But the children haven't even arrived! How much do I organize before they come? Am I being possessive of the environment? Am I able to let go more? How can children feel ownership in a classroom I have already created?

I continued to struggle with these questions as I planned and ordered the space. I wanted to find a balance—setting the stage to make clear that beauty and order are important while leaving the space open to children's work and ideas over time. Writing in my journal, I reassured myself:

> By displaying the materials beautifully I have given the children a starting point, a frame of reference on which we can build further. One of my personal talents happens to be room arranging/decorating, and all teachers, I believe, should bring their particular talents to the classroom. It is a place for the teacher as well, and I would not want to give children the message that their interaction with the room is significant but mine is not. But what I have done is temporary and subject to change by the children.

Getting to know one another

With Laurie, the other kindergarten teacher, I planned an open house for the children and their families. Our goal was to make this a gentle, positive way for children to meet their new teachers and to entice them into wanting to come back. We wanted the children to make something they would leave in the room and find again on the first day of school. We agreed on the idea of small ornaments, each with a child's name on it, to be hung outside the classroom door. Cutting out ornaments was inappropriate, however, since some children could not cut yet.

Laurie had ideas for alternatives. I didn't, but none of hers felt right to me. An activity such as cutting out paper apples, something I had done in the past, I felt was meaningless. What goes through a child's mind when such a task is her first school experience? And what do apples have to do with starting school?

It took me a day to rethink *my* purpose for the open house. What did I want to explore in the first weeks with my new class? The children—their lives, their feelings, their fascinations.

Eventually we agreed to invite the children to paint self-portraits at the open house. They could choose from a variety of skin colors and then sponge paint to create skin and hair and use cotton-tipped swabs to add a face and shirt. We mounted the portraits on color ovals, added a name badge, and hung them outside the door, where they remained all year as a well-loved testimony to the importance of the people inside. (The next year at the open house, all the adults who worked in the classroom made portraits of themselves too.)

Waiting for themes to emerge

During the first months of school, I waited for themes to emerge and struggled to define for myself the role of teacher as researcher and co-constructor of knowledge. My only experience to date was with themes that were teacher chosen, integrated topics for study. These might not have anything to do with the children's lives.

I wanted to uncover children's passions. But I didn't know how to go about discovering what really captivated the children in my class. And when something with potential occurred, I floundered, not sure of what to do with it.

Even as possible themes arose and I made choices both wise and unwise, I was never quite sure what was really inspiring to the children. I had moved from being completely in charge of the curriculum to stepping back and just waiting for something to happen. Neither approach was very productive with the children.

Early in the school year, I wondered when the emergent curriculum would start. In truth, it already had, in subtle ways. I expected the dramatic and was getting simplicity. After reading *The Little Engine That Could* (Piper [1930] 1998), we cut out train cars. Some children walked around the room proudly displaying theirs as they finished. Sean Michael was saying, "Mine's an Old West train that carries gold." I took him over to the computer and asked him to repeat his story. We keyed it in, and at once everyone else wanted a turn. So at choice time I asked the children to tell their train stories.

The next day we put the train cars in the middle of the room for the children to graph different colors, then types. I was hoping someone would suggest making one long train. Thank goodness for Skyler! He suggested that we hook them together to make one train and hang it up in the classroom. If we had a train, we would need tracks, and this led to discussion about creating a mural complete with hillsides, a sky, and so on. I put everyone into focus groups, and the next day I met with the grass/hillside group to plan the first part of the mural.

Although I had begun to understand for myself the construction of one's own reality (Piaget 1954), it didn't carry over yet into my practice as a teacher. It's not an emergent curriculum when the teacher has an expected outcome and tries to lure the children to discover it (Bredekamp & Rosegrant 1992). Although making a train was an idea Skyler voiced, I had already thought of it. So from that point on, I owned the activity.

I should have stopped leading the children and asked them how they thought we could put the train cars together. I needed to get inside their heads and capture their visions. Then taking this path, I could have helped them talk about what a mural is and what we needed to do to make one. Instead, for the rest of the year, only Skyler periodically mentioned the train mural, no one else. He was the only child with real investment in it.

I wrote in my September journal:

They play wonderfully, eagerly, messily. Today Sean Michael and A.J., who tend to dominate the block area thus far, asked me for more railroad tracks. "Can we get some from another classroom?" they said. "The other kindergarten is using them," I answered, moving on. When I came back later, A.J. beamed at me and said, "We made our own." He had taken several long flat blocks and created extra tracks.

Never underestimate the ingenuity of children! If they need something and don't have it, they create it, without encouragement from me. I think I could learn something from that.

In October I wrote,

I need to make a list of everything that seems to matter to the children. Adults are a big interest right now. The school is so new, so exciting. They love to yell a hello to Mr. Gregory (the custodian) and Mr. Potts (the librarian) when they see them in the hallway. But what else? I am so busy every moment that it's hard to watch for themes that emerge.

Had I made this list of the things important to my children, and really paid attention to it, might I have started something? In retrospect it seems obvious to me that they were still fascinated by the workings of school. But in my plan we had covered that, and I assumed we were ready to move on.

What more did the children want to know about the adults in the school? And was it just about the adults? What else mattered to them? We went to a pumpkin patch one brilliant autumn day, and the children were mesmerized when I read a book on pumpkins, later even turning our playhouse into a pumpkin stand. Bunkbeds too kept coming into our group discussions. The children talked about getting such beds, putting them together, sleeping in them. Should we build bunkbeds for dramatic play? Equipped to explore these questions and topics that kept popping up, I could have set out on a path of investigation. I could have found answers to what I agonized over for a year: how to know the passions of my children.

Zippity, the hamster

"We're getting a hamster tomorrow," I wrote in my October journal. "I need to seize the moment." The children named her Zippity. They created a playhouse out of blocks for Zippity and then watched to see where she would go. Some children used our materials for inventions to build furniture—a television set, a table, a food dish—for Zippity's house.

One day Zippity rolled around the room inside a plastic hamster ball. This was very exciting for many children! I grabbed a notebook to document our conversation:

Skyler: Teacher! This is like Hamster OMSI! *(Oregon Museum of Science and Industry)*

Mrs. S: Hamster OMSI?

Skyler: Well, it's gooder than plain old OMSI!

Lisa: Better, you mean.

Megan: Zippity's taking a bath in there.

Mrs. S: How do you know?

Brianna: She's licking herself!

(Zippity rolls about, bumping into things and getting out of tight places. The children rush to make tunnels with their legs for the hamster to go through.)

Christopher: I'm not sure I can go down much farther. *(He's almost doing the splits.)*

Jessica: She's spinning herself around in circles! I wonder if she'll go under the table?

I recorded this happening in the class journal and, to the children's delight, included a copy in the parent newsletter.

Zippity remained a fascination in the children's play all year, and new ideas would come and go. We read books about hamsters, and stories about Zippity recurred in our classroom journal. Some children wrote

letters to our hamster in their journals, and others were constantly building playrooms. Zippity became a continuing means for facilitating language and play.

A week before school was out, Zippity died in her sleep. Although death had first come to our classroom when Jonni's uncle died, followed by Sean's grandpa, with Zippity we all experienced death's finality. The funeral service the children planned for her was somber and poetic. They put gifts in a shoe-box casket and placed Zippity under a tree in a flower bed where children don't usually play at recess. Some cried. Some said a few words. On top of Zippity's grave, we planted a violet. We sang to our hamster and then quietly filed back into the classroom.

In spite of all the hamster events of the year, I never considered Zippity a real project theme. Within a few weeks of Zippity's arrival, I had written in my journal:

> When the hamster came, I thought this was it. The children voted on names and created a playroom out of blocks. Activity escalated, but after a few days it tapered off. Is this because I throw too much at them? Possibly I'm too impatient, and we're all teetering on the edge of a big happening or a big "drowning."

I realized later that I was too focused on the details to see the big picture. Also I was preoccupied with my need to turn interests into lessons. For example, when the hamster playroom building first began, I found myself thinking about doing mini-units on measurement and having the children design a hamster playroom on graph paper, with specific criteria, and then go on to build it from their plan, using boxes and junk materials. Yet we didn't do this, because I guess I knew at some level that this was not how it should happen. The children's fascination was not with the mathematics of designing hamster play spaces but with the drama of hamster behavior in these spaces. At this point, obstacles and amusements were the attraction.

Later, as Zippity started skidding around the room, it occurred to me that until now we had made only small playrooms with the blocks, and I wondered if we could build a giant hamster playroom in the room? I thought that maybe we could eventually explore the idea of an obstacle course for Zippity or even visit Hamster OMSI on a field trip to the Oregon Museum of Science and Industry. But I did not pursue the obstacle course or field trip ideas any further; each seemed more like another isolated idea that didn't fit into a meaningful whole.

What is the meaningful whole?

I was beginning to grasp how to sustain meaningful experiences for children, but our day together still felt fragmented. Most of it was structured into isolated experiences that rarely seemed to overlap—journals, word cards, shared reading experiences, math stations. The children were absorbed in each, but I kept asking myself, "Why? Why are we doing this? Is it the best use of our precious time?" I wrote in my journal:

> During play—or choice time—the children are independent, decisive, resourceful, confident, assertive, responsible. That's 40 minutes a day. They do not fall apart the rest of the time, but it doesn't feel the same. I do not have the same exuberant feeling of standing back and watching them tackle thinking.
>
> Is choice in my room too strictly confined to choice time? What would happen during activity/center/instructional time if I said, "I want you to figure _____ out. You know where the room materials are. You may solve it however you wish. Now begin." Is this too loose for 5-year-olds? Maybe the answer would depend on the problem.
>
> I am concerned that the process of children's digging deep inside themselves to find answers and seeking out others to help is not happening enough during work time. I do see these things during the children's play. I don't want to lead them through every activity. I want them to take over the room. Somehow projects are what I envision.

I found myself fumbling for a way to connect all the loose pieces, but this seemed like a backwards and unworkable approach. You cannot expect to take pieces and fit them together meaningfully into something. Instead, when a larger purpose is identified, routines like journal writing and word cards take on new life. I kept looking for a larger purpose, a *real* project.

Exploring sand

In March I brought back some beautiful sand from the coast, and consequently my kids began inquiring about beaches. We examined sand in several exploratory ways. And then, getting the idea from an article about the Reggio approach (Forman 1989), I asked the kindergartners to write what sand is and diagram their ideas of where it comes from. Their responses amazed me and revealed how important it is to start with children's thinking and what they know. Most of them had already decided that sand was crushed up rock or lava, or even salt. I was fascinated to find out where they thought sand originated. Most of the children believed that people smash rocks with hammers or machines to create sand and then ship it to the beach in trucks.

At the time, I was reading Kieran Egan's *Teaching as Storytelling* (1989), which suggested a next step to me. The next day at school a letter mysteriously appeared outside our door. It was from a sea animal asking the children for help (since it seems that the sand on the Oregon coast is disappearing). The animal challenged the kids to find out where sand comes from so the animals could have more of it. I had invented a provocation, "a stimulating event or activity that gets the children thinking about the topic" (Edwards, Gandini, & Forman 1993, 255).

My intention was to have the children further explore the sand and its origin. But the letter evoked an interest in the charac-

ter: Who was this animal writing a letter to us? There was excited inquiry and letter writing by the children in return. But after several letters, interest waned, mostly because I didn't take their energy further. For some reason, I had the notion that our big idea lay in the sand itself.

So we studied sand. We measured sand's volume and duration, "painted" pictures with colored sand, viewed different kinds of sand through microscopes, interviewed people to find out what makes sand, and so on.

My kids loved sand. They were very happy investigating it, and I had reams and reams of ideas for activities. But I kept struggling, asking myself: Why are we doing this? What's the point? Without an overall purpose, this study felt like a randomly chosen theme. We had done a lot of small projects to support our learning, but shouldn't the children be ready for something big to sustain them over time? What? I kept seeing sand castles.

Sand is a huge topic. It was only from watching and listening to the children that I learned that the most important part of sand is getting to play in it. Had I been paying closer attention, I would have realized this sooner (it's all in my notes—my research on children).

Finally one day I told the other kindergarten teacher that I wanted to do something with sand to tie up this unit and be done. I told her I couldn't get past seeing sand castles. She suggested that we dump a load of sand at the school and make a sandbox for outdoor play at recess.

There it was! Brilliant! This would mean something to the children, something very much. Why couldn't I have thought of that sooner? The other activities might not have changed, but I would have had a sense of peace in knowing our eventual purpose.

I tried to capture the children's expressions of interest in the sandbox idea for a parent newsletter I sent home during this time. Here's an excerpt.

After our reading of *Tar Beach* (Ringgold 1991), I commented to the children that we are lucky to live near the ocean and get to play in the sand. Skyler said he has a sandpile in the yard. Michael added that he has a sandbox in his yard, as do Taylor and Lauren.

The deep table in our kindergarten room doesn't hold a lot of sand, and we always seem to have too many people wanting to play there. "Let's put the sand outside!" someone suggested. "You mean the whole deep table?" I asked. Several chimed in, "Skyler has a sandpile, why not the school?"

Christopher and Sean Michael said it would be fun to play with dump trucks in it, but cats couldn't go in it. (Nicholas mentioned that his cat ran away yesterday.) Megan said that we could build a sandbox with a lid. Erik asked, "What kind of lid?" Jessica asked, "What if somebody steals it?"

Kayla wondered where we would get the sand. Children's ideas included, "From the ocean," "We could make it with rocks and hammers," "From our deep table." Brianna suggested we make the sandbox a rectangle shape. Chance suggested we do jobs at home again to earn the money. Debra suggested we wash cars, and others offered their piggy banks.

Working in pairs, the whole kindergarten class designed sandboxes. They used modeling clay, pipe cleaners, toothpicks, Popsicle sticks, and so on. Their ideas, when let loose, were amazing. Some made two-story castle sandboxes with flags flying on the battlements; others made guard dogs to keep cats out. Kindergartners excel at fantasy. In this instance their ideas were so inventive, so incredible, so unrealistic. How could I bring them down to earth again to the idea of a basic sandbox with four sides and a simple lid?

Planning a sandbox

Faced with the challenge of organizing the whole class to complete a major project in a limited time (it was early May, and the sandbox needed to be built before school ended in mid-June), I fell back on a familiar structure—rotating committees with teacher-assigned tasks. I asked the children to volunteer for one of four sandbox planning

committees: Moneymakers, Lawmakers, Landscapers, Designers. I explained that the committees would work together all day, doing different activities. Each group would have a turn with me every day to plan its work on the sandbox project. I tried to create a feeling of interdependence, encouraging each committee to be responsible for all of its members.

The Moneymakers got us going when they decided we should raise money for the sandbox by collecting soda pop cans. Brianna used invented spelling to write a letter to the school about our intentions (see her letter below), which she keyed in on the computer. The committee members decorated the letter, and I duplicated copies. Posters were printed and mounted on colored paper. The committee members delivered copies of the letter to every classroom and hung posters in the hallways throughout the school. We had begun.

This committee's responsibility was to make financial reports to the parents, which I included in our weekly newsletter. On ½-inch-scale graph paper, the children worked in pairs to picture the daily and weekly total collection of pop cans. I enlarged these and added the children's dictated explanations.

The children thought we should ask lumber companies for donations of materials. Letters were written but never sent, because one local company offered to donate recycled discards.

to or clas mats at wlamit primeriy scool,

we or coletig pop cans and plastic pop bodels to rays muniy to mayc a sand box four the scool. if you hav eni cans put them in the gorbij cans out side of room 20 Mrs. stigers klas room.

We were excited. Recycled plastic lumber was the perfect material for our sandbox.

The Lawmakers brainstormed a list of rules to follow in using the sandbox.

- Do not let dogs come in and drool in the sandbox.
- Do not let people ride their bikes in.
- Play safely.
- Don't bring jump ropes to the sandbox or whip people with them.
- Wear old clothes like jeans.

Their original list was much longer, and we discussed the difficulty of remembering long lists of rules. I helped them with the challenge of simplifying and categorizing. They acted out the rules and then began to practice drawing symbols to illustrate our rules sign. We talked about universal symbols (so, the children thought, animals and babies could read them) and made up some of our own, which we used on our sign. These symbols included a thumbs-up for DO rules and a thumbs-down for DON'T rules. Each rule's symbol had a circle around it; the don'ts had a slash through the circle. The children decided all this.

The Landscapers determined the perimeter of the playground, using people as their standard of measurement. They lined up kids and counted how many it took to fill each of the four sides. As a child was counted he or she would run around to the end of the line until the side was filled. The children liked this best when I was also involved in the counting and running. The counting took about a week to complete. Then we drew up a blueprint on ¼-inch-scale graph paper, with each square representing a person counted. Children took turns counting the squares and drawing the lines for making the playground.

When the playground blueprint was drawn up, we were ready to decide on a location for the sandbox. We walked around the playground and discussed the possibilities. The next day the principal came to our room to meet with this committee and then went outside with the children to discuss possible sandbox locations. Afterward, the Landscapers brought the whole class outside to show the kids the location agreed on and the approximate dimensions of the sandbox. I think it was five people by six, with arms somewhat extended.

We began the playground model. I had some clear-plastic planting trays, which worked perfectly because we could lay them over the blueprint and trace the size. Children poured dirt and planted grass seed, collected sawdust from the playground, and used rocks for the pavement. They enjoyed keeping the dirt moist with a sprayer each day. The grass began to grow quickly, and the children made playground equipment out of Popsicle sticks, straw, and clay. They enjoyed inventing and playing out new ideas for the model each day.

The Designers' job was to sort through all their peers' wonderful ideas and come up with a single design. I wasn't sure how to help them do this. What is the next step toward reality when you've experimented with all the possibilities? I thought, "Should I give the children a narrower focus, asking them to redesign the

The Lively Kindergarten

sandbox within certain limitations, or make the criteria more and more narrow until reality is approachable?"

I thought we could begin by deciding on a shape for the sandbox. We went outside with rolls of yarn and tried out different shapes: circles, rectangles, squares, triangles. The group thought they liked best the circle and rectangle shapes. Using equal lengths of yarn, we estimated which shape would hold the most sand. Next we made the two shapes on graph paper and counted the squares to figure the total area of each shape. All this felt somewhat fragmented, and I was directing the process, not the children.

I contacted an engineer. He was willing to meet with the children and draw up a sandbox blueprint for us. He wanted to know the height of the sides, the sand depth, whether to construct a bottom, and the dimensions of the sandbox. The committee decided to interview other classes at school and get students' advice; several members had older brothers or sisters in the school. Each Designer took a few questions to ask and, paired with a Lawmaker, set out to a higher grade classroom. An adult or fifth grader went along with each pair to take notes.

We compiled the responses, recognizing many patterns. On a chart, under headings of Yes and No, we made a list of the things we wanted and the things we didn't want. We went outdoors to the site for the sandbox to measure the size we wanted, again using a people count as our measurement standard. The children decided that 21 kids should be able to play in the sandbox.

Mike, the engineer, met with the Designers committee on a Friday. The principal, who was working on a project to encourage business partnerships with public schools, wanted to videotape this meeting. The committee members knew by now what they wanted. They were informed, self-assured,

and eloquent. They took Mike to the site, answered his questions, and showed him exactly what they wanted. He followed up by sending us a blueprint plan.

Building the sandbox

After much rescheduling, we decided on the date for building the sandbox. It would be the day following the last day of kindergarten, the final day of school for all other grades. This was the only day I could get enough helpers from the community of parents and friends. A parent volunteered to be our master builder, following the engineer's blueprint and directing the work crew in creating the form with our recycled plastic lumber. We met at 9 A.M. and had the sandbox built by 11:30, amid rain showers, laughter, and a scramble to temporary shelter. The dump truck poured our eight cubic yards of sand just as the rest of the school filed out of its final assembly. Several classes stopped to watch.

When all the sand was dumped, kids immediately jumped in. They played joyfully. Earlier by newsletter I had begged my parents to try to stop by on a lunch break or in the evening, so all the kids could play in the sand. I saw about 12 of my kindergartners. It was over, and I was exhausted.

Thinking about this year

Many times throughout the year, I felt I had failed in my original idea of documenting the creation of a play-based curriculum for children. I intended to observe children's play and academically support the themes arising. Often I lost sight of my goal, but I plugged on anyway. At times this job overwhelmed me, and I thought "I'm not cut out for teaching." I would tell myself I would just make it through the year.

Trying to wade through the layers of self-protection to find who you truly are almost feels like therapy. The real teacher in me has been buried by years of conscious and unconscious educational indoctrination. Only in a release from the past can I honestly give myself to a play-driven curriculum. In my heart I believe this is how children learn, but in my mind I'm unable to accept it. Parts of my past still shout out about accountability and remaining true to preestablished systems, which were born of adults trying to force learning onto children, placing importance on finding the main idea of some drab piece of literature rather than discovering the magic in a fairy tale.

I sense in myself an unresolved tension between demands I've internalized to *teach-the-curriculum* and my evolving understanding that children must construct knowledge through action. It's hard to act on this understanding, and the sandbox project leaves me feeling I didn't really succeed even though many good things happened. I have to renew my belief in children and the workings of their minds. I must trust in their learning, never underestimating the power of it, and not overestimate the power of teacher-directed lessons that interrupt children's own investigations.

These thoughts are not new for me. But it is always easier to compromise; though how easily it corrupts! As I shed each layer of the past, these ideas reoccur ever more starkly and confront my weaknesses, challenging me to risk, to believe, to defy convention.

LEARNING FROM CAROLYN'S STORY

Perhaps the biggest risk in teaching is trying too hard. Above all, Carolyn was committed to her own creative vision—as a teacher she sought "to restore the voice of the artist in myself." Through her own background as a dancer, she understood the vision and discipline required to achieve an aesthetic outcome.

Letting go of expectations

Carolyn yearned to be an authentic teacher, co-constructing with children a shared and shareable product of their year's work together. Awed by the quality of projects at Reggio Emilia programs in Italy, teaching in a school where competition for beautiful bulletin boards was the norm, and setting herself the task of achieving a new way of being with children, she faced the daily challenges of meeting school expectations within the limitations of a short half-day, plus pullouts and school bus schedules, and a class of 25 with only volunteer assistance. And she was isolated in her school, with no interested colleagues to think with. How could she possibly have done it all?

Reflecting on her experience, Carolyn was the first to acknowledge that her own vision kept getting in the way of her ability to attend to children's needs. In Reggio Emilia, which she so admired, the primary reason for documentation of children's activity is "to understand what the children understand" (Fraser 2000), not to display their work to impress others. Displays are a culmination, the bringing together of the community to celebrate with the children, the end of a long process of collaborative inquiry. Within the constraints of much of American education, however, there is almost no opportunity for collaborative inquiry or even for taking children's interests seriously. There is too little time, too much to be covered, and no expectation that teachers need to talk with each other to understand what they themselves do understand and do not.

Carolyn had the energy, the vision, and the theory. She knew her first obligation was to observe children, and she did that. But she also knew that teachers and children in school are supposed to produce *products*—to work, not just to play.

This dilemma has been brought up again and again in dialogue within our group—the teacher/writers of this book. In the dialogue that follows, Kay, secure in her teaching setting, questions Carolyn's expectation, and the rest of us continue the thinking.

KR: I was wondering why it was necessary to build a sandbox? On their own the children couldn't have built a sandbox; they designed great fantasy sandboxes, though. You, recognizing that the children saw sand as something to play in, had visions of sand castles. Why did these visions turn so quickly into a project that had to be constructed by adults?

CS: I felt our class was ready to put its energies together and accomplish something as a community. We had explored a variety of emergent themes all year. I think having a project with a goal to work toward can be invaluable—as important as the process. The sandbox was an opportunity for the children to dream and to see that dreaming realized.

KR–Kay Stritzel Rencken, **CS**–Carolyn Stringer, **BJ**–Betty Jones, **MW**–Marsha Williams, **KE**–Kathleen Evans

BJ: When you asked Laurie for ideas about sand, her first suggestion was to dump a load of sand on the playground. Her second was to build a sandbox. Can you remember what went through your mind? Why did you build rather than dump?

CS: I've asked myself that question often. And most often, I have pleaded the lack of time. It was April. But I also wanted the children to leave with something that would symbolize what we had strived for in that year—something they could contribute to the world around them. The sandbox was their humble contribution as well as a lasting reminder of our time together.

KR: Perhaps the more natural progression would have been to dump sand, explore all the issues raised by a mountain of sand on the playground, and allow the ideas to transform themselves, involving all the children of the school. Over time, such an experience might have helped to create an atmosphere in the school in which classrooms interchangeably toss around challenges.

MW: I'm skeptical about that. I think a pile of sand would have been viewed by other adults as a mess, raising health concerns as well issues of control (control of both sand and children!). I get anxious if the principal or colleagues pass by when my children appear to be messing about. Classroom activities are supposed to look *intentional*—a word our superintendent is particularly fond of. When I get caught up in this anxiety, it's hard for me to listen closely to children and hear their themes, much less explore their themes in the face of curriculum demands.

CS: You're right. A sandpile would really have been exploring the unknown, with no clear outcome and many risks. Instead I think I was seduced by certainty. Building a real sandbox was a very clear goal, and my teaching experience had taught me to put the goal in the center.

MW: I admired your ability to integrate academic objectives into the committee work, with lessons on area designing, measuring, and all that counting.

CS: Yes, but that was the heart of my dilemma. I kept taking over from the children, reverting to teacher control; yet I'm not a control freak, very much the opposite in fact. Looking back, I realize how unconsciously I had bought into the pervasive assumption that the teacher is above all responsible for dispensing knowledge.

KE: I'm wondering if there isn't another issue here: our culture's expectations for children. An upscale community like the one you were teaching in is especially not patient with 5-year-olds being five and doing the small, messy things 5-year-olds do. So teachers get hooked on doing ambitious, impressive projects. I used to do that stuff. I was a wreck, I was mean to the kids, I didn't like the way I behaved for the sake of getting it done. It was largely a show to prove to myself, the parents, and the administrators that I was a good teacher. The children got left out of the equation. They were doing *my* work, not their own.

KR: Remember my decision not to take over the display in our room of children's house drawings? I was tempted; it would have looked so much nicer if I had done it. When 5-year-olds tack up their own drawings, one on top of the other, the result is not impressive to adults. But from my perspective, their work was of extraordinary quality. It was *theirs*, and they were most definitely learning. I chose not to take that away from them, but not without a lot of inner conversation about my choice.

CS: Reggio educators write about *reciprocity*, "a central principle that involves mutual guidance of the educational process by teacher and learner and responsiveness in circular paths of communication, caring, and control" (Rankin 1993, 191). I couldn't be fully reciprocal in my practice because I kept trying to balance the required kindergarten curriculum with an emergent curriculum without recognizing what I was doing. I simply had not acknowledged my deep-seated assumption that the teacher is the source of all knowledge. So recognizing meaningful experiences was one thing, but keeping them meaningful was another. The real problem was not so much my controlling as my not recognizing *why* I was controlling. I don't think a teacher can truly change her practice if she has not looked at and questioned the assumptions that drive that practice.

KE: You're speaking so clearly to a basic principle of John Dewey's. Somewhere he wrote something like this: The teacher needs to be responsibly, wholeheartedly reflective, uncovering the assumptions which drive practice. Without reflection on our practice, we cannot be responsible teachers. And we have to be honest about who owns the learning.

—BJ

Introducing Kathleen Evans

Kathleen has taught kindergarten at Garfield School for seven years, having moved into the public schools after 16 years of teaching and directing in early childhood programs. Garfield is a large inner-city school in Oakland, California. Its neighborhood is a richly diverse community, where recently arrived immigrants and refugees from Mexico, Central America, and Asia settle in with more established African American and Mexican American families.

This school of 1,300 students, preschool through grade 6, struggles to provide a coherent educational program in an environment of ever-shifting demographics. With 95% of the students qualifying for free lunches, and over 30 different home languages spoken by families, Garfield is not unlike many urban schools in California. The school provides bilingual or sheltered-English classes for children who speak Spanish, Cantonese, Vietnamese, Cambodian, Mien, and Lao. The school is truly a global village, where staff, students, and families are constantly challenged to address diversity issues in caring and respectful ways.

At the time of her story, Kathleen is a Reading Recovery teacher in the mornings, working with individual children at risk of failing to learn to read in first grade. In the afternoon she teaches a four-hour kindergarten, with one hour of assistance provided by a Mien-speaking aide. Most of her 27 kindergarten students are members of the Iu Mien people, a hill tribe uprooted from Laos following the end of the Southeast Asian wars. In coming from refugee camps to Oakland, the Mien people were introduced to formal schooling, literacy, and a wage economy for the first time in their long history as a people.

The introduction of Kathleen's students to literacy and the unavoidable acculturation issues related to moving from an oral culture to literacy are perplexing challenges. Her professional passions range from the place of play in the development of literacy to the technical aspects of reading and writing, the training of literacy teachers, and the creation of democratic classrooms in which critique, dialogue, and empowerment are valued as models for communities of readers, thinkers, and writers.

Holding On to Many Threads: Emergent Literacy in a Classroom of Iu Mien Children

Children have two visions, the inner and the outer.
Of the two the inner is brighter.
—Sylvia Ashton-Warner

All but seven children in my classroom were members of the Iu Mien (ee-mee-EN) culture, a tribal people from the highland provinces in South China and Laos. Looking over my class list before school began, I realized that this new year, working with children from a culture so far removed from postindustrial influences, would require my making some adjustments in the classroom.

The name list was unlike any I had ever received. A few different first names were repeated in a variety of ways; nearly all last names began with the prefix *Sae*. There appeared to be six or seven different root surnames. Although a naming system was apparent, it didn't seem to be based on gender. Naming became the first of many Mien customs I would learn about from these children and their culture.

Beginning with children's vision

During the first days of school, I invited parents to stay to help ease the children's adjustment to school. Despite a few children's tears and my gesturing to extend this invitation to Mien parents, none of them came inside. Later in the month at the back-to-school night, the parents stood in the middle of the room smiling at me. The younger-age parents, those who have been educated in this country, helped translate my description of what we were doing in the classroom and the questions other parents had about what the children would be learning. My assistant, who is Mien, explained to me that most parents, because they have not been to a school, feel unsure about their roles in the classroom and at meetings.

I didn't speak the language of the Mien parents, and they didn't speak mine. I quickly learned that written communication to most parents was ineffective. Any message I had to get to the class was efficiently transmitted if I asked my assistant or one of the English-speaking Mien parents to stand at the door and relay it to the parents when they came to take the children home.

As a group, the Mien children, who seemed at the first to be unnaturally quiet and compliant, stared up at me from the rug, and I wondered just how I was going to provide a curriculum that engaged and stimulated all the children. I had a lot to learn about them, what they were interested in, and what they thought about. I wondered how I could create a curriculum that would reflect their culture and provide a supportive transition into American culture—a completely different way of looking at and being in the world.

In reflecting on that beginning, I realize there had been the option to carry on and conduct a traditional type of class. This was the kind of structure the children's big brothers and sisters had prepared them for. I'm sure the children would have been good and also happy about doing worksheets and coloring pictures. I had observed Mien children in other classrooms, with the teacher as the center and the children appearing to work happily in whole-group activities and doing what they were told when they were told. But I had never taught this way, and I felt that the spirit of these children—or any child—was too precious to waste on meaningless, empty work. The group of Mien children in my class seemed so curious and thoughtful. I was confident they would thrive in a classroom in which action, talking, and thinking were expected.

Becoming culturally aware

The Iu Mien families I was learning to know were undergoing a drastic acculturation shift, given the differences between village life in Laos and an American urban setting, plus the trauma of life as refugees and their adjustment to inner-city, northern California living in general and an urban public school in particular. To me it seemed very important to have a classroom that both reflected Mien cultural values and prepared the children as much as possible for success in school beyond kindergarten.

Because the Mien culture's language is spoken, not written, I felt I needed to be clearer in my mind about how the Mien oral tradition and other cultural practices could support literacy learning. The children still lived in group settings in which families shared childrearing, food preparation, and religious ceremonies. Hence I felt I must be very conscious of the ways my teaching promoted collaboration and cooperation and be careful not to undermine cultural values by creating unnecessary competitiveness. The broad differences in Mien and American traditions and values as well as the fragility of the Mien culture as foreign within a hostile, dominant culture, made me wary of any undermining actions on my part. A Mien colleague, Tom Schao, wrote to me, "The Mien have really just boarded a train that carries a technological and educational advancement that is at least 200 years ahead of their time, and they are beginning to feel a bumpy, but progressive ride toward an American destination."

Through Mien culture classes offered by the school district, my associations with Mien teachers (two in the district at that time) and instructional assistants from the Mien community, attending all cultural functions I was invited to, and reading whatever I could find, I learned about the culture of the children I was to teach.

Who are the Iu Mien?

The Iu Mien, the Hmong, and other hill tribes have been referred to as Yao (*outsider* in Chinese) in China and Laos, where their status has been not unlike that of Native Americans in the United States. In Asia the Mien were slash-and-burn farmers most noted for their elegant dress and intricate cross-stitch needlework. During the Indo-Chinese wars, Mien soldiers were collaborators, first with the French and later the United States. They were fierce, brave fighters whose acts of courage won their commanders' great respect.

When it became impossible for the Mien people to continue inhabiting the regions of Laos where they had settled, they crossed the Mekong River into refugee camps in Thailand. Later the U.S. government, designating the Mien as "guests" in gratitude for their help in the war, relocated them to the United States and provided welfare assistance and low-income housing in inner-city neighborhoods. In some ways this level of support eased their transition from tribal life to a wage economy. In many more ways, however, the lives of the Mien people were transformed and disrupted profoundly.

Bringing Mien culture into the classroom

Mien storytellers believe that in the days when the Iu Mien lived on the land, the elders would go into the forest to commune with the spirits before selecting a site for a new village in order to decide if the children would be safe in that place from evil spirits. So it is with ghosts that my classroom story here begins.

Around the time of Halloween, in most kindergartens across the country, there is much talk of ghosts. Artwork, stories, and conversations often center on ghosts. Each year at our school a rumor would develop among the first- and second-graders that a ghost resided in the custodian's closet next to our classroom. Bloodcurdling screams and the scampering feet of the older children escaping from the closeted ghost often interrupted us.

At circle time one day following such a ghostly visitation, I asked the children what they would do if a ghost came into their houses. "No problem," said Sarn, one of the Mien children. "All we have to do is call the priest." Thereafter, the children attributed any unexplained occurrences to the spirit world. A cloud passing in front of the sun

and casting a shadow on the rug was noted as a significant event. Likewise, a classroom problem was often given a spiritual or supernatural explanation. When one of the favored penlights used for chart reading turned up missing, the children, sensing my distress, suggested that I imagine the missing light and then I would surely be able to locate it. "Do you really think this will work?" I asked. "It might," they offered.

Once when a great flood was prophesied by the shamans, each Mien child wore an amulet to protect her from danger. My assistant thought perhaps I might find this custom strange. But I told her I came from a very devout Catholic family, and I brought in the brown felt scapular my mother had given me at age 7 to protect me from harm. As a child I had an unwavering belief in my guardian angel, and I still pray to St. Anthony whenever I lose my keys. The beliefs of the Mien children resonated with my own recollections of being 5 and still secure in the protection of my mother and her saints.

Near our school is a beautiful park, rich in the history of our city and named after the patron saint of lost keys—San Antonio. In California's early days there was a corrida for bullfights. The trees are old, and the gentle slopes provide for views of the bay, the freeways, the trains, and the downtown skyline. In the morning the Chinese elders come to the quiet of the park to do tai chi chuan. On weekends Spanish-speaking soccer leagues hold matches from dawn to dusk. There is a Head Start program and recreation center as well as an organized tennis program.

But some of the bad things happening in the neighborhood also went on in the park—drug deals, drug users shooting up in the bathrooms, homelessness, violence, sex. Over the years the children have told me stories of the bad things they've seen happen there. It seemed reasonable for the community's elders to believe there were evil spirits in the park, for indeed there were. Still, the children navigated these streets every day. The park was part of their world and belonged to them. If we went there in a large enough group, we could be safe from the evil. So we did go to the park as often as we could, usually with many parents and even many of the elders.

On one trip to the park, Donna ran out of the bathroom shouting, "There's a monster in the bathroom." I went in with her to check, hoping to reassure her but being aware that it was certainly possible someone might have eluded our careful surveillance and slipped in unseen. Finding the restroom empty and remarkably tidy, I said, "See, Donna, there's no monster here." "No, Ms. Evans, it wasn't really a monster. It's a ghost." I certainly was not about to deny the existence of ghosts to someone as convinced as Donna. About this time Kao and Scott entered our conversation. Kao said, "There is a ghost. See, it is moving your hair." "But, Kao," I said, "perhaps it is just the wind." In an instant he licked his forefinger, raised it, and pronounced gravely, "There's no wind." An imperceptible breeze moved the swings ever so gently. And Scott, without saying anything, pointed to them.

In a way, the children in our Room 2 lived in a world not so unlike the one I inhabited at age 5, one full of spirits, both good and evil, guarding our safety *and* tempting us into dangerous places. Last year when one child's preschool-age sister was killed by a car, the children said, "It was not that lady's fault. The spirits put their hands over her eyes, and she just couldn't see Linda."

But urban public schools are not very magical places. And more and more American children are pushed to abandon magical beliefs for the sake of efficiency, technology, and progress. In contrast, spiritual life is a strength and one of the special gifts the Mien children brought to our school. Holding on

to it is one of the struggles they must take up to survive in this society.

Author and educator Sylvia Ashton-Warner writes that inner vision is "the vision that burns brighter." What she calls *inner vision* is what I felt I needed to understand and honor in order to connect the children's learning to their inner life and also to sustain as the children became more acculturated.

A conflict of visions

When I observed the Mien children at play, cultural difference was obvious. It was not unusual to see two or three boys collaborating, with very little conflict, to build one car out of Legos. Children rarely played alone. And until a Mien child had been at school for a while, he would not draw himself alone on a page but always depicted a child surrounded by others.

This year our story dictation took on a sense of community. One girl began the story: "Erica got a lollipop. Kathy don't got a lollipop. Kathy cry." This same theme and a related picture story was told and retold with many variations for several weeks, each version becoming a more in-depth exploration of the feelings of the characters, presenting different resolutions to the problem, and incidentally investigating more complex explorations of English syntax. A later story involved balloons, a dilemma, and a happy resolution: "Me have a balloon. And Kathy don't have a balloon. And she crying. We buy some balloons. And Kathy happy."

Unfortunately many teachers appear unable to grasp a cultural context in which sharing, taking turns, and cooperative effort are the norm and don't have to be taught at school. Teachers in upper grades complained that Mien children chattered constantly, were unable to work independently, and cheated by giving the answer to children who were having difficulty. The children saw many problems as having an explanation in an unatoned past bad deed or perhaps a curse.

American concepts of blame and fault are not considered in resolving issues. The Mien reach decisions through the consensus of wise people, following discussion that continues until most can accept the reasons. A vote about which nearly half the group is unhappy hardly seems a very sensible way of determining rules for living together. Membership is regarded as the benefit one receives from living in accord with the customs of the community.

So many of the discipline procedures in schools, such as stickers and points for good behavior, would seem quite silly to the Mien community for whom rules are clear and simple. The community decides on the rules, which mutually benefit the members. If a member is unable to abide by these rules, the community is offended. The offending member must fix the problem if he or she wishes to continue to enjoy the reward of living in a supportive community.

As I learned more about how the Mien community works, I saw more clearly the obvious and subtle ways in which competition is inherent in our schooling in this country and how destructive winning and losing can be to developing a community of learners. Most non-Mien children who came into our group fit naturally into this cooperative way of being in the world.

Brittany, a bright, energetic African American child placed in my class midyear because she was considered a discipline problem in her previous, more traditional class, told her mother at the end-of-the-year conference how much she liked being in a class where no one called her names, everyone shared, and nobody hit. Another African American girl cautioned a new student about the class: "There's no punks in here." I wondered if I might be seeing a common cultural thread linking the Mien and my urbanized African Americans and the recapturing of the idea of *community*, having roots for the latter in Africa and America's rural South.

Into the world of print

The challenge for me was providing children with what Lisa Delpit (1995) calls "the culture of power" while supporting them in retaining what is beautiful and useful about the Mien home culture. The greatest challenge centered on literacy. Historically, since the Mien people had no written language, the priests, who traditionally were the only ones to read and write, did so in Chinese. According to legend, however, the Mien language once was written, but because of Chinese domination the women hid the writing in their needlework where its form was lost or forgotten.

In the Mien's homeland, education involved teaching children the community work of the tribe, the traditions, the stories of the people, and spiritual beliefs. From my observation of the ways the Mien children approached new learning, the teaching method children experienced before must have consisted of watching, chatting among themselves about how the task was to be done, and attempting the task when feeling confident to try without failure. The body of knowledge taught by the Mien has effectively withstood years of oppression, domination, war, and dislocation. For the Mien it maintains a strong, vibrant bond with the past, strengthens their solidarity today, and provides a common foundation as they look cautiously to the future.

Reading and writing is something very new for the Mien people. Many parents can only sign their own names, and they do this with great difficulty. After I posted the class chart of children's names (our main tool for teaching beginning phonics), including each child's picture, Yang Ta's mother spent each morning practicing the names of the letters in her child's name, so she would be able to help Yang learn to write it.

Nai Chow's struggle to learn to write her name illustrates the Mien approach to learning. On the first day of school Nai Chow's older sister made it quite clear that she wanted me to get the spelling of Nai's name corrected—the office had Nai Chao instead of Chow. Next she brought up her concern about Nai's letter reversals and mirror writing. It was obvious to me that every person in Nai's family was working with her on name writing. One day I observed Nai at the name chart very carefully tracing and retracing her name with her finger. By December she had perfected her name. Her self-portrait in September had been a small face immersed in a sea of colored squares, like very soft pillows. She repeated this theme in drawing and painting for nearly three months—practice for perfection indeed being a cultural value.

Cultural conflicts

Supported by family values, quite a few younger Mien parents have graduated from an American high school and have attended community college. A very few have university de-

grees. But young children's strong sense of place in the family more often is eroded as Mien youth move into middle and secondary school, where dropout rates are very high. Within families and the community some divisions develop as Christianity, materialism, loss of respect for elders, and exposure to rational, logical beliefs about the cosmos become more widely accepted by the young people. Disaffection with school and the estrangement of adolescents from the tribe— "bicultural ambivalence" (Krashen 1993)— are serious problems in the Mien community. I wondered, given these influences and forces of change, if literacy was a positive or destructive force for this culture, for my students?

Further confounding this dilemma of acculturation are widely held popular beliefs that good readers come from homes in which they have "spent over a 1,000 hours actively engaged in some kind of reading and writing" (Cunningham & Allington 1994, 22) before entering kindergarten; that literate children come from homes full of books and magazines; and that the mystery of print has been explained to them. Since these conditions are seen by many schools as the only way children become literate, this leaves little room for children from the Mien culture to become members of the community of readers and writers.

Rather than give in to this deficit model of needing more, I tried to support the literacy strengths I saw embedded in the Mien culture and to build on those. I saw a group with a rich oral tradition, and children with the ability to memorize and recall long and complicated stories. I saw a group of children whose involvement in art and music and with math materials indicated a complex understanding of pattern and the ability not only to re-create, but also to create. I saw a group of children who worked together well, so the strong foundation necessary to create a community of readers and writers already existed. Valuing these competencies and taking care to plan my instruction in ways that reflected how children learn at home, I tried to re-create in the classroom the environment of a literate home. In this way I was able to dispel literacy beliefs built on a deficit model.

Many of the activities we engaged in during this school year focused on the importance of the children's Mien culture, the stories about home and family transcribed in their journals and class-made books, their descriptions of activities on the documentation boards posted in the halls outside the classrooms, the little rituals at the ends of our themes, and the big performances to celebrate special events. These all served as cultural bridges. Such passages back and forth between the culture of home and the culture of school—the Americanizing institution—demonstrated that both traditional beliefs and the requirements of modern culture can coexist in one person. I believe a curriculum that is generated from the cultural values of the community and that offers insight and skill necessary for survival in the dominant culture supports young people struggling to find ways to become bicultural.

Creating curriculum—The threads are time and structure

How is it that seemingly opposing needs and demands became coordinated in a meaningful program for 5- and 6-year-olds? The clearest way for me to explain how this happened is through the idea of an emergent curriculum. Through my observation of the children, chats with them, group discussions in the classroom, my alliances with Mien

adults, and my own reflections, I searched for ways to bring both the children's home culture and the skills of empowerment into my classroom. An added challenge was doing this without violating sacred things that rightfully do not belong outside the boundaries of home and tribe.

The beginning of the year, even the beginning of a new phase in the school year, started with reflection, chats, and a review of observation notes, children's portfolios, and other work samples. I also considered the developmental scales and district curriculum expectations, which are part of my practice. To me it seemed most logical to begin with the familiar and move into the exotic as the children became more grounded and better skilled.

Veteran kindergarten teachers begin by focusing on the child and family, moving to the larger community, and then finally exploring larger topics such as ocean life or dinosaurs. The validity of such practice is in needing to create a functioning community of learners, and to do so it is essential that each child feel valued for his or her unique contribution to the community. Even children whom the class may view as troublesome feel they have talents and skills to contribute.

If my Mien children were going to view membership in the tribe/community as worthwhile and if the rest of the tribe/class were to accept them, then all had to spend time getting to know each other. I had found this practice of moving from familiar to exotic even more useful in working with English-language learners whose vocabulary and usage were constantly evolving from the everyday things they were able to name to the more abstract subjects they would yet learn.

When planning any curriculum, I now have a rule for myself: proceed thoughtfully and very carefully. Before I followed this rule, my teaching was harder work and less successful. Once I would brainstorm elaborate webs around interest areas, with many activities in every subject area and all selectively and obviously connected to each and every other activity planned for the week. My knowledge of every topic I covered during the year was in great breadth and depth. My theme boxes and binders bulged with materials and content. But I was so exhausted and the children so overwhelmed that the joy of learning was lost.

Planning became more of a shared process with the children, although probably not as obvious as when a group would ask, "This year can we learn more about snakes?" Although at times I chose the theme, planning was shared in the sense that I divined a topic that seemed of great interest through observation, chatting, and reflection. I field-tested ideas by putting out a tub of books on the subject, reading aloud other books on the subject, and displaying pictures or posters and watching for a response. If there was enough conversation (in Mien or English or both), if there was noticeable curiosity or interest, then perhaps this could become a community project. After this preliminary engagement, I began the planning process—still checking responses, extending invitations, and making adjustments for the best fit.

Houses as a cross-culture theme

I was determined this year that as a class we would take a walk to each child's house at the beginning of the school year. This was my way of initiating a *house* theme and also building community. If a non-Mien child and a Mien child lived near one another, I thought, they might not even realize it. My hope was that cross-cultural play would happen in the neighborhood. To introduce the houses theme, I used a variety of storybooks and poems. What we observed and recorded during our several days of walking around the neighbor-

hood generated many of the questions we explored during this theme.

In children's art and block play, I observed their ideas about house and neighborhood beginning to evolve. Block play, which began as individual children building isolated structures, evolved into group play as children connected their structures with roads and walls and passages. The children went on to refine their play and add to it. In their paintings of houses, which started out as rectangles with triangular roofs and chimneys, more and more details appeared as the children looked at and thought more about the different houses they saw and the finishes and trim they noticed that set one house apart from another.

As the children played, painted, and drew, their conversations included more and more words and concepts about houses than were evident when we began. In pursuing the house theme, I was able to incorporate basic mathematical concepts and key skills in the kindergarten curriculum, such as graphing, estimation, geometric shapes, measurement, and counting.

Why my practice changed

The difference in my practice as a result of my new approach to curriculum was a slowed pace. Now I noticed and augmented spontaneous learning as well as modified my plans when what occurred spontaneously proved more meaningful and important to the children's learning (for example, children thinking about houses in new and different ways). Another difference, I believe, now that teaching was less work and more satisfying, was that I had undergone a process of decentering—my ideas, my creativity, and my timeline were no longer the preeminent consideration. Instead, in a community of learners, my participation was there along with the contributions of all the other members.

What brought about this change? Was it only a result of my unique situation, one in which my cultural values were so unsuited to the Mien children in the classroom, the resources on which I usually relied for communicating about our classroom activities were useless, and the expectations of parents for what they wanted for their children—a loving and safe place where their culture and beliefs were treated with respect—were so clearly communicated nonverbally? Perhaps abiding pleasure in watching 5- and 6-year-olds play and learn, despite my accumulated experiences of frustration (with the system), led me to believe that teaching could be better. Perhaps it was a fear that if I didn't make some changes, I would join the ranks of those who stay in public school long after the joy of teaching and learning has gone. These challenges caused me to look hard at my practice and to change.

I looked at how I planned curriculum and what this has to do with closure; before, a curriculum theme would usually just die a natural death because I had exhausted it. Now I saw how very important it was to have a culminating event and product. Rituals resonate with 5-year-olds, and for Mien children ritual was so much a part of how they lived each day. An ending ritual, such as the release of newly hatched butterflies at the park, a family party to unveil a class book or mural, or an informal performance of frog songs and poems we had learned, seemed a more natural way to close—a kind of cushion—rather than arbitrarily ending a unit of study simply because it was time move on to something else.

While indeed it was time to do something else because the projects, theme, and learning had covered as much as could be man-

aged and new, more interesting questions were surfacing for most of the class, a ritual closing celebrated our community of learners. Formally closing our study gave a sense of value to all our efforts and a clear, comfortable passage into the next phase of the school year.

The flow of the day

When I think about the very best type of kindergarten, I think of one with the natural rhythms of a home but with more toys and kids. The image I have has something to do with how I structure the environment and the day in my classroom—emergent environment, emergent scheduling. The environment happens first, I imagine, because so much of our professional development has to do with creating environments that work for children. I spent a great deal of time finding ways for the Mien children to work and play in the room and to manage this well without adult intervention. These independent activities allowed me more freedom to work with small groups or individual children to observe, note, and scaffold children's learning and to promote their sense of independence and responsibility for their own learning.

Allowing time to transit

In an overcrowded public school, time was a great challenge for me. Transition times were tense and unpleasant. Through my informal research I could see clearly that nearly all unresolvable discipline problems occurred at transitions. Having to stop rich and wonderful work, interactions, or play to do something less significant caused me distress. To avoid this I created a time period for adjustment when my class of Mien children first began school and a transition period each day when they arrived in the classroom. In my yearlong plan, this beginning period of several weeks had a curriculum that included learning the room, adjusting to being in a group, and following rules for cleanup, sharing, making responsible choices, and so on. Transitions ended when it seemed that things were working well.

Reading on the rug

In my daily plan, one period of adjustment was called *reading on the rug*. During this time children recorded on a chart and filed the work they had done at home, recorded their presence on the attendance chart, greeted friends, as well as engaged in independent *reading*. These independent activities freed up my time for talking with parents and checking on children who were having problems, which ranged from missing lunch to being pushed in line. This start to the day also gave me time to observe and note children's book-handling skills and reading behaviors. Following these activities was our opening ritual, which changed very little in structure from day to day.

Changes in the content of the opening ritual occurred as children appeared to have mastered what was offered and could manage more complex activity. Shifts in complexity were based on my observations, conversations with the children, and reviews of their work samples. As it appeared that most could handle a new level of complexity, I made adjustments to the content of what was happening during whole-group activities. I kept in mind both state and district standards and expectations.

Relaxed writing

After our opening we had another long, relaxed time for writing. During this period kids would *write*, date stamp and file

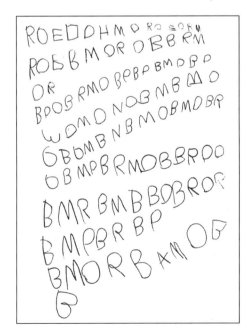

their writing, and work on literacy-related activities of their choosing in several centers. While children were busy with their important work, I had my work—collecting Mien oral language samples, taking story dictations, assisting with writing, and meeting with specific children one-to-one on letter identification and handwriting. I often completed some portion of our district-mandated English Language Development Assessments. To close this part of the day, another whole-group ritual happened as we moved into toy time. We called it *choice* or *center time* in Room 2.

Our day moved in this fluid way nearly every day. After I made changes in the environment and scheduling and ensured time flow rather than time limits, I found the children's play had greater richness and depth. In turn, this gave me many more classroom ideas for meaningful play and project work connected both to the Mien children's home lives and the idea of *the culture of power* (see p. 148).

Creative emerging ideas

Ghosts and spirits, fishing, sewing, caring for babies, cooking, and constructions all emerged as curriculum areas to include that reflected the Mien children's home culture. The office, bookstore, hospital, shampoo factory, as well as space exploration, all emerged prominently as aspects of learning to share in the culture of power. Our reading and writing, including even children's artistic representations as sign systems, became ways for us to explore, document, and preserve Mien cultural activities. As I watched and listened to the children and collected documentation, I decided what were the recurring cultural themes and confusions.

Fishing. From Mien children's drawings, dictated stories, and chats with the children, I found out how important fishing was to the families. At the water table I added fishing poles, magnetic fish, rubber sea creatures, rocks, shells, and tin buckets. This became an engaging, important place to play. Unfortunately it only had room for three, and many more wanted to fish. So, from construction toys the children invented fishing poles—the long, deep-sea kind. On pillows, which functioned as the bank, they sat, fished, laughed, and joked for an extended period of time.

The playhouse. The way I set up and stocked the playhouse provided some interesting insights into the Mien children's culture. I had included a high chair, even though I had never seen a high chair in a Mien home or a Mien child sitting in one. I just didn't think this through. Before I knew it the children, not the dolls, were sitting in the high chair. And before I thought to remove the chair, it was as broken as the wee bear's chair.

More successful accessories in the house were the Chinese dishes. Toward the middle of the year a group of children had taken to carefully arranging the dishes, the flowers, and artificial fruit into a shrine and then kneeling to pray. They did this without self-consciousness, in a most natural way, completely unaware that my team teacher and I had noticed them.

Sewing was something I initiated, and Mrs. Saelee, my assistant, supervised the activity. On small burlap squares the children drew designs, which they then stitched by hand. I had observed the Mien mothers using this same sewing technique as they did traditional stitchery—something they often engaged in as they chatted with each other and watched the children.

At first this was an activity chosen by girls, although the non-Mien boys also chose it. After a few of these boys risked trying, some of the Mien boys thought it might be interesting, though none pursued the sewing very long. The mothers were very pleased with the small, fine stitches the children made. I was truly amazed at the fine-motor skills they demonstrated and the beauty of this first needlework. Mien mothers fear that the younger generation will lose this skill, and they appreciated this connection between home and school. I regret that I didn't take the opportunity to discuss why the boys had abandoned the activity so quickly.

The bookstore was another idea that came from the children. As each of our days began with reading on the rug, children's choices were wide. The options included reading picture books, big books, child-authored books, and books at various skill levels available in the team book boxes; using flannel board stories; and listening to story tapes. Each day a small group of children would take nearly all the picture books from the low shelf and arrange them on a round table. There would be a great deal of chattering and discussion back and forth in Mien and English, children leaving with several books and returning within a few minutes to get another stack.

Although I typically used this time to observe literacy behaviors, the children did not appear to be particularly engaged in books or reading-like behaviors—that is, not until I asked just what they were doing. "We're having a bookstore," they responded and then asked if we couldn't have a bookstore for a dramatic play center. I am certain that very few of the children had ever been in a bookstore, and there aren't many bookstores on television. I'll never know the seed for this idea, but it was a rich learning opportunity for several weeks, not only in literacy but also in math—children counting and making change.

The hospital was a dramatic play center I included each year after the third month of school. Most of the children had had fairly significant experiences with hospitals, either visits of their own or those of a sibling. To meet the pediatric health problems in the Mien community, Children's Hospital in Oakland had developed a full-service clinic. Most Mien parents still used traditional forms of healing, however, along with the services of the clinic, so children had an array of issues to resolve about the hospital.

To accommodate the children's new dramatic play area in our room, we moved one of the round tables nearer the playhouse. The book area was the waiting room—providing the opportunity to read while waiting for the doctors. Doctor kits and other props enriched this play and suggested the language used in the area. Prescription pads, calendars, and other resources that gave opportunities for writing were also included in this center. The children transported the dolls from the house to the hospital with a great deal of commotion, discussion, and excitement. Both girls and boys acted as physicians.

Our debriefing after a period of play usually included updates on the condition of each patient and what operations the doctors had to perform. As 5-year-old Kenny wrote in his school memories book, "My hero is a doctor at Children's Hospital. She saved me when I was very sick." One of our earlier discussions had concluded that heroes are strong and brave; they save or help people and can be a man or a woman. Hence Kenny selected this pediatrician without regard to gender stereotypes.

Play—The material of literacy

Play activities served as rich opportunities for the children to use language. One class observer noted how fluidly the children slipped between English and Mien as the play or players warranted it. This talk was more important to the children's development of bilingualism than any other activity or lesson I could have provided.

To document the Mien children's development of English language skills, I used samples of their dictated stories over time. Within a single story I could see the ways a child constructed his use of personal pronouns. "Me have candy. Shirley don't have candy. And him sad. And I buy for her. Now she happy." Our storytelling sessions were always watched by a number of children, each contributing ideas on English syntax. One child added, "It's not *him*. Shirley is a girl. Say *she*." This contribution from one member of our community of learners assisted our storyteller as he constructed the unfamiliar language.

Books supporting learning

Read-aloud books, stories on tape, poem and song chart reading, and flannel board stories are all important literacy components that support children in learning English sounds, vocabulary, and syntax. After so many years of working with second-language learning, I realized that there is no systematic approach to the task. Providing a variety of opportunities to use oral, visual, and rhythmic cues was the most effective way to help each child construct the new, very confusing language.

Choosing materials requires careful thought. Read-aloud books need to contain repetition and pattern to give children lots of opportunities to practice the sounds of English and to predict appropriate words. These include simple stories with engaging language so that the children are interested in the story as well as successful at understanding the meaning. Some examples are *Heckedy Peg* (Wood 1987), *We're Going on a Bear Hunt* (Rosen 1989), *The Elephant and the Bad Baby* (Vipont 1969), *Hattie and the Fox* (Fox 1992). All are books that work well with English-language learners.

Rereading a few stories and reading them quite often resulted in lots of retellings of popular books that were read aloud. Again, this provided the children with many opportunities to practice constructing English syntax, developing vocabulary, and strengthening the meaning of the language. In our class here is how Meuy retold the story of "Goldilocks and the Three Bears":

> Mother Bear and Baby Bear go for a walk. Papa Bear too. And Mother Bear and Baby Bear and Papa Bear go home. Then they get home, and they see Goldilocks. And Goldilocks run away.

While Meuy was still having trouble with English tenses, she had mastered the personal pronoun *they*. A few weeks earlier Meuy had still been listing each one of her characters in every sentence because she was unable to put *they* to use.

Brenda took retelling to another level with her variation of the "Goldilocks and the Three Bears" story:

> Baby Bear cries so the three bears go for a walk. Papa Bear see a little rabbit. Mama Bear see a cat in the window. Baby Bear sees a lot of labybugs and tells his Mommy.

Brenda tried orally to resolve uses of tense, using modifiers, conjunctions, and prepositions. Somewhere in her memory of stories in English, she had heard the way it should sound, and now she attempted to make her language match those remembered patterns of the language.

Retelling stories as a variation occurred through the use of our class books. Our class made its own big book called Yum Soup which was a variation on *Yuck Soup* (Cowley 1986). The children's book was created as a cookbook following a soup-making project. Their refrain, "In go some _____," introduced high-frequency words, and the pictures the children painted of the vegetables they'd brought from home provided the cues for the less-familiar English words for the various ingredients. The ingredients themselves provided a multicultural stew, with everything from potatoes to bok choy, and provoked a discussion of the Mien names for each of the vegetables as well as why some could not have a Mien name. A silly wall story we created on the same theme was "Yuck Pizza." Anyone familiar with a 6-year-old's sense of humor can just imagine the unmentionables that go on a yuck pizza.

Traveling books. Toward the middle of the year the children began taking books home to read to their older siblings, parents, or grandparents. These books on an early emergent-reading level included simple sentences and print that was large and well spaced to allow for easy word pointing. The text, while repetitious and predictable, was in a natural language, pleasing to read aloud. The pictures gave obvious cues for the difficult or unfamiliar words, provided the child had enough English vocabulary and/or conceptual knowledge to interpret the picture.

I introduced the early reading books to the children by establishing the pattern of the story text and through a walk through the book discussing the pictures and their relationship to the words. Choosing the books was a collaborative effort between the child and myself, seeking at least one new challenge and one guaranteed success. As children returned the books, they placed them in the team book box so others could then share these books with their friends. With amazement I watched the children reading on the rug, reading their books to each other, sharing special books with a group of friends, and making book choices based on recommendations of a friend.

Flannel board stories were another great support for developing children's story retelling and English-language patterns. "Five Little Ducks" was one of our favorites. It was on a song chart, a story tape, and in a storybook in the book boxes. We sang its words frequently and with great emotion, particularly when "poor Mother Duck" went out to find all her children missing.

Jerry and Billy, who broke into song (the "Five Little Ducks") while playing with blocks and walking to the cafeteria, came to me one day hoping to make the story on the flannel board. "Unfortunately," I told them, "I only have six little ducks. Could you tell the story with these ducks?" "No," they said, "those ducks aren't good. They are all the same size. The ducks in the song are five babies and a mother." This was, of course, accurate. So I suggested using the baby ducks from the farm flannel board set and the big duck from the other group.

The two boys agreed and went off singing to set this story up on the flannel board. By the time they had gotten to the fifth little duck, they had found that the Mother Duck I'd given them just wasn't going to work out.

"Why?" I asked, wondering what could possibly be wrong. "Look," they said, "this duck you gave us is very happy. Mother Duck is sad. Do you have a sad-looking duck?"

The incident involving Jerry and Billy illustrates that, with support for different ways of representing and using a song, children with little facility in English can display a level of interpretation quite solid and well developed for 5-year-olds.

Integrating reading with writing

As English-language learners begin to develop beyond the stage of single word utterances, it is critically important to provide them with as many rich opportunities as possible for developing language. Through emergent writing children often begin to integrate what they have heard in read-aloud books, songs, and poems with the print they have seen in the environment, emergent-reader books and in messages written by the teacher. It is really here that the sounds they have heard and the symbols they have seen begin to connect in a useful way.

I believe that delaying emergent writing slows down the second-language acquisition process significantly. Children *write* every day from the first day of kindergarten. For most of them this means drawing pictures to tell a story. If they choose to dictate the picture story, all but a few dictate just one word as a label—*tree, flower, rainbow, star*—although their drawings contain quite elaborate scenes with lots of action and characters.

By the end of the first kindergarten month, I began to see a great deal of pretend writing by the children. Did this come from learning to write their names, watching me write in the classroom, participating in the shared writing experience in our class-opening letter, or seeing older siblings do their homework? I was not sure I would ever know the answer. Rune-like symbols occurred in this stage and rapidly evolved into real letters placed randomly on the page. Often there would be a familiar word or two from the class-opening letter, such as "Hi Boys! Hi Girls!" followed by a complete page of scribbles, because real writers fill pages.

What I did observe at this stage was left-to-right progression, line return to the left-hand side of the page, and continuation of line after line. In homes filled with books and opportunities to see family members writing and to practice writing, preschoolers develop literacy skills over a period of years. With my Mien kindergartners I saw the developmental stages of writing condensed into a short period of time in spite of the fact that direct literacy instruction occupied less than 10 minutes of our school day.

Models of writing. I began to demonstrate how words are formed and can be manipulated to express ideas and thoughts. Most of the children relied on these models, such as "I will play," "I will write," "I will ___ today" for their writing. Some were able to change words around or add new words to make their own meaning. Second-language learners seem to need these aids to begin to grasp enough about the workings of print and the new language before they are able to risk using what they know about the sound/symbol relationship to create their own words, sentences, and meanings. Reliance on high-frequency words, environmental print, and written models of English syntax seem to be the scaffolding these beginning writers require to move into invented spelling and more fluent independent writing.

Created sentences, symbols, and labels. About a third of the children in our class got to the brink of creating their own sentences. Another one-third developed some sound/symbol connections and a grasp of a few high-frequency words but as yet not the ability to coordinate their knowledge for use in writing. The final one-third were just beginning to dictate one or two sentences in English, form some words, apply some labels to their drawings, recall how to form some high-frequency words, and copy the sentence models but still had confusions about how sounds related to letters and words. In spite of this the children's writing portfolios all showed marked progress in the development of early writing.

To have each child consider how he or she had grown as a writer over the year, I reviewed each portfolio with the individual child, from the first writing in September to the final sample collected in August. The question I asked after we completed this review was, "What do you think of yourself as a writer now?"

Scott: I like writing, because it is fun. I write by myself. Before I cannot write my name. I write my name. I write what I see.

Peter: I am a good writer. I can write a lot of words. I can tell stories about my friends. I want to write a silly story.

Kao: Because I like to write, I can write words. I can write animal names, because I like animals.

Children come to school with rich histories of using words. Their growing ability to take social action through narratives and other genres helps children develop a sense of control and agency and in addition a sense of connection with others . . . . Because there are sociocultural differences in family and community uses of written and oral language, educators use the metaphor of a cultural bridge . . . . Gradually educators can introduce new ways of using the language.

—Anne Haas Dyson (1989)

Jason: I copy the room. I copy about toys. I can write my name. I can write my friends' names.

Erica: I like writing. I can write a word and put jokes. I learned to make words.

Cindy: I can read what I write.

Sarn: I like writing because [it is] to think. Then I can write a whole lot of stuff.

This reflective evaluation showed the children's own development as writers.

Valuing language skills. As the children saw their conversations and thoughts transformed into words, sentences, and stories, they were conversely able to read the words of others. As they used books to find answers to their questions and to expand their knowledge of the world and used writing to record the important events and items of their everyday lives—from snack choices to wish lists, party invitations to classroom events—the value and usefulness of writing and reading became clear to them.

Now that a movement exists to transliterate the sounds of spoken Mien into readable text as a means of preserving the words of the language and the stories of the elders, Mien literacy is indeed an essential skill. Acquiring this skill supports the Iu Mien as they continue their struggle in the inevitable process of acculturation.

Conclusion

The only way I saw for our classroom to manage the very complicated challenge of acculturation was to provide an emergent curriculum. The Mien culture sustained its people for a very long time through some very difficult struggles, but Mien children needed to learn how to function in modern America. They needed to become fluent in English; they needed to read and write well. Most of all, I believed it was best if they continued speaking their native language.

So the question becomes, Who owns the learning process? If teachers and children bridge cultures carefully and thoughtfully, if the curriculum emerges from the needs, questions, and requirements of the individual situation, then it is the learner who owns the learning. As teachers we can still meet standards and expectations and work within guidelines and frameworks. But the topics, ideas, and questions we pursue must emerge from the community of learners, grow out of the interactions among children, and expand between teacher and students. This is the only curriculum that can be culturally relevant.

In teaching children whose culture is very different from that of urban America in which their families now live, Kathleen finds emergent environment and emergent scheduling necessities. Within this fluid, slow-paced structure, she has designed many ways for children to work and play in the classroom without her active supervision. This design frees her to observe and learn from the children as well as to work flexibly with individuals and small groups while the life of the classroom goes on.

A structure for bicultural learning

So many North American schools faced with large numbers of children whose first language is other than English try various strategies, including English immersion, sheltered English, bilingual instruction, and primary reading instruction in a child's home language. The Mien language of the children in Kathleen's classroom, however, was not spoken by school staff other than paraprofessionals from the community, nor did it have a written form until recent transliteration by Christian missonaries.

Kathleen approaches her complex task with a commitment to support the biculturality of the Mien children and their families— to validate the place of home culture at school while introducing children to the language, literacy, and numeracy demanded by the culture of power with which they must come to terms. The effects of acculturation on Iu Mien culture are highly destructive. To counter these effects, Kathleen believes in teaching American values in conscious and explicit ways, always questioning their fit with traditional Mien values.

By using short sessions of group instruction, balanced by much longer periods of play and choice, Kathleen applies her in-depth knowledge of literacy learning to respond to the particular needs of her second-language learners. While 1,000 hours of being read to before age 5 are currently prescribed as ideal preparation for becoming a reader, Mien children may have no read-to hours at all. Yet they bring to school many strengths that serve in their growth toward literacy—a rich oral tradition emphasizing memory, understanding of complex patterns, and much practice in cooperation.

Kathleen's classroom builds upon these strengths from the Mien culture. She also offers clear, consistent, and explicit teaching of the conventions of print that most children who have been frequently read to manage to figure out for themselves. For example, she explains, "During shared reading children usually sweep along a line of print without regard for the individual words. For children who haven't been read to, this inattention to words as individual units of speech can become a source of several confusions in reading. Scaffolding a practice of children's pointing at each word in a text takes no more time and clarifies for the inexperienced how text works."

Kathleen's classroom is carefully provisioned to include play themes from Mien and American cultures to help children become grounded in both. Through rich and varied opportunities for dramatic play, children develop a knowledge of English vocabulary and practice using English syntax while continuing to use their Mien language.

In the next section, Kathleen shares details about her classroom as a setting for emergent curriculum and her theory about the process of orchestrating it.

—BJ

I have taught in other classrooms, with other children, many of whom did share my background, and I do not think that teaching children from a culture not your own is ultimately different from teaching children you believe you understand more easily. The differences are less important than the similarities. From the vantage point of teacher research, as I understand it now, teaching children that you know you don't always understand is an advantage—the problem comes when you think you understand. For a teacher-researcher, what is important with all children is to find the challenge to your understanding.

—Cynthia Ballenger

PART III

Making Classrooms Work

The Setting for Emergent Curriculum: Space, Time, and Materials

The teacher's contribution to play always begins with the physical environment, with stage setting. Developmentally, physical knowledge comes first. Children need the physical stuff of the world, the [David Hawkins] "It" out there beyond the "I" and the "Thou."
—Elizabeth Jones and Gretchen Reynolds (1992)

Like improvisational theater, emergent curriculum doesn't just happen. Only the thematic content and details of plot and character are unpredictable, growing as they do out of the classroom community—who we are as its members and what interests us individually and collectively. This section describes the stage on which emerging curriculum is played out.

Setting the stage

As the instructional leader in this community of learners, I set the stage, being responsible for planning and shaping the space and time in which we learn together and the interactions through which this happens. In this very active role, I draw on everything I know about learning environments (see "Using the Environment as a Tool," p. 80) and about children.

This practical knowledge base is vital for a teacher to maintain control of the classroom and responsively teach every child. For myself I choose a challenge very different from that of teachers who decide to teach all the children the same thing at the same time and accept as inevitable that some children just won't get it.

Organizing space and materials

Young children learn through action, through interacting with materials and people. Five-year-olds are still young children. Through the observation of children, teachers' understanding of them begins. To play and learn, children need materials, space to move within, and time to carry out their ideas. As Harriet Cuffaro explains, materials are the texts of early childhood classrooms.

The materials we choose to bring into the space of our classrooms reveal the choices we have made about knowledge and what we think it is important to know. How children are invited to use the materials indicates the role they shall have in their own learning. Materials are the texts of early childhood classrooms. Unlike books filled with facts and printed words, materials are more like outlines. They offer openings or pathways by and through which children may enter the ordered knowledge of the adult world. Materials also become tools with which children give form to and express their understanding of the world and of the meanings they have constructed. (1995, 33)

Young children begin their research into the world by investigating materials of all kinds.

I choose materials carefully, and I organize them with great care. Years of experience teaching in early childhood programs enable me to take the elements of such organization for granted, to the point that I sometimes forget to explain it to others. Betty Jones once commented to me that when she visited my class, the structure appeared "so seamless as to be invisible," with the children and me "flowing spontaneously through space and time." She guessed, however, that behind the scenes I'd put a great deal of thought and energy into planning and arranging.

That's right. I learned from Liz Prescott, one of my mentors, that environment predicts behavior (Kritchevsky & Prescott 1977). I've really tried to listen for her voice. I've spent many years refining my room setup to make it predictable, easy for children to restore to its original order, and inviting. (See also "Looking in on Another Early Childhood Classroom," p. 82) I often stress to student teachers that the number of chairs at a table and the amount of equipment in an area are nonverbal cues to children about how many can use a place at a time.

I also hear my mentor Elinor Griffin's (1982) admonition not to overstimulate the children. While my room is rich, it is not crammed full of stuff. It is easy to see where something belongs. I rotate materials and equipment as I observe which ones aren't being used. Children may remember some things that aren't out at the moment and know they can ask for them.

Many, many places and materials in our room lend themselves to dramatic play: little ponies with combs, brushes, barrettes, and rollers (a My Little Pony set) next to the big blocks; sea creatures and shells in the water table; teddy bears in the math area; small dinosaurs in the playdough. Puppets, of course, inspire play, as does the collection of rubber snakes, lizards, snails, and the like. Dolls in the house/dramatic play center and a two-family dollhouse on a small table invite children's pretend play. The plan book calls it English language development, but the way I see it, dramatic play offers scores of ways for kids to act out their worries, dreams, and hopes and to use their home language and their newly acquired language to express these.

Using the Environment as a Tool

• The learning environment can be a powerful teaching instrument at the disposal of the teacher, or it can be an undirected and unrecognized influence on the behavior of both teachers and children. . . .

• Knowledge of the relationships between physical surroundings and actions is a practical tool the teacher can use for many purposes.

• Teachers can predict behavior in classroom settings. They can teach through the environment and its materials.

• This releases teacher time from management and gives more time for productive interactions with children.

Source : Reprinted, by permission of the publisher, from C.E. Loughlin and J.H. Suina, *The Learning Environment,* p. 5 (New York: Teachers College Press). © 1982 by Teachers College, Columbia University. All rights reserved.

Choosing materials and defining their use

As kindergarten begins, *open* tasks should predominate over *closed* tasks. Open tasks offer every child an opportunity to be successful. They offer me the opportunity to observe children's risk taking, dominant learning styles, ways of interacting with others, and individual approaches to solitary

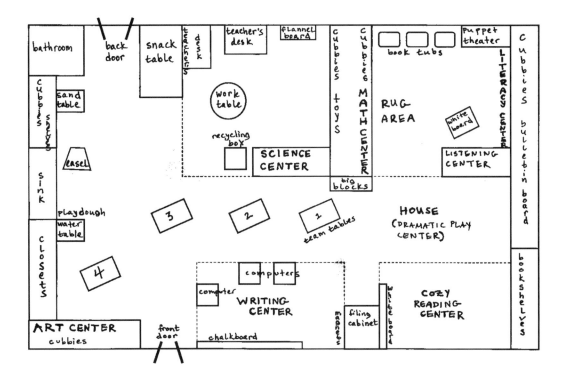

tasks. (See "The Open/Closed Dimension in the Classroom," p. 83.)

A teacher can, of course, determine how any material will be used. The relatively open materials, for example, may be messed with (explored), played with purposefully (such as in "I'm going to build a house"), or converted into a teacher-directed task (for example, "Make a pattern with the blocks that matches the pattern on this card"). The versatility of such materials as unit blocks and pattern blocks makes them particularly appropriate for 5-year-olds, who are in transition from initiative to industry (Erikson 1950)—from play to work.

In play, children invent their own rules. Teachers who are convinced that kindergarten is for work, not play, may tip the balance toward closed activities with adult-made rules to follow. In developmental sequence, however, exploration and play precede learning to play by other people's rules (Jones & Reynolds 1992). Children need to explore each new material—"What does this do?"—before they are ready to play with it—"What

can we do with this?"—or to use it competently in directed task—"Can I do what my teacher wants me to do with this?" When teachers don't allow enough time for children's self-directed exploration, the school's learning objectives get derailed, because most children must know the full potential of any material before they can learn from it without becoming distracted.

School is where children learn to play games with rules, not just those in four-square and soccer but all the rules that underlie reading (left-to-right, phonics) or math or not getting into trouble at school. Children ready for these challenges approach them with confidence, experiencing them as meaningful tests of competence. Children still finding their way are more likely to find such tasks lacking in a personal sense—just things your teacher makes you do. Under these conditions it is difficult to maintain classroom discipline.

As teachers trying to build theories to inform our practice, we are not all that different from the children or any other

Looking in on Another
Early Childhood Classroom

Kathleen's classroom organization is very similar in style to my kindergarten (shown below). My room is a large, light- and plant-filled environment with centers arranged for block building, math/computer use, art, reading, house play, science, puppets, and so on. There are pillows and stuffed animals, mats and blankets, rugs and curtains to add softness. Our tables, easels, playhouse furniture are all movable. Equipment is arranged for easy access by adults or children. The space design encourages small-group interaction, exploration of materials, and children's responsibility taking.

Storage areas are neat and kept to a minimum. Everyone helps pick up the room and keep it clean. If the kids don't feel responsible for an orderly space, the whole thing can fall apart for me. Certainly I am not about to keep it this way all by myself or by being a dictator.

—*Kay Stritzel Rencken*

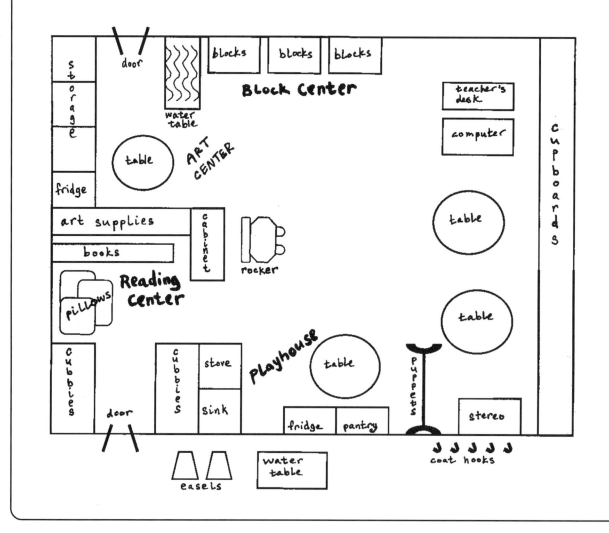

learners. Theories are like materials. We must explore, rename, and transform them before they become our own.

Organizing time

In my schedule, play is of central importance, though there are some limits on choices, and sometimes we all do the same thing together. In teaching Iu Mien children whose culture was different from my own, I continued learning to communicate. For many, English was a language that was unfamiliar. I built shared understandings best by watching them at play, then introducing activities that connected with what they already knew and did—what was truly important to them. Giving them choices and relying on the competencies they brought to school, I greatly reduced discipline issues in my classroom and was freer to pay attention to the children and curriculum.

By building my theory through experience and experimentation in structuring the day, I have learned several important things:

1. The time provided for play/choice/self-selection must be long enough for children to fully engage in their chosen activities. By midyear, for fives, about one uninterrupted hour is needed.

2. The schedule must be flexible, consistent in sequence but not dictated by the clock, in order to acknowledge and, as appropriate, sustain rather than interrupt the unusually productive activity that may happen on some days.

The Open/Closed Dimension in the Classroom

Looking at materials, the open/closed dimension describes the extent to which restrictions inherent in a material impose a clear and arbitrary solution. Water, paint, dough, and sand are open; puzzles, workbook tasks, tracing patterns are closed. A lot of other things fit somewhere in between.

Closed: Both the goal and the mode of relationship among the parts are constrained. The number of alternatives is exceedingly limited. Examples: puzzles, matching games, arithmetic worksheets.

Relatively open: Either the goal or the mode of relationship, but not both, is constrained. The number of alternatives is greater, but not unlimited. Examples: floor blocks, Tinkertoys, Cuisenaire rods.

Open: Neither the goal nor the mode of relationship is constrained. The number of alternatives is unlimited. Examples: dough, collage, sand, water play.

Source: Reprinted, by permission, from E. Jones and E. Prescott, *Dimensions of Teaching-Learning Environments: A Handbook for Teachers in Elementary Schools and Day Care Centers* (Pasadena, CA: Pacific Oaks College, 1984), 24.

We value space because of its power to organize, promote pleasant relationships between people of different ages, create a handsome environment, provide changes, promote choices and activity, and its potential for sparking all kinds of social, affective and cognitive learning. All of this contributes to a sense of well-being and security in children. We also think that the space has to be a sort of aquarium that mirrors the ideas, values, attitudes, and cultures of the people who live within it.

—Loris Malaguzzi (to Lella Gandini)

3. Transitions, which interrupt focused attention to play and work, should be kept to a minimum and be orchestrated in a way that makes them manageable for every child.

Untiming the curriculum

Children's in-depth engagement in projects in early childhood programs in Reggio Emilia, Italy, has gained international attention. Susan Fraser describes the setting, "Routines are minimal . . . the children are not interrupted by unnecessary transitions from one activity to the next, as so often happens in schools in other parts of the world. In a Reggio Emilia classroom, there are times to eat and sleep and meet with the group, but there are few unnecessary interruptions in the children's day" (2000,10).

A predictable sequence of events offers children security. Flexible timing of events from day to day enables adults and children to pay attention to what is really going on in the classroom. In contrast, Carol Anne Wien and Susan Kirby-Smith describe the origins of inflexible scheduling common in schools:

> The desire to offer children unhurried time and sustained attention in activity is . . . threatened by production-schedule organization of time . . . [which] emerged with the rise of factories. . . . Schools adopted the production schedule organization . . . with separate timed periods for each activity and sharp breaks between them. . . . A rigidly kept time schedule undercuts support for children's play, for children's decisionmaking and ownership of their activity, and for giving children the opportunity to assume responsibility for their actions. (1998, 8, 12)

Flexible, consistent scheduling offers autonomy to teachers and children. Teachers, like children, can make spontaneous choices—to observe, to scaffold, to introduce a guided activity as one of the children's choices, to work with an individual or a small group. Such teacher folk wisdom as "You've got to get 'em trained" applies as much to a developmentally focused classroom as it does to a teacher-directed classroom. In the former, it is training in independence and social responsibility that predominates. The work of the class is expected to go on whether or not the teacher is managing every minute; in a democratic community, everyone is responsible.

The details of such a structure vary with the experience and style of both children and teacher. In the teaching I have done with children who have high cultural competence in cooperation, oral memory, and pattern-making but low exposure to English language and literacy, I believe it was important to immerse them in print—a new experience—and to encourage collaborative work that built on their interpersonal competence.

Developing a workable schedule (see "A Teacher's Day in Kindergarten" opposite) for a three-and-a-half-hour teaching day required more conscious thought on my part than did arranging the space and provisioning it. I wanted to avoid the rigid scheduling in which some children have to be hurried to finish and some have to be amused while others finish. After considerable experimentation I developed a schedule that satisfied me with an appropriate variety of choices, time for in-depth play, and opportunities for specific teaching of skills to small groups and individual children. There were long

---

Knowledge is constructed not in isolation but within the social group. [The environment] needs to be designed to provide opportunities for the people involved to interact with one another and with the environment to co-construct knowledge.

—Susan Fraser

The Lively Kindergarten

A Teacher's Day in Kindergarten

What the children are doing	What I am doing

11:30 A.M. INDEPENDENT READING

- coming into the room
- filing homework, putting a sticker on the chart
- looking at, choosing, and talking about books
- relocating books in proper storage pots and on shelves

- spot-checking homework
- talking to parents
- chatting with kids about yesterday's unresolved problems (personal or homework)
- observing children's book skills

11:50 A.M. WHOLE-GROUP WRITING/READING

- singing a calming song
- exploring interactive writing (our opening greeting)
- reading together

- singing with children as a calming down time
- writing the greeting; noting letter identification, formation, use of initial sounds; anticipating the next teaching point; observing reading behaviors
- reading with children; observing their reading

12:05 P.M. DRAWING/WRITING TIME

- drawing/writing individually, with friends, with the teacher
- date stamping and filing writing after it has been checked
- playing in literacy centers
- sharing individual stories in a group

- working with a team on its story dictation or shared writing
- spot-checking children's writing
- noting what's going on in literacy centers
- reading or leading a music activity

12:45 P.M. FREE CHOICE TIME

- being the Person-of-the-Day to choose an activity
- choosing what to do and doing it
- working individually with Mrs. Lee, the classroom assistant

- announcing centers for choosing
- observing children at play
- leading special activities

1:45 P.M OUTSIDE TIME

- carrying out cleanup tasks to prepare for going outside
- playing outside

- helping in the cleanup
- observing children at play

2:20 P.M. WHOLE-GROUP MATH

- participating in a group math activity

- leading the children in the activity

2:30 P.M. MATH TEAMS

- engaging in team math activities

- working with one team of children
- observing /noting the progress of other teams

3:00 P.M. CLOSING CIRCLE

- sharing their stories and constructions
- giving the news as the Person-of-the-Day
- singing a closing song

- writing the news of the day
- giving homework
- singing with the children

Note: Times are approximate and variable.

blocks of time for children to work, and they could continue working or move to new choices when their work was completed. Short whole-group meetings on the rug let us experience transition while emphasizing classroom community; the ritual things we did together balanced the choices we made for ourselves.

Teacher time and choice time

Earlier in discussing the central role of play in my classroom, I explained the rhythm of our day and the flow between teacher choice and children's choice. It would go like this.

Independent reading—The start to our kindergarten day

As children come into the classroom, they show me their homework, file it, and put a sticker on the chart. Then they go to their team tables and get books from their team's book pot or from any of several book pots around the room (art books in the art area, math books in the math area, science books in the science area, theme books in a theme display, Big Books in the big book rack, as well as photo albums and class-made books). Children move around the room, take books wherever they like, read on the rug or at any table, talk to friends, use pointers to read song or poem charts or Big Books, go to the theme or math or science center to get books.

What's a book pot? In New Zealand, where Reading Recovery was invented, teachers use the word *pot* for any sort of container—basket, box, tub, or real pot. I trained as a Reading Recovery teacher, and I like the word.

This time allows children to straggle in and me to speak to parents without interruption.

It enables me to chat individually and in small groups with kids who have unresolved problems from the previous day. Sometimes I meet with children who have had a hard time with the homework. I also spend time observing children's book-handling skills and early reading strategies (a district-mandated assessment I do easily through observation and by using a class checklist and anecdotal notes). Later in the year I also use this time with children who appear ready for guided reading in early emergent reading books.

This is a wonderful time in a community of readers and writers. Children share books, do spontaneous choral reading, and engage in lively chats everywhere in the room, anticipating our day together. During this time of day, I notice that themes for emergent curriculum are often germinated as children get each other excited about a new topic.

Whole-group writing/reading

As arrivals come to a close, I turn off the lights and begin a song for calming down. This signals the time to gather on the rug. Whole-group gathering follows a specific ritual and functions as a centering time. From the first day of our kindergarten, the whole-group time ritual would begin with interactive writing—our opening greeting. (This teaching strategy is often called *morning message*, but our kindergarten was afternoon.)

I write the daily greeting on a dry-erase board. Children take turns sharing the pen with me and doing as much of the writing as they can. Everyone participates. Children who are unable to form letters handle the equally important jobs of holding the spaces between the words and putting in punctuation. By this process I teach the children how writing works, how reading and writing are interconnected, how letters are formed, and the conventions of writing in English. This group

---

Developmental Stages in Encounters with Materials
Toddlers: *Again and again, I do what I do with this stuff.*
Threes: *Hey! Look what this stuff can do!*
Fours and fives: *What can I make this stuff be?*
　　　　　　　　　　—*Margie Carter and Deb Curtis (1994)*

> Dear Students,
>
> Today is Thursday.
>
> Today we are going to the park.
>
> ♡ Ms. Evans

> Hi Girls!
>
> Hi Boys!
>
> Today is Monday.
>
> ♡ Ms. Evans

activity sets the stage for the individual writing that follows.

On the first day of school, and for as much as half the year, the letter we write reads, "Hi Girls! Hi Boys! Today is Monday. ♡ Ms. Evans." I say each word slowly; the children say it with me. I invite volunteers to write any letter they hear, and I refer them to the nearby name chart as a cue for letters. We reread the greeting as each word is added. The first day I do nearly all of the writing, but by day two there are several volunteers.

The format stays the same until most children have mastered some writing and all of the reading. Then I add to our opening a second, varying sentence, which we have spent some time discussing: "Today we are going to ___."

Later on I change the salutation to include new words that children like the sound of. "Dear Kids" is an example. (My class in "Kathleen's story . . . " [Part 2] was especially fond of "Dear Students" for some reason.) Even later we negotiate further on what the text might be.

To discourage copying, I erase the greeting after we read it and before I send children off to write. Copying fosters dependency on a model and delays the development of independent writers. I want children to take the risk of using whatever they know about writing to construct their meaning in their own way, even though they may not immediately produce what looks like real writing.

Whole-group time also includes shared reading from a Big Book, a chart, or a mini-lesson on some fundamental aspect of reading. Like the greeting, these activities model the conventions of print. But from the first day I also model the different ways children write—drawing, scribbling, making random letters—and we continue to talk a lot about how all of these are fine ways to write in kindergarten. All efforts at *driting*, a combination of drawing/writing, are valued and shared.

Driting is a term Anne Haas Dyson uses to describe the symbolic representations of emergent writers. She explains,

> Initially print may simply be an interesting object to investigate or a useful prop for dramatic play . . . When children first begin to use written language to symbolize their ideas, print may continue in a supplemental role. For example, they may write stories by "symbol weaving" . . . by intertwining written words with talk and drawing. (1993, 79)

I know teachers who have abandoned drawing and story dictation to focus on writing. But, while some children use drawing and dictation in order to avoid writing, I find these activities invaluable in assessing children's English language development as they practice using story grammar and construction. I also gain insight into each child's interests, fears, and worries and acquire readable symbolic representations of their thinking.

For children who see few adults writing, observing word-to-text matching is a wonderful opportunity. A teacher taking dictation must carefully repeat each word as it is recorded to maximize the learning.

Even in very young children, we see pretend writing before representational drawing

---

It's up to adults to provide enough space, enough materials, and enough time, by arranging the environment so play can happen.

—Elizabeth Jones and Gretchen Reynolds (1992)

Seven Stages of Writing Development

Young children's understanding of writing develops in predictable stages:

1. Children are unable to differentiate between drawing and written language.
2. Children start differentiating between drawing and written language.
3. Children begin to use symbols that are part of the culture's system of writing. They may just write strings of letters, but when someone asks them to read what they wrote, they go on and on.
4. Children try to create an alternative correspondence between spoken and written language; for example, the written response may be the length of the spoken utterance according to the child's own reasoning.
5. Children begin using the syllabic hypothesis, one symbol for one syllable.
6. Children use both the syllabic and the alphabetic hypotheses; the alphabetic assumes a relationship between letters and sounds.
7. Children break the code. They are now on their way to developing their written language according to the way adults use written language in their culture. This is when they begin to grapple with invented spellings and discover the conventional spellings used in our orthography (Ferreiro & Teberosky 1982; Flores & Garcia 1984).

or organized scribbling. I look for examples of developmental stages (see "Seven Stages of Writing Development" above) as I review children's driting. One drawing example of a birthday cake had wavy lines going left to right down the length of the cake. Other drawings included invented symbols—

letterlike, but not real letters of the English language. As children make the transition from pretend to real letters, they rehearse what they know—their names, then words in their environment, and strings of letters as well. It's at this stage that they begin to apply phonetic principles.

In our class the opening greeting serves as daily practice in hearing sounds in words and recording them. I have found that judicious use of sentence frames and word walls is an effective scaffold at this point to help children move into greater independence.

Driting time

From the whole group, children move out to their team tables, where blank sheets of legal-size paper (I think lined paper inhibits the development of writing at this stage), crayons, pencils, and markers are available. Writing activity begins at the table but often ends up on the floor, in the office play area, at the science table, or anywhere there is available print and space to write.

At the start of the year, I always hope for at least name writing or an attempt at it (to help me identify a child's future work) as well as whatever else a child is able to do given his or her stage of writing development. If a child can't hold a pencil, much less form letters, I am happy with some dedicated scribbling as appropriate practice for future writing. If a child who can draw representationally just slaps something on the paper to get done, I send him back for a better effort. By the end of each year, several children get to the point at which they know lots of high-frequency-use words and have enough experience saying words slowly and recording the word sounds they hear by spelling phonetically that with some coaching they can put together a sentence or two.

As the year progresses I ask children to rehearse what they want to write. At group time I ask, "What do you think you'll write about today?" and then help them focus their story and rehearse it. The process also helps to stimulate other children's ideas. As writing is finished, any children who want to pretend read their writing to me or to the class are invited to do so. The children complete their writing, date-stamp and file their works (I keep the file box on the table at which I am working), and then are free to go to any one of the various literacy centers in the room (see "Literacy Centers"). The children and I revisit the writing files at the end of each month to choose writing samples for portfolios.

Most children write for at least 10 minutes; some stay with it for the entire driting time—about 40 minutes. There is lots of conversation and movement around the room to find words or get help from a friend.

During this time I work with one team of children per day, taking story dictation and sharing the pen with children who are ready. These work samples give me the opportunity to assess each child's English language development (a district requirement), notion of story language, and conventions, and to note what ideas and themes are on the children's minds. I work with the small group or with individual children for nearly the entire time except for the inevitable interruptions, which are minimal as children become more competent in managing their learning.

It takes at least the first three weeks of school to get this period of the day organized. By the end of the year I am not needed to keep it going, except for help in spelling words; it has a life of its own.

The closing ritual for writing time is either a read-aloud from a book or the sharing of children's stories (if there are children who want to share). A short movement or music activity may follow, and then it is "toy time" —an hour of choice.

Literacy Centers

Literacy centers offer additional skill practice during writing time. They provide activities that children haven't tended to pick during choice time and that support their development of fine-motor skills, letter recognition, sight vocabulary, and oral language. Not all activities are available every day; I vary the offerings.

ABCs: everything has alphabet letters— books, rubber stamps, puzzles, felt letters, magnetic letters, letter templates, sandpaper letters, an ABC lotto game.

table toys: puzzles, bead stringing, sewing cards—all help fine-motor skills.

puppets: puppets and a flannel board to explore oral language.

office: typewriter and office supplies.

overhead projector: a class poem or a sheet of handwriting is projected onto large sheets of paper tacked to the wall, and colored markers are there for "rainbow writing."

bookmaking

sentence strips

read-the-room: song and poem charts from our shared reading are posted around the room; a variety of pointers are available.

write-around-the-room: blank paper, clipboards, and a variety of writing tools for writers on the move.

laptop writing: small chalkboards and dry-erase boards.

Book pots are in all the literacy areas.

Free choice—"Toy time"

Children make more limited choices among activities at several other times of our day, but during this hour everything in the room is available to them for self-selected work and play. They call it "toy time." Some children choose to continue a literacy or math activity; others move to the art tables, rug toys, and dramatic play.

Our transition from the previous activity begins as I go through the choices for the day, pointing to each of the icons I have created to represent the areas. The child named Person-of-the-Day has the first choice—the activity or materials he or she would like to play with—and goes off to play. We continue quickly through the options until all have something they would like to do.

The key to setting up this activity is having more choices than children (see "Setting Up a Choice Time"). If a child doesn't get a first choice, another will work perhaps. Some children stay with their initial choice, others don't. But the number of available spaces at an activity is clear from its setup and is restated whenever a child chooses an area. The children become quite competent in finding places without disrupting the play of others. They are also free to negotiate a change of places. Further, the children become aware that more materials are located in the closet behind my desk, where they are allowed to snoop, window-shop, and take things out if they ask for and get my permission.

During the children's toy time, I use my time several ways. I might call a few children away from their activity to work on "have-tos," such as a special activity missed by a child who has been absent. I might direct a small cooking, science, or art activity that requires adult supervision. I might lead a theme activity. I am always listening to the children and observing their play to uncover emergent themes, issues, and ideas. Debriefing following choice time helps me figure out if what I've seen is truly important to the children. For example, I might say, "I noticed a lot of you trying to get a turn at the water table where I put the fishing poles, shells, and sea creatures. Why don't you think about finding a way we could make a bigger fishing pier tomorrow?"

Mrs. Lee, our classroom assistant, arrives each afternoon near the end of free choice and begins to work one-to-one with children on letter identification. Thoughtfully she

Setting Up a Choice Time

Choice centers (with the number of child places at each indicated) can include some of the following:

water table (2), science center (4), art table (6), playdough (2 to 4), easel painting (2), theme center (4), table toys (6), little dollhouse (2), playhouse (4), dramatic play (e.g., store, hospital, restaurant) (4), rug toys (6 to 8+).

Below are details for three examples.

Science center

• animals (seasonal): caterpillars to Monarchs, silkworms to moths, and snails, lizards, frogs, fish, rabbits

• rocks, seashells

• magnifying glasses, bug boxes, lenses, balances, and so on

Art table

• materials for making collages

• materials for 3-D sculptures (cardboard mailing tubes, paper towel and toilet paper rolls, stiff paper)

• tools such as scissors, small pinking shears, yarn, string, ribbon, brads, hole punches, plastic needles, staplers, glue, tape

• paper in a variety of sizes, shapes, and textures

• art media such as watercolors, pastels, charcoal (after each medium has been introduced)

Rug play

• blocks, large pattern blocks, Legos, Space Construx, animals, family dolls (many cultures), superhero figures, dinosaurs, and so on

---

Note: Art materials vary with the season and with what children bring in. I organize collections of materials to encourage new creative combinations. Many of our rug toys come from friends, thrift shops, and flea markets.

looks for children on her list who are between activities rather than interrupting those who are presently involved. Because the children so look forward to her arrival, at least a couple of them always hang out just to watch her working one-to-one and benefit from her instruction as well.

Children clean up, with help from the adults. A quick song or fingerplay gets everyone to the rug as an ending to choice time. From here we head outside for 25 to 30 minutes.

Outside time

At the school described in my story (Part 2), I had very little control over our outside time and space, a shared playground on which I had wanted us to have exclusive use of the climber without big kids interfering. Typically I use outside time to observe children's large-motor skills, play interactions, and play themes. Are these the same themes I see in their stories and indoor imaginative play? Are there big concerns or worries?

Often when the weather is nice, the area outside the classroom becomes a place for outdoor art making and more elaborate water play. We come inside and the children settle down to my story (if I haven't read one before) and singing or a calming dance activity.

Whole-group math

In our whole-group math lesson, I use the calendar in a variety of ways, for counting, numeral recognition and formation, patterning (sticker arrangements on the calendar), saying the names of days of the week, and counting off days until some big event. Graphing or estimation is one activity we work on each week, relating it to our current theme development or

an emerging topic (e.g., How many people are going to have what kind of sandwich at our upcoming picnic?). One popular theme—teeth—is a topic that works well when nearly everyone has lost a tooth. Our graphing activity goes like this:

Inquiry. Who has lost teeth? How many teeth have you lost?

Data collection. Day 1: (homework assignment) Draw a picture of the teeth you have lost. How many have you lost?

Data representation. Day 2: Cut out a big tooth, and write on it the number of teeth you have lost.

Graphing. Day 3: Put your big tooth on the graph in the column with your number on it.

Analyzing. Day 4: Look at the graph. Tell me what you notice about how many teeth kids have lost. (As a record of their mathematical awareness, I write the children's comments in speech bubbles drawn on the graph. Predictably they talk about which number column has "won" (most lost teeth) and which columns have zero.)

Conclusions. Day 5: What else do you notice on our graph? (I reread their Day 4 comments and encourage them to take the analysis further. Children make various

How many 🦷 did the children in our class lose?

comparisons, and we record them on the graph. The tooth graph goes in our Save box, and I pull it out in a few months after we've done another tooth graph to ask, "How has our math picture changed since February [or whenever]?"

Our estimating activities occur over a week's time. I change the amount to be estimated each day and tell the children if I have added or taken away: "There is more today" or "There is less than yesterday." I usually start with about eight items in a jar, thinking that *eight* might be the limit of number sense for many beginning kindergartners. We don't do this activity every week; I feel it might get boring.

At the end of whole-group math, the children join their math teams.

Math teams

Like the writing teams I created, math teams are based on where children sat on the rug on the first day of school! Occasionally I change the team makeup. I make minor adjustments, or children decide after one of the breaks in our year-round cycle that it is time for a change. Interestingly, however, the teams end up much the same as they start out. Best friends get on teams together; some teams are predominantly boys or girls. It's up to them.

Math team activities rotate through the days of the week. Each day one team works with me on an activity that involves manipulatives, and this enables me to assess their mathematical thinking. One other team works with the classroom assistant on skill-focused activities such as numeral writing, counting, and measuring. Another team listens to a math-related story tape of books such as these at the listening center—*Mouse Count* (Walsh 1991), *Millions of Cats* (Gag 1977), and *Five Little Ducks* (Raffi 1999). When the tape finishes, they illustrate the story and retell it to one of the adults, the class assistant or me. One team has free

choice to explore manipulatives in the math area or the blocks and other construction toys on the rug.

Closing circle

We close the day with a sharing of math stories and constructions (either the actual construction or the child's drawing of it). I discuss homework. In the group gathering, the Person-of-the-Day dictates the news of the day to me and then gets help in illustrating it in our news book (an oversized sketch pad). The rest of us finish our debriefing of our day. We reread yesterday's news, sing a song, and then go home.

So long, it's been good to know you,
So long, it's been good to know you,
So long, it's been good to know you,
We've got to be traveling on.

The process: A cycle of teacher behaviors

Once the stage is set in the classroom, with materials organized for children to explore and a schedule prepared that gives them time to explore, the teacher's main challenges are, first, to pay attention to children's interests and skills and, second, to orchestrate the possible strands into a multifaceted curriculum. Orchestration is a complex process grounded in the teacher's trust that she will be able to meet required objectives in a program that responds to children and their interests.

Paying attention requires a knowledge of children—their family/cultural experiences, their behavior and its meaning, and the developmental sequence of their growth (Bredekamp & Rosegrant 1992). In learning to pay attention in this way, the study of child development, plenty of practice in focused observing (Reynolds & Jones 1997), and opportunities for dialogue with other adults are all important elements.

As a preschool teacher, I learned my profession in a child development framework. More recently, as a Reading Recovery teacher, I have learned to look at how curriculum emerges in the smallest ways. In Reading Recovery (Clay 1993) we call it "taking the child's lead" in deciding how to teach and what is next. My teaching decisions in developing the literacy curriculum for one child are different from those I make when I'm working with a whole class, but in each circumstance decisions happen within an emergent curriculum process. I like thinking about what happens as steps in a cycle of teacher behaviors in support of emergent curriculum.

Paying attention to children and orchestrating their learning seem to include all these steps in more or less this sequence:

noticing what is happening with children, at school and in the world around them

inviting children to pay attention to the happenings and to become involved in exploring them

responding to children's apparent interests; encouraging their responses in a variety of ways

provisioning the classroom with materials to further children's exploration

connecting everyone to the exploration, connecting past explorations and experiences in this new learning, and leaving avenues for further connection

conferring with children about what's happening

reflecting—as an adult, with other adults, and with the children—on children's learning

What does each of these steps look like when it is happening? In writing this book, we have been dialoguing intensively as we try to sort out what we know and how to explain it. A sample of our dialogue about our experiences with this cycle of teaching behaviors follows in the next section.

Young children learn through their actions and interactions with material things and with people. In preparing a learning environment we begin with things—furnishings, materials, objects.

From space and time to people

Things stay where we put them, at least temporarily, and they don't have minds of their own. They serve as the children's first message about this place called *school*. If, as Kathleen describes, the nonverbal cues are clear and there is more than enough for everyone to choose and to do, children learn to negotiate the environment without dependence on teacher direction.

Schools run by clocks. Clocks are useful tools in coordinating organizational tasks, but clock time and child time don't always match. Clearly defined but flexible scheduling offers children a second message about school—that our days together are predictable and all these things will happen every day. They learn that you won't be interrupted every time you start something really interesting, that in this place there is enough time as well as enough stuff.

Schools are full of people. Kathleen says that the very best kindergarten would "be like home but with more toys and more kids." More kids mean more possible friendships as well as more possible squabbles. Making friends and solving squabbles are a central part of what happens at school, where we all are practicing life in a democratic community and everyone is expected to be responsible.

Responsibility implies critical thinking about such basic issues as fairness and friendship. There is also room for feelings—hurt and anger, delight and love. In the classroom, feelings get *represented*—in talk and storybooks and paintings and playdough—just as facts and spatial relationships do. Learning is full of relationships of all sorts, and it takes place in *community*.

—BJ

Thinking about Teacher Behaviors That Support Emergent Curriculum

On the empty stage a play is born; so too children and teacher turn the classroom environment into an active community of learners. How this happens, how curriculum emerges is a process that starts with paying attention and follows through to full orchestration. What happens are steps in a cycle of teacher behaviors.

Capturing the essence of what we did

To explore how the steps in this cycle have played out in each of our experiences, we decided to talk together, share reflections and insights on the stories we have told in Part 2, and offer constructive evaluation of our teaching practices. This dialogue netted a richness of ideas that follow, grouped by steps (noticing, inviting, responding, provisioning, connecting, conferring, and reflecting) in the cycle of teacher behaviors.

Noticing

Teachers need to *notice* what is happening at school and in the world around. "The best care, whether by a parent or a physician or a teacher, is founded in observation. . . . If we can learn a deeper noticing of the world around us, this will be the basis of effective concern" (Bateson 1994,109).

BJ: Looking back on your teacher stories I think some of what you all were noticing were curriculum possibilities, not just children's current interests. You were asking yourselves, "What's going on around here? In the neighborhood? In the media? In children's families?" "Is it something we should explore in our class?"

KR: That sounds familiar. Our school moved to a new neighborhood, and I checked out its possibilities before school even started. There were lots of interesting houses. Later in the year they became a compelling class project.

KE: Back in the year of *Jurassic Park*, I noticed that dinosaurs seemed to be everywhere. I wondered then if I needed to bring them into the classroom, if they were influencing children's lives.

BJ: When I was raising my own children, I was always alert to the presence of

---

BJ—Betty Jones, **KR**—Kay Stritzel Rencken, **KE**—Kathleen Evans, **MW**—Marsha Williams, **CS**—Carolyn Stringer

construction sites within walking or driving distance. How roads and buildings and bridges get built is interesting to children *and* to me. Watching building projects is something I enjoy doing with kids.

MW: Our family goes to the beach at a nearby state park, and on these family trips I've gotten ideas to bring back to the classroom. (Luckily for me, K–1 in our district must do oceanography as a science unit.) Carolyn, did you go to the beach to get sand for your classroom, or did you go to the beach for you?

CS: For me, definitely! But when I was there, noticing surf and sunsets and sand, I realized that sand could be transported—and that it's a really neat thing to share with kids.

KE: These are all *potential* interests for children, but also I urge teachers to notice children's *actual* interests, which may be more subtle, revealed in their chats, stories, or drawings. I think we need to pay close attention to these.

MW: I think so too. Say more about how you all do that.

KR: I schedule long blocks of time, indoors and outdoors, in which children are free to choose activities and I am free to watch them and listen. I pay attention to their dramatic play and their conversations and their drawings. I notice what these are about. I begin to look for and find themes and patterns.

CS: I did that sort of noticing pretty well, I think. I took notes about the children's interest in all the people working at our school. I noticed a lot of interest in bunk beds. I noticed that the children liked having a store for selling pumpkins. But I didn't know when to take it further. I

didn't know what interests to follow up on. And when I did try, I kept taking over.

I made the assumption that I needed to do something with what I noticed—to fill the learning space. Parker Palmer (1998) writes about preparing a learning space that is open. This requires a lot more skill than filling it does!

KE: It seems to be hard for inexperienced teachers to know what to do with what they notice. They don't know which events are significant and which are extraneous. You're an experienced teacher, Carolyn, but perhaps not in this kind of teaching.

CS: I wrote in my journal, "Had I been paying closer attention . . ."

KR: You *were* good at noticing, but what about the other steps in Kathleen's cycle—in the whole orchestrating process? What comes next, Kathleen?

Inviting

Teachers need to *invite* children to become engaged in the project of building the classroom.

KE: Regie Routman (1991) introduced me to the concept of *invitations*. "Would you like to ____?" "What would happen if you ____?" Invitations are particularly important for children who are unsure about school or find my room unlike what they have heard about school. I use invitations to get them into the environment and also to help me decide whether a potential theme is worth pursuing or when to let go of an idea.

Those dinosaurs, for example, when *Jurassic Park* was big—as my invitation I got all my dinosaur books together into a pot, left them with the other books, and watched to see what happened.

CS: What were you watching for?

KE: To see if the children just ran through them and went right on to other books or if they pored over them, talked with their friends about the pictures, asked questions about them of each other and of me. As I watched, it was clear that they were wondering about dinosaurs.

KR: Are your invitations the same as what conventional lesson plans call *motivations* and teachers at Reggio Emilia call *provocations*?

BJ: I've always thought of motivations as manipulations, because they omit the step of watching the children to see what their interests are. The curriculum is prescribed by teacher or textbook, and the teacher is supposed to motivate the children to be interested in what they have to study.

MW: I was supposed to motivate them to study oceanography. However, some prescribed curriculum makes sense because of where we live—on the ocean. Ocean would be likely to emerge as a spontaneous interest of our children.

KE: If I were ever stuck with a have-to theme, I'd do my level best to see what piece of it really resonated with the children. And that's the piece I'd do. Any theme is rich and varied in the approaches one can take, so this always seems possible to me.

CS: I do like the word *provocation,* used at Reggio. I think of a provocation as an event of any kind that catalyzes children's passions. It can come from anywhere, not necessarily from the teacher. Provocations happen in the classroom all the time, and at recess. Our hampster Zippity's death was a provocation—in my class.

KR: That's interesting; you've broadened the definition to include unplanned as well as planned events. But it was your "sea

animal," Carolyn, that I experienced as provoking rather than inviting. It introduced play acting and magical thinking, which wasn't necessary to motivate the children; they were already fascinated by sand itself. The sea animal was a cute teacher idea rather than an authentic part of the inquiry.

BJ: Carolyn, what do you think?

CS: I agree with Kay. The children were truly fascinated with sand, but I hadn't had enough experience with emergent curriculum to know where to go with that interest or how to keep our investigations *open.* I played teacher by inventing—first, a sea animal, and later, a sandbox. I kept looking around for closure, for answers, instead of continuing to ask myself, "What are the children's questions?" This question should have been at the center of my research and practice, but all I knew was the traditional motivation approach. Some days I would stumble onto something real, and the next day I'd be back imposing things again.

KR: And as it turned out, you didn't follow through with the sea animal. So maybe you recognized it as unnecessary after all.

BJ: Carolyn, you mentioned that your train activities began with reading, *The Little Engine That Could* (Piper [1930] 1998), and your pumpkin patch stories and play began with a field trip. Are books and field trips different kinds of invitations? Can emergent curriculum begin with these as well as be moved along with them?

KR: Oh yes! I do that too, especially at the beginning of the year. For the last few years, I've introduced a watermelon theme by reading a watermelon story (Parkes & Smith 1986) in the second or third week of school. Watermelon is in season—it's

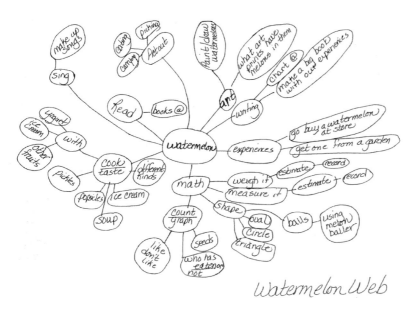

Watermelon Web

KE: Having noticed the presence of dinosaurs in the media and their spin-offs, then inviting the children's response and receiving it, I mentioned to the children at our group time that it was clear they were wondering about dinosaurs. "Let's do a chart," I said. I used my K-W-L (know/wonder/learn) chart (Staley 1998, 22), set up with three columns headed with these questions:

What do you already *know* about dinosaurs?

What do you *wonder* about dinosaurs?

What do you want to *learn* about dinosaurs?

I saw that the children had learned a lot from looking at the books (and I remembered that my questions about the world, when I was 5, came from poring over the pictures in *National Geographic*). I acknowledged how much they knew, and I said that we'd be thinking about what else we'd like to know about dinosaurs. For homework I sent home a pictograph: Three Questions Your Child Has about Dinosaurs. There were frames on the page to invite drawings as well as words. Older brothers and sisters helped, and all the children were able to complete the task. The questions that came back were wonderful: "Do daddy dinosaurs take care of the baby dinosaurs?" "Do dinosaurs cry?" "Can a dinosaur climb a tree?" "Do dinosaurs chase people?" All led to important investigations.

something the children all know about—and it offers many possible areas of study. I can concentrate on the children and follow their interests rather than focus on a new curriculum theme.

KE: With young children it's important to begin with what's real. I take the children walking to every child's house at the beginning of the year. That's another sort of invitation; it introduces types of houses and gives us a common experience to take off from. If the children show interest, I respond.

Responding

Teachers need to *respond* to children's apparent interests and to look for their responses.

If teachers were to approach their classes with an appreciation of how much their pupils already know, helping to bring the structure of informal knowledge into consciousness, students would have the feeling of being on familiar ground, already knowing much about how to know, how knowledge is organized and integrated.

— Mary Catherine Bateson

MW: Since the Romeo and Juliet play was genuinely the children's idea, not mine, the first thing I did was to respond. The invitation that preceded this had nothing to do with my noticing *children's* interests; I just noticed how soon Valentine's Day would be upon us. My questioning "What do you think we should do?" led to Elizabeth's answer, "We could do Romeo and Juliet."

"Why Romeo and Juliet?" was my response. But the children seemed to know why, even if I didn't.

BJ: Marsha, you're describing your verbal response to children's ideas. You began there too, Kathleen, and then you went right on to pull out more ideas from them, using your know/wonder/learn chart. So did Marsha, with class brainstorming at every step of the process. Is this what you all mean by responding—conversations with yourself, spontaneous planning, conversations with the children, and then representing what is said?

KE: Yes. Different things can set off the conversation. And other people such as parents can be included. Sometimes it's really just noticing. I began to realize how important fishing was to the Mien families by paying attention to the content of children's drawings and dictated stories. I responded with comments like this: "I see you've drawn a fishing picture every day this week. Do people in your family fish a lot?"

KR: You were responding to the child's invitation to his topic, weren't you, instead of inviting him to respond to one you chose?

KE: Yes. I could introduce children to American cultural themes but not to Mien cultural themes. I had to rely on the children and their parents to teach me about things important to them. So I did a lot of noticing and offered children invitations (providing drawing materials and opportunities to tell their stories, for example) to bring their home experiences into the classroom. Then I could respond by acknowledging, planning, and provisioning for dramatic play, art activities, science explorations.

CS: It seems to me that true responding requires us, as teachers, to believe in the wealth that is in children and always take care to watch for the truth they have to offer us.

Provisioning

Teachers need to *provision* the classroom with materials for children's further exploration.

BJ: Is *provisioning* a real verb? Shouldn't it be *providing*?

KE: I hope it is, because *providing* isn't as descriptive of the process—"getting in provisions" is something children can participate in. I brought in fishing poles and magnetic fish and rocks and shells for the water table to encourage fishing. But when there were more fishers than fishing poles, children solved the problem by cheerfully improvising more poles from construction toys and rearranging the book area to become a pier.

MW: Creating a play involved us all in collecting and making props, creating a stage set, and producing programs. That's another kind of provisioning. We relied heavily on parents too for boxes as props, and for costumes and help in making them.

KR: You mentioned the provisioning you did, Carolyn, when you told us about the children creating a hamster playground. You provided a construction table as well as blocks, didn't you?

CS: Yes, with all sorts of junk—cardboard tubes, boxes, all the stuff children can construct with. And tape and glue and rubber bands to hold the pieces together—I have those available all the time.

KE: Oh, that reminds me of our mouse traps! For a while our classroom was overrun with mice. We couldn't open a cupboard without running into evidence of their presence. Through story dictation I realized that the mice were on the minds of the children just as they were on mine. In each of Jimmy's stories, a character called Monster Mouse showed up.

Jimmy was a *master player* (Reynolds & Jones 1997), and he and his friends decided it was time to build mouse traps. I suggested that they draw some plans so they would know what supplies they could bring from home and I would know what I might need to find. We also have many loose parts in the classroom, provisions right there for the using.

At the beginning of each day, more and more loose parts arrived from home. From the sketches made each day during writing time, more and more elegant mouse traps were constructed during choice time.

(Unfortunately they never trapped a mouse, although we had lots of evidence that the bait attracted many mice.)

MW: Did that become a whole-class project?

KE: No, it remained a small-group activity. And I wouldn't have encouraged it to expand; I was getting very tired of mice. It was just a few boys who worked pretty independently on it for several weeks.

KR: What an original way to become superheroes! Mighty Mousecatchers versus Monster Mouse!

CS: Can we talk about *connecting* now? I'm not sure what you mean by it.

Connecting

Teachers need to *connect* the children to the exploration, connect past explorations to this new learning, and consider opportunities for future connections.

KE: I'm thinking of several questions: (1) How does everyone involved get connected to the topic, the project? (2) How does this connect to what we've done before and to what we'll do in the future? and even (3) What's the connection to the basic question, What's worth knowing in kindergarten?

CS: Getting the whole class connected to a project was the only way I could think about it. If only one or two kids were truly interested in trains, then in my mind somehow trains weren't a real project.

KR: I notice that in three of our four classrooms we've

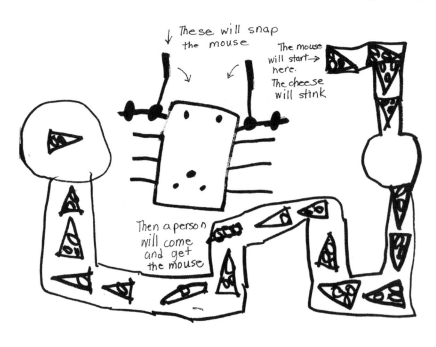

These will snap the mouse

The mouse will start here.

The cheese will stink

Then a person will come and get the mouse

been talking about whole-class projects—my houses, Marsha's play, Carolyn's sandbox. Our whole class kept going on walking field trips, looking at houses, and then coming back and discussing and drawing them. Marsha took the whole class through the plot and characters and staging *Romeo and Juliet,* and many of her children's choice activities during that time were related to the play—making hats, costumes, and castle windows. Carolyn organized her class into committees, and committee work took over her day.

MW: I guess Elizabeth and Ben and Michael and Chester could have had a Romeo and Juliet project as a small group instead of involving the whole class. But there wasn't another adult available to work with them regularly, and I don't think they would have gotten very far on their own. Certainly some of the children were much less involved than others, but they had other choices except during class meetings. They didn't *have to be* preoccupied by the play.

KE: Carolyn, How would your project have looked different if the small groups had tackled it the best they could?

CS: I didn't consider that. I worked with each committee in turn, while others worked independently. But by creating committees, I required everyone to participate in the sandbox project, though some children were more actively interested than others. It was my value that they be involved in the sandbox production and in the academic activities I purposefully brought into it.

KE: I guess I'm the exception. I didn't feel any need to develop a whole-class project other than our continuing focus on language and literacy. For my children, that focus was the overall purpose of school. But I did identify and support specific play themes, and I documented and shared these with the whole class and with parents. They became interest focuses. I made an effort to integrate the interests into our day without overwhelming the everyday rituals, activities, and play.

KR: What about your houses, the start to your year? That's whole class too.

KE: That was my idea, not the children's. It was a community building activity, giving us shared experience on which to build in drawing, stories, and play. It connected the children to each other in the two contexts of school and family. They could talk about it. They could find each other—for playing after school or walking to school together.

KR: So one question has to do with connecting people with each other around a common topic. Your second question asks about connecting to past and future activities. Are you thinking about other topics or about skill learning? Vocabulary building, classification, graphing and measuring, reading and writing and drawing—all the measurable objectives to which we're supposed to be teaching?

CS: I was constantly aware of the need to integrate the mandatory teaching into whatever we were doing. That anxiety got in my way a lot.

MW: I found that connecting with skills learning kept happening without my conscious effort. Counting and measuring, shapes and colors, and vocabulary really are all part of the interesting activities in our world beyond the classroom. If learning has purpose, it becomes authentic, and children retain it longer.

BJ: Skills are worth learning; we're agreed on that. What content is worth learning? That was your third question, Kathleen. I've found it useful to think about the big ideas that human beings need to grapple with at any age. "Playable big ideas" that John Nimmo and I generated in *Emergent Curriculum* (Jones & Nimmo 1994) include caring for each other, going places, gardens and harvest, lights in the darkness, and lots more.

KR: Then what are the big ideas we've been talking about in our stories? How about the idea that people need places to live?

CS: The earth has a history. Sand doesn't just happen. I didn't tell you much about our class investigation of sand and where it comes from, but many of the children really did have ideas about that.

MW: Is this a big idea? Ben said it in our Romeo and Juliet post-play discussion with the audience when someone asked about memorizing the words, "We talked a lot about what words mean and how you can use more than one word to mean the same thing." It sure felt like a big idea to me when I heard it. It's what I had wanted the children to understand: people use language to communicate, and language is complicated.

BJ: And *connecting* is a complicated concept, isn't it? It includes the teacher's ability to link and synthesize multiple worlds of concern (skills, relationships, what's worth knowing, children's interests, adults' interests) and layer them in a cohesive curriculum (Carol Anne Wien, personal communication 2000).

KE: Oh yes! And what we're doing here is an abstract, grownup version of what we need to do with children too: it's *conferring*.

Conferring

Teachers need to *confer* with children about what's happening.

KE: To me, this is the evaluative piece (in the cycle). What has been learned? What will be tackled next? What happened? What risks were taken? What mistakes were made? What joys were experienced? How does this connect? This evaluation can be done in writing, face-to-face, with a partner, in a small group, or one-to-one with a teacher.

MW: Not in a large group? We conferred all the time in our class discussions of Romeo

---

Teachers' Collaborative Research on Children

Always the teacher remains an attentive observer and, beyond that, a researcher.

The teacher's observations and transcribed tapes are taken to colleagues for group reflection.

They produce discussion and conflict within each educator's self and the group at large, and these are as important as the preceding conflicts and discussions among the children.

The teachers' reflections then modify, at times radically, their thoughts and hypotheses about the children and, even more important, their interactions with the children.

———————

Source: Reprinted, by permission of the publisher, from C. Rinaldi, "Emergent Curriculum and Social Constructivism," *The Hundred Languages of Children: The Reggio Emilia Approach to Early Childhood Education,* eds. C. Edwards, L. Gandini, & G. Forman (Norwood, NJ: Ablex, 1993), 106.

and Juliet. "We can't make the cone hats stay on—what shall we do?" And someone said, "Don't put them on your heads, put them on the castle." The kids thought that was pretty funny, but that's what we did.

KE: Yes, you certainly used conferring as group planning and evaluation. And you even did it in front of an audience, inviting them to be your outside evaluators, so to speak.

KR: Kathleen, in conferring are you trying to introduce the idea of self-evaluation by children? As teachers we aren't expected to evaluate the work of the whole class (except when a class test-score average gets thrown back at us). But we have to assess each child's progress. Do all of you confer with children individually?

MW: I've always thought we shortchange kindergartners in this area. They are capable of self-assessment if we provide time for it in our daily work. "How did you do that?" "If you did it again, what would you add?" (To do this really takes time; that's one of the luxuries of an all-day kindergarten.)

KE: At the end of the year as I close our portfolio process, I ask each child, "What do you think of yourself as a writer now?" This is an open-ended, kindergarten question, not an analytic question of the sort one might ask older children. But the children's responses are insightful: "I write by myself. Before I cannot write my name." "I can write animal names, because I like animals." "I can read what I write." These children are recognizing newfound skills, the importance of motivation, and the fact that writing is designed to be read.

KR: I was surprised by all the conferring that went on among my children about the house drawings, as they compared their drawings with our photos and with the real houses. When we devised a comments list, everyone had something good said about their drawings. These were not comments contrived by the adults; in every child's rendering of a house the children saw good points to highlight.

CS: You know, I also needed to be conferring with other teachers. The children in the classroom, working together and talking with each other, kept learning from each other. Isn't that basic Piaget—that people learn from action on objects and interaction with peers? I didn't have any peers. I didn't have anyone in my school to bounce my ideas off of or to tell me whether they were good ideas or not. Until we all started writing and talking about this book, I had to figure out things by myself, and that's a slower process.

KE: You've taken us right to the next step in the cycle, Carolyn, what I call *reflecting.*

Reflecting

Teachers need to *reflect*—as adults, with other adults, and with children—on children's learning.

KE: Reflecting has to go on all the time. It is an essential element in noticing, inviting, responding, provisioning, and connecting.

KR: And we can't just do it by ourselves. We don't have enough ideas by ourselves! John Dewey told us that. And Jean Piaget emphasized *disequilibrium* as necessary to stimulate new thinking—and there won't be enough disequilibrium unless some of it is coming in from other people's reactions. That concept may be the most important thing Americans can learn from the Reggio Emilia approach—that schools don't get wonderful unless they regularly provide for teacher talk.

BJ: And schools don't get wonderful unless the climate for teacher talk includes trust and tolerance for conflict, for genuine arguments among people with diverse experiences (Jones & Nimmo 1999). This exchange is basic to the principles in John Dewey's ideas about the richness of democracy—that dialogue with an exchange of diverse views creates the best thinking and problem solving.

Summing up

BJ: Can we sum up the steps? Kathleen, this cycle of teacher behaviors is a fine example of teacher theory building. Reflecting on your teaching practice, you invented a classification scheme to which we've all been adding examples from our own experiences. And we've been going off on tangents, of course—that's how thinking happens. It's how both curriculum and theory emerge.

KE: Yes! When I am teaching, I pay attention and I orchestrate. And that includes noticing, inviting, responding, provisioning, connecting, conferring, and reflecting. From this, curriculum emerges.

Every teacher must learn the art of stage setting, unless she or he is wedded to having desks in rows and to top-down control of the class as a whole. Every teacher who wishes to share genuine responsibility with children must also develop strategies for building a democratic community in which children care about each other and value each other's differences. And every teacher who values children's individualities must also pay attention to the family and community from which the children come, building community with parents as well. We discuss both of these challenges in the next section.

—BJ

Building a Community of Learners

In the sort of classroom we are trying to create, there are two underlying principles:

> Each child is important.
>
> Respect for others is important.

As the previous section illustrates, we orchestrate space, time, and materials to provide a setting supportive of these principles. Manipulating the setting is much easier and more respectful than manipulating children. We experiment with the organization of space to provide in reasonable balance the space for coming together, for small-group cohesion, and for privacy. We invent time schedules flexible enough to enable important projects to be sustained until they are done.

A classroom is both place and people. Our rules for the use of space and materials encourage choice, interaction among children, movement, and conversation. Large-group meetings offer both shared rituals and opportunities for solving the real problems of living together.

More problems surface in democratic classrooms than in authoritarian classrooms. Thus there are many more opportunities to practice listening to other points of view, asserting oneself, and learning to respect both self and others as people with rights and voices. Learning to live together in community, day in/day out, is basic curriculum.

In this piece we share some of our strategies for building community within the classroom and building community with families, the most important people in children's lives. We also look again at the ways in which each of us, the four teachers in this book, has interwoven classroom and community by taking children outside the classroom and bringing other people in.

Children's getting to know each other is basic: Who are you? What do you like to do? What are you afraid of? Whom do you love? In our classrooms each of us matters. We are similar, and we are all different from each other. And since adults as well as children are egocentric, our differences often cause surprise, disbelief, and even hostility. We ask ourselves, How can we learn to respect and even enjoy our differences? Can that respect accommodate individual cultural, language, and gender differences as well as support us in collaborating on a project?

The stories we each tell here include dialogue with our co-teacher/writers. Theory building, as we experience it, is a collaborative process. When colleagues question, wonder, offer stories different from our own, we grow in our ability to name and classify our experiences and eventually to present them with some confidence as principles that other teachers may find also useful. So we sum up each of our discussions with the question, What's our theory?

Kay's story—

Building classroom community: Beginning with self and others' selves

Building a community of learners in the classroom starts with the children and their teacher and their own most immediate concerns. Many activities are designed to increase the children's awareness of each other.

A democratic classroom

Democracy, the most lauded American value, is often the most ignored, especially in schools. In as many ways as I can, I try to practice democracy in my classroom. The children have many chances to act as a democratic society. We vote on many occasions. Some actions involve decisions that are important for us to make, and some do not. We vote to choose between two activities that occur at the same time; we vote to name our baby dolls; we vote to name books that we've made together.

I start the year with the children's names. Every child comes to kindergarten knowing his or her name. So we get to know one another's names. Activities enhance each child's knowledge about his or her own name. This focus builds community as well as literacy; it demands that children pay attention to significant details about each other. We look at who we are, how each name looks, how we can create art that includes our names, how we learn our names, and so on.

Our room is full of writing tools, which are available as choices every day. We use these tools in many planned activities that involve names.

Most classrooms post the alphabet, but generally the letters are identified by commercial pictures. The posted alphabet on our classroom walls lists the children's names under each letter:

M—Maria
　　Mark
　　Marcos
　　Michael

Starting the Year with Children's Names

Name book

After we talk about names, I send home a letter asking for the origin of each child's name. We make a class book, with a page for each child that includes a photo, the child's name, and what the parent said about the name.

Clapout

Using name cards showing each name divided into syllables, we clap out the children's names. These cards are available during choosing time, and children practice names by clapping out the syllables or using a rhythm instrument.

Name shapes

Children draw a line around the letters in their names to discover what shapes they make. The name card and a blank card can be a matching game.

Name graph

Using cubes, one for each letter, children graph the length of their names. They compare their names to look at concepts of *longer, shorter,* and *same.*

Body letters

Using their bodies to form letters, a group of children creates the letters of a child's name for the other children to guess.

Sign language

At the beginning of the year, we sign the initial letter of each child's name. Later we make name cards showing the sign for every letter.

Name songs

Children sing and personalize name songs, such as "Mary Wore a Red Dress" ("Feuy Wore a Yellow Sweater," etc.). We make a class big book of songs, one verse for each page. I also write out all the name songs on charts.

Reliance on commercial alphabets wastes a wonderful opportunity to make us all aware of each other and to practice reading words that really matter.

I, not the children, choose to use names as our beginning focus; that's my purposeful stage setting. From experience I know that every child's first concern when they come to school is to get their name on something. Names are safe; every child can recognize her own name or elements of it. I want each child to learn to recognize everyone else's name as well. This is a very appropriate literacy objective for kindergartners. Because names of the people in one's community are what Sylvia Ashton-Warner (1963) calls "key words," they carry the power of relationships. My goals are literacy development *and* community building.

Each room at our school has the names of the adults posted on the door or wall outside. In the first week the children and I put up a sign with all our names on it to show that we all live here.

My colleagial teacher/writers comment:

KE: I chose visiting children's houses in the same way, as a *beginning* designed for bringing us together and getting to know one another. When we don't yet know the children, we can't draw curriculum from specific knowledge of their interests.

BJ: I'm struck by the fact that both you and Kathleen teach basic skills from the beginning (Kathleen has said before that her children begin writing from day one, even if it's drawing), and you do it in ways that keep children connecting with each other as well as with their own personal concerns. Would you both say, as Dewey does in effect, that you are building the collective on the egocentricity of young children? By acknowledging each *me* publicly,

you root each child in the group, while insisting that the group has many *me*'s and you will pay attention to every one.

In John Dewey's vision, democracy is built on reciprocity among strong egos ([1916] 1966). To build democracy in a classroom there must be many opportunities to choose and to play—for children to find out who they are and what they care about, to decenter, to learn that other people are not like them. It is a place of constant negotiation—practice in the politics of getting one's own way among all those other folks with ways of their own.

In a progressive, developmentally appropriate classroom, the basic skills of literacy and mathematics are taught within the context of community building. Learning these skills—talking, writing, reading, counting, estimating—enables young members of a community to become more effective thinkers and communicators and sustains the community through shared meaning.

MW: You know, that picture is really different from what I myself remember as a child in school. As I look back, it seems to me that our teachers made it clear that school wasn't *our* place. We were big kids, big enough to stop doing what we wanted to do and instead do what we were told. It was a whole new world of following directions, keeping quiet, being controlled.

BJ: My most controlling teacher—in sixth grade—used to lecture us all the time about self-control. But as we'd sing "America the Beautiful," we used to laugh whenever we got to the line, "Confirm thy soul in self-control," because in her class *she* was in control, not us. I still see that in most schools.

KE—Kathleen Evans, BJ—Betty Jones, MW—Marsha Williams

Messages that count

Beginning activities like those Kathleen and I describe here give each child an immediate teacher message: "Yes, I know you're here. I'm glad you're here. We are paying attention to you. You're an important person in this group." This message frees the child from having to make a bid for attention. Attention is clearly a given in this place.

I've found that acknowledging children in meaningful ways like these motivates them to *want* to be responsible and self-controlled. School is a good place in which they have a presence. They don't want to mess it up. Ignoring bad behavior seems to be the least effective way of bringing children around to the idea of community. Noticing and acknowledging each child is what's necessary to get community going.

Not only are children present in this sort of classroom, but also they are absorbed. There's a lot of good stuff to do here; there's enough time and attention to go round. A curriculum that is active and interesting creates a much more relaxed classroom than does control through discipline alone. In a group of children, control can either be established top-down—the teacher being really bigger and smarter and meaner than the kids, at least in kindergarten—or bottom-up, through mutual caring.

If school is a production enterprise—Get those test scores up!—then top-down control is most efficient. But if it's a nurturing enterprise (Noddings 1992), in which competence is built on self-esteem and mutual esteem, then I believe I have to develop relationships step-by-step among us all. We all—the children too—have to own the problem of keeping things manageable. It means we all need to give the bad kid a wide berth when he's having a bad day, knowing that we all, even the teacher, will be given some leeway on our bad days.

Dilemmas teachers face

I've been teaching this way, valuing democracy, for so long that to me the worth of it seems self-evident. To be helpful to other teachers, I realize that I need to be able to analyze what I know intuitively. Carolyn reminds me, not for the first time, that problem-solving skills take a lot of learning, by teachers as well as by kids. Here's more of our group dialogue:

CS: In my classroom I kept trying to invent systems that would work to keep things under control and, as you say, to involve the children in ownership of them.

That January, I wrote in my journal that I had "finally (for now!) resolved a continuous, escalating problem" in my classroom. Choice time had been going like this: Kids would go where they pleased, switching when they liked, with no limit on numbers at any place. At cleanup, materials were strewn everywhere, and I really had to push the children to get items picked up. This was true even after I designated a child as checker, who walked to each area and showed either thumbs up or thumbs down. At first it worked beautifully; kids would go finish cleaning their area if they got thumbs down. But later no one budged except for the few children who always like to see things right even if they aren't responsible for the mess.

The children and I discussed the problem thoroughly, and they always came up with the same solution: Close choice time indefinitely and entirely. It's so absurd! Don't children realize their own right to play in a classroom?

Since their solution was inappropriate, I decided to impose my own. (I guess that's my right as teacher.) I wrote each choice on a card that I posted on the whiteboard with a magnet. The children have name

---

CS—Carolyn Stringer, **MW**—Marsha Williams, **KE**—Kathleen Evans, **KR**—Kay Stritzel Rencken, **BJ**—Betty Jones

magnets, which we use to count attendance each morning. I called a few children at a time to post their names under their choice. It worked nicely. I thought it would also be fun to comment some days on the graph this made—to know, for instance, how many chose Library? Playhouse? Easel? Zippity the hamster?

I noticed that five children put their names by the paint easel (which holds only two at a time), and four put their names by the computer (which has two chairs). I didn't intervene. I watched while kids at the computer negotiated for turns and those at the easel either watched or helped a friend paint.

MW: I like the way you waited to see what would happen. Sometimes I think I'm just being lazy when I do that. But often that's when I learn the most about how children think.

KE: When they said, "Close choice time," weren't they just reacting in the way they see adults react all the time? "If you two can't get along, I'll have to put that toy up"—in other words, stop the play.

When stuff like this happens in my classroom, I ask the children, "Aren't there any other solutions?" Someone will surely have one, and then the discussion of several alternatives can begin.

KR: You know, Carolyn, it sounds to me as if cleanup wasn't their problem, it was yours. They didn't have ownership in keeping the room picked up, except the few children who wanted things tidy (or wanted to make their teacher happy). If we ignore the children's solution, we avoid the challenge of building their investment in the problem. You wanted a solution, not the messiness of collective problem solving, which takes longer but works better

> WHAT DO YOU THINK WE SHOULD DO?
>
> How could both of you use the cash register?
> Clean-up isn't happening. What shall we do about that?
> What shall we do when we get to the park for our picnic?
> How could you get that bike wheel unstuck?
> Do we have enough pop-tops saved to buy what we need?
> What do you think we should do instead?
> I've noticed that many children have been arguing about blocks this week. Is that a problem? What could we do about it?
> Aren't there any other solutions?

in the long run. I sympathize! Democracy is hard work.

CS: Suppose they had said, "Close choice time," and I had said, "Okay, we'll try your idea." And the next day, no choice time. How would I have handled that?

KR: Well, after whatever usually comes before choice time, you could have called a meeting. And you could have explained to the children that usually this is choice time, but the class has agreed we shouldn't have choice time anymore. So, you ask, "What do you all think we should do instead?"

Five-year-olds don't always really get the connection between words and reality. They can say, "Close choice time," without really anticipating what that will be like when it happens.

CS: And when they find that out, what would they say?

KR: I don't know. That's what makes teaching kindergarten interesting! But they would certainly have new ownership in the problem. And you would learn more about how 5-year-olds think.

BJ: You know, Carolyn, you do understand all this; you keep putting it into words. "Finally (for now!)," you wrote, "I resolved a continuing problem." Your words, "Finally (for now!)," make the basic point. There are no finallys. In any classroom with life in it, problems will keep right on cropping up. That's why an intelligent adult can keep teaching 5-year-olds year after year without losing enthusiasm, because she is "researching children"—words you used earlier. Children are unpredictable. They create the dramas that keep us learning together. Good teaching is always *learning* to teach.

A Day in the Classroom

Occasionally a quarrel erupts in the block center. Wherever these boys take their passion, arguments follow. I watch and wait to see how they solve it. Sometimes I intervene by removing the object of heated debate and asking them to discuss the problem together. They usually come to me minutes later to retrieve the object of the debate, the issue completely resolved.

Today there is no object in question. The boys are chanting at Lauren, who is standing over them with a mixed expression of amusement, embarrassment, and frustration.

"Skyler loves Lauren! Skyler loves Lauren!" It switches quickly to "Taylor loves Lauren!" They go through a list of names.

Lisa leans over to Hayley and says, "They watch too much *Ninja Turtles.* It's sick." Some kids begin to look upset. I walk over. This time I don't talk about hurt feelings or respecting others. The boys know. Their faces have a guilty look. They had just gotten carried away. This time I make them listen to Lauren's feelings, and I demand that the taunting stop.

Endless negotiation. It's never a surprise or an inconvenience because it is an integral part of the curriculum. They are learning most from working through problems of how to manage the sand at the deep table. It's action-packed adventure every moment. A substitute teacher commented on their negotiation abilities. She seemed amazed that they take it upon themselves to speak their feelings without adult intervention.

The fluidity is constant. Old routines vanish and newer, more appropriate ones take their places. The children dictate these changes, and I try to keep up.

—CS

MW: But I don't want to be learning everything all the time—that's exhausting. I want some things firmly in place, as habitual behaviors I don't have to think about. That frees my energy for the new challenges.

KE: Maybe at this point it's worthwhile to reflect on what you must have in place—for me it was the environment and scheduling—and what new challenges you eagerly anticipate. Then you can consider how these challenges connect to your curriculum for children.

CS: Do you know, I found I could do some of that once I established a system. A few weeks later I wrote about it in my journal on a weekend at the Oregon coast (see "A Day in the Classroom").

What's our theory?

What do teachers know, collectively, about community building in the classroom? Here's a statement of four principles that guide my practice.

1. A developmentally appropriate curriculum in kindergarten (a) builds directly on the skills, knowledge, and curiosities each child brings to school; (b) continually asks the children to pay attention to each other's needs, interests, and competencies; and (c) creates a world of activities and experiences that bind the group in purposeful learning and play. Thus the democratic community grows.

Kerstin Moore writes about individuality as a social process—John Dewey's view of the purpose of education:

> If we believe that children are egocentric in the sense that they want to know who they are in relationship to others, that they seek to define their individuality in terms of their differences in contrast to others, and that they desire to contribute their uniqueness to group life, then individuality is a social process. For Dewey, the purpose of education is to support this process—to transform individual capacities, interests, experiences, points of view, and ways of being into a common understanding. . . . Awareness of another point of view [does not] require abandoning one's own idea and adopting someone else's. It simply means awareness of other points of view in contrast to one's own experience as part of an ongoing process of deepening one's own understanding. (1998, 9)

2. Learning requires interaction with peers. School is for talking—that's how language develops. It is also for making friends and having power struggles ("You're not my friend"). It's for generating the social and intellectual disequilibrium out of which new schemas are constructed.

Action and interaction generate problems. Without problems to be solved, there is no authentic curriculum. Problems do not necessarily represent the teacher's failure to control; they represent teachable moments. Collective meaning is created through endless negotiation.

Class Meetings Build Community

I use class meetings for many purposes, all related to community building. There might be

- a group problem to solve,
- a shared experience,
- a skill to be explicitly taught,
- a ritual, or
- announcements of importance to everyone.

Coming together on the rug centers the group, enabling children to make the next transition calmly and with adequate information about what's coming next.

The theory building that teachers help children engage in can be about academic and technological problems as well as social problems. That's how I usually approach graphing, one of our whole-group activities.

I try to make graphing relevant to classroom events. I would say, for example, "We need to know who wants what kind of sandwiches for the picnic. Let's make a mathematical picture of it, so you can easily see who wants what and I can easily tell what to buy."

—*KE*

---

3. Problem solving is among the best reasons for large-group meetings. Most individual problems can be solved on the spot: How could you get that bike wheel unstuck? How could both of you use the cash register? What do you need in order to paint this box? But some problems affect everyone, and those problems are worth the time spent in group discussion.

Class Meetings: Time for Talking

I have five class meetings during our six-hour kindergarten day that starts at 8:30 A.M. with the Pledge on the patio for entire school:

1. 8:40 A.M. — Morning circle
9:00–9:45 A.M. — Outdoor time
2. 9:45–10:00 A.M. — Planning circle
10:00–11:00 A.M. — Choosing time
3. 11:00–11:20 A.M. — Story or Spanish
11:20–12:15 P.M. — Lunch
4. 12:15–12:30 P.M. — Story or discussion
12:30–1:00 P.M. — Rest and story
1:00–1:30 P.M. — Specialists' visits
  Monday/Tuesday — Movement
  Wednesday — Library
  Thursday — Computers
  Friday — Music
1:30–2:10 P.M. — Committee time
5. 2:10–2:30 P.M. — Circle time

The beginning meeting is to take care of "What is happening today?" We take attendance but in a variety of fun ways that keep the children attuned. And we talk about what we'll be doing that day.

This is what we do at the other class meetings:

• Planning circle is when children make their choices for choosing time.
• Just before lunch we have a story or a visitor/resource teacher.
• Just after lunch is another story, a chance to cool down before resting.
• After resting there is another story, talking, and sharing.
• Just before going home we come together for singing, dancing, games, story, and talking.

I do very little planning for these meetings, other than choosing what books I will read. There is a lot of time for talking, and I can't plan for that in advance.

In my opinion, many teachers misuse class meetings, especially the first circle as a long discussion of the calendar. I use the calendar very sparingly with the whole group, primarily when we are anticipating an event (field trip or holiday). Daily I post what we are doing that day on a board marked with the days of the week. There are also calendars in the playhouse and near my desk.

I think that whole-group writing and guided reading are not effective uses of group time; they can be done with small groups much more easily. When I read a story to the whole group, we talk about it, but I don't use it for a reading lesson.

—KR

As many teachers have noticed, whenever class meetings focus on genuine problems in which the children feel ownership, young children have remarkably long attention spans (see "Class Meetings Build Community, p. 111" and "Class Meetings: Time for Talking" on the page opposite). In this process the teacher—the group's leader—takes responsibility for identifying shared problems and concerns and guiding children's theory building about them. She does so by asking questions to which she does not know the answer (see "Getting to Know Each Child," p. 127) and taking children's answers seriously as evidence of how they think and how she can scaffold their further thinking (Paley 1986). To hold the problems and the solutions, in memory, the teacher represents them by means of speech, written symbols, diagrams and pictures, and models. (See children's sandbox rules, "Carolyn's story," in Part 2, p. 52.)

4. Class meetings also create shared rituals and collective memory—
the elements of a group's culture. Marsha read *Romeo and Juliet* at class meetings, and children collectively learned about its themes. Linda Torgerson (1994) and Catherine Wilson (2000) both describe the care with which a teacher may choose stories with common referent and vocabulary to be shared with a class for the purpose of creating dramatic play and dialogue.

Kathleen's story—

Building community with parents: The people who care most about the children we teach

In early childhood especially, parenting and teaching are complementary roles (Katz 1980). Parents' investment in their children is personal and even irrational; a child represents the family's future, its hope. Children should be a credit to the family, and a joy. In contrast, teachers have a professional, thoughtful obligation to balance the needs of all the children in the class. Parents and teachers have much to learn from each other about the children whose care they share. Kindergarten, the child's first brush with real school, lays a foundation for the rest of the family's experience with schooling.

Building cross-cultural relationships

Teaching children from a culture with which I had no prior experience, I consistently relied on the extended family to share responsibility for keeping the children safe and connected. Walking trips to the neighborhood park, where many urban evils could be found (but which, as I explained earlier, are part of the children's world), were made safe by the presence—at my invitation—of many of the culture's elders.

It must have been very hard for Iu Mien parents to drop their child in my room on the first day of kindergarten. Here was a teacher who didn't know the child's language, who didn't look like anybody they knew, except maybe a social worker. What in my voice, my face, my demeanor could reassure them that I would take the very best care of their most precious child? What in the room and the songs and stories could reassure the children that this would be a great place to be for three hours every day?

The Mien have people endured rudeness and inconsideration even to get as far as my door. There was often a lot of confusion about legal addresses, immunizations, custody, birth certificates—even about names. People at the registration table may have been loud and brusque—characteristics seldom seen in a Mien person in a public setting. A translator may or may not have been available. So when they arrived at my room, I tried my best to look reassuring. I invited parents to stay for a while if their child seemed unsure, and I connected them with parents I already knew from previous years. From the children's enthusiasm for this wonderful place set up just for them, most parents were able to hope it would be good.

Parents with a long family history of school success may not need the same reassurance. For nearly every parent, however, there is anxiety: Will the school be a good place for so precious a child? But higher anxiety must be the common immigrant experience, especially when there are language barriers. African Americans experience aspects of anxiety as well. Those viewed as outsiders by people in official roles have a hard time. Parents who have the confidence to be active advocates may articulate doubt about the reality of the school's commitment to teaching their children.

When we first introduced more developmentally appropriate practices at our school, teachers were afraid that parents would be unsupportive. But when parents saw children's enthusiasm—children who used to cry and cling on arrival now running in to join the others, children who used to be "sick" in the morning now bouncing up early to be sure to get to school, and children whose parents feared they would be bad now eagerly joining the group—their support flourished.

For me teaching in the Mien community has been a wonderful challenge. My previous experience had been mostly with children of European American and African American cultures with which I am very familiar. Mien culture was altogether new to me. But I found the Mien people forthcoming about sharing their cultural beliefs and practices, and I simply asked if I was unsure of something. On issues of death and funerals, it surprised me to learn that Mien people don't practice protracted grieving rituals because they believe that the longer you grieve, the more difficult you make it for the departed to go to the next world.

I would ask, observe, visit! I risked cultural blunders and noticed when I blundered. Whenever I was invited to weddings, birthday parties, cultural events, I'd go. I would step outside the school system to help families get mental health services, legal advice, and citizenship classes. In teaching adult literacy, I learned more and more about life in the refugee camps in Laos and Thailand.

I've learned that, as Bateson says, "Living in a society made up of different ethnic groups offers a paradigm for learning to participate without knowing all the rules and learning from the process without allowing the rough edges to create unbridgeable conflict" (1994, 153). Clearly I am going beyond the boundaries of the classroom in

---

The boundaries of the cultural bridge inevitably blur inside the children's worlds, because from their points of view, school is not one social sphere. The issue thus becomes not how children make a transition from the home world to "the" school world, but how they find themselves—how they compose a place for themselves— amidst the diverse and potentially contradiction-ridden world of the classroom.

—Anne Haas Dyson (1993)

defining my obligations as a teacher. But I am very concerned that children get skills, and I cannot be an effective teacher of children unless I know what is meaningful and engaging to them. Skills learning can occur in the midst of any topic, theme, or activity; it must, however, be grounded in what is important to the learner.

There are classrooms that include children from many different cultures and languages—more than any teacher can become truly familiar with. Some teachers are neither knowledgeable about the cultural realities of the families in their community nor committed to the complexity of becoming culturally aware. Our dialogue on cultural issues raises some questions about communities and classrooms different from mine.

BJ: Some parent involvement emphasizes who the family is. The teacher asks families: What do you celebrate? What could you lend us from your treasures? Could you come in to tell the children about life in your country? This approach seems genuinely welcoming in many classrooms, but it may not go beyond tokenism in others (especially if only the children from outside the White middle-class mainstream are thought of by the teacher as having a culture).

CS: What do you mean by tokenism?

BJ: I think of some displays labeled Multicultural that I've seen in early childhood classrooms. They seem to have no real purpose other than to serve as evidence under the "Multicultural" heading on the program review checklist.

KR: A tourist approach. That's very easy to do with a flag, a few pictures, and an object or two from a particular culture. It is much more difficult to have experiences with children that genuinely represent another culture. I try to integrate other cultures into the curriculum throughout the year with books, songs, phrases, manipulatives, and food.

BJ: I remember visiting a kindergarten in which nine different languages were spoken in the children's homes. The teacher said to me cheerfully, "Our basic curriculum is language! What are all the different ways people can say things?"

MW: At my school in an affluent neighborhood where it appeared that everyone was trying to be alike, the issue wasn't really "How are we different?" I really care about involving parents—I need their help! So I guess my approach could be called something like "How can you help the school educate your child?"

CS: Oh, that's an interesting way to think about it. I used the same approach in recruiting parent volunteers. And I put a lot of energy into my newsletter to let parents know what was happening for their children at school and to encourage conversation about it at home.

Homework as home/school communication

A second issue about which we dialogued is that of ways to communicate with parents about what's going on at school.

BJ: These days the primary mode of communication seems to be homework, even in kindergarten. (See "Homework Ideas," p. 116.)

CS: Do you think that's the reason for homework? The teachers I know assume it's for further skill practice.

BJ—Betty Jones, **CS**—Carolyn Stringer, **KR**—Kay Stritzel Rencken, **MW**—Marsha Williams, **KE**—Kathleen Evans

Homework Ideas

Names

I ask parents to tell the story of how they named their child. I take the collected stories and put them in a book that we keep in the classroom and read again and again.

Pennies

I ask families to send us 10 pennies and to count them with their child before giving them to him or her to bring to school.

I collect pennies after reading to the children *A Chair for My Mother* (Williams 1982). We also use them repeatedly for math activities. (I begin with a general request for pennies but may later ask for subsequent specific amounts.)

Card games

I teach a number of card games to the children: slap, more (war), numbers (eights), and so on. Many years I am able to get free decks of cards from a casino, and I send these home with rules for the games and a chart on the math learnings in each game.

Baby

When my grandson Gregory was born, I told the children how long he was and how much he weighed. The children wondered how much they weighed at birth, so I asked parents to send in their child's length and weight.

We had already measured ourselves in class, and the papers representing current height were hanging on the wall, so we were able to superimpose a new paper length—length at birth. We compared weights too.

What is your favorite?

We often have a pizza restaurant in our playhouse, and a discussion of *favorite* comes up. I send home a letter describing the play and ask that parents send back the name of the family's favorite pizza. We create a graph, and I send copies home. I've done the same with favorite peanut butters.

Calendars

At school we use a calendar to count down to an important event like our jumpathon, a field trip, and so forth. I ask families to post calendars and use them in a similar way.

Math bags

Children take home a set of pattern blocks, a blank book, stencils, and markers. With these they demonstrate their favorite designs for their families. I ask families to write a story about this to send back.

BJ: Frankly, I think that's counterproductive. My old-fashioned view is that most homework is mindless and that young children will learn more if they're free to play after school. But that doesn't seem to be how our society is organized these days. So my question for you all is this: Does homework have potential advantages for home-school relationships beyond the notion, "Parents should help children with their homework"? Are parents reassured when schools give homework?

KR: Our district has a homework policy, but I haven't read it in years. I have my own homework policy, first developed when I worked in a federally funded preschool program in which we did home visits.

There I really learned to make homework an integral part of what's going on at school. I call it work the children and their families do at home.

KE: At our school we were required to give homework four days a week, and for several reasons I chose not to argue with that policy. I gave a different job each night: handwriting practice (which, as kids learned letter formation, could be replaced with a phonics sheet), math skills practice (a workbook page I didn't have to do in class), data collection for graphing or a K-W-L (see a description of know-wonder-learn charts in the previous section, p. 98), and reading.

I even gave children homework stickers when they brought their work back to school. That was part of a compromise I made with the parents. They wanted concrete evidence that they and their child were getting credit for doing the right thing, so we (like every other classroom in the school) posted a homework chart. Parents checked it. Some children's older brothers or sisters picked them up, and they would check the chart too.

MW: That's part of playing school—doing homework, getting stickers. Parents like being reassured that their child is in a real school.

CS: How did you find time to keep that up-to-date?

KE: All I did was stand at the door with stickers in hand, greet the child, spot-check the homework, and give the child a sticker to put on the chart. If a child didn't seem to have gotten the homework, I'd set it aside for Mrs. Lee to help them with it. They filed the assignment in their own folders unless the homework was data collection for some-

thing we were doing. I set that aside to bring to the group meeting later.

CS: Did the children do the chart accurately?

KE: Sometimes. Often they put their stickers in someone else's place. But I didn't have any trouble letting go of accuracy in this activity. It was a quick way to dispatch something I didn't really care for. And parents were vigilant in straightening it out.

What's our theory?

Traditional schooling may include a parent education component in which parents receive the offer of expertise by professional educators in support of their childrearing task. And many schools depend on parents for fundraising, supervising homework, volunteering for prescribed tasks in the school, but not for input into the curriculum. In contrast, an emergent curriculum in early childhood incorporates parents' knowledge of their children and parents' desires for their children's learning as well. In low-income communities especially, parental anxieties that their children are not valued as learners may have a basis in fact. I believe,

1. Parents and teachers need each other if curriculum is to be built to include the interests of each child and the culture of his or her family.

2. Teachers can initiate any of a wide variety of invitations to families to participate in their child's life at school, depending on the community. Home visits, school visits, field trips, celebrations, newsletters, homework designed to elicit parents' special knowledge, volunteering in the classroom have all been used by the kindergarten teachers in this book.

In fact the steps in a cycle of teacher behaviors in support of emergent curriculum (see p. 92–93) can be applied to parent involvement as well. Teachers are challenged to pay attention to families by noticing, inviting, responding, provisioning, connecting, referring, and reflecting.

3. Parent communities may have very different expectations of the school and of teachers, depending especially on their educational and class backgrounds (Lareau 1989). Some entitled, privileged parents are active advocates for their children at all times, even ignoring the needs of the classroom community in their urgent concerns for their own child. Some may be inclined to regard teachers as servants rather than as independent professionals.

In contrast, for other parents the dictates of the school are to be accepted. Since they may see teachers as functionaries of an oppressor class, these parents may feel the teacher knows best and the child's obligation is to obey without question. On the broad spectrum between these extremes, there are many challenges for teachers and parents.

* * *

Kindergarten in the community

Home, school, and community are traditional emphases in kindergarten social studies. Do these topics of study emerge even if they are not prescribed, because they are in fact central in young children's lives? In the classroom stories of the four of us teacher/writers, no one covered the familiar topic of *community helpers* nor were there visits to the fire station (though there could have been). It is typical of an emergent curriculum to have less breadth, more depth, and variation one classroom to another.

Taking the children into the community

Curriculum depth was our experience. We describe this here, with added comments by our colleagues.

KR: I had no idea when we began walking in the neighborhood to look at houses that we'd meet those interesting people as well. Emergent curriculum is often serendipitous. The construction workers turned out to be a wonderful resource. So did the woman with the backyard farm and all the animals. Both of these encounters provided experience in appropriate public behavior and much stimulation for dramatic play, discussion, and drawing.

KE: I took advantage of the extended family, including elders as well as parents in our frequent neighborhood walks. This made it possible for us to claim the local park as one of our play places. We were free of the tyranny of bus transportation; all our families lived within walking distance. Our community was rich and varied in opportunities for learning.

These forays into the community were particularly educational for student teachers, who were likely to understand poverty and inner-city life in a one-dimensional way. This experience also grounded me in the day-to-day reality of the families and children I worked with. We were a third-world community existing in the first world. That political reality was important for me to continue to recognize.

Bringing the community into the classroom

CS: "Tyranny of bus schedules" describes our experience! It wasn't practical for us to leave the school very often, but our school was a comfortably small one, and we could

---

KR— Kay Stritzel Rencken, **KE**—Kathleen Evans, **CS**—Carolyn Stringer, **MW**—Marsha Williams

The Lively Kindergarten

easily connect with the variety of people who worked there. These people were an active interest of my children early in the year. I wrote then, "The school is so new, so exciting. Adults are a big idea right now. The kids love to yell 'hello' to the custodian and the librarian." Later I realized that I could have followed up that interest by asking the children what more they wanted to know about the adults in the school.

One of the strengths, I think, of the sandbox project was the ways in which it connected us with other people in the school and the community. Children distributed letters to other classrooms, went out to measure the playground, and interviewed students in other classes to get bigger kids' opinions about sandbox dimensions. We even invited an engineer to come to school to meet with us and discuss our ideas so he could draw up plans for us. This visit delighted the principal, who was trying to develop school/business/community partnerships.

MW: I've always relied heavily on parent volunteers. Our need for props for our Romeo and Juliet play drew further on community resources, mostly by way of parents, although the cone-hats parent wasn't one of my kindergarten parents— her son was in the half-day class. (I knew her from last year in preschool.) The actual performances drew in not only parents but also extended family members and other classes in the school.

KE: I chose to move actively within the island of the children's neighborhood, while deliberately sheltering them from those aspects of the school itself that I felt would be overstimulating or threatening. I scheduled our outside time to avoid competition with bigger kids for playground resources. I refused to take our class to school as-

semblies, instead collaborating with another kindergarten teacher to have small, short assemblies more appropriate for 5-year-olds.

I have been very conscious of my role as bridge builder between home and school cultures. There is a lot of evidence that children of immigrant families are more likely to do well in school if they experience their home culture and language as a safe haven, a source of identity and pride, and as the foundation on which to build their new identity at school.

My first task was to extend that safety to school, to establish it in our classroom as a haven; then I could go on to provide many opportunities for children to explore. These happened through sociodramatic play, the arts and language, and the varied dramatic experiences in their lives. Thus I always introduced the hospital as a dramatic play center—the instituuion of Western medicine being one of those places of power where Mien people experience great cultural conflict. Children introduced other themes—fishing, even a bookstore. There was provision for many re-creations of the children's community experiences in our classroom as well as for American themes.

What's our theory?

Children learn through emergent curriculum! We have learned these important points:

1. The people, places, work, and everyday occurrences in the school and community are an important source of emergent curriculum.

2. A preplanned curriculum on community risks superficiality and obvious omissions. Rather, the question is, What are *these* children curious about, at this time, and how much can we learn about that?

3. Depending on circumstances, community studies can take place within or outside the classroom.

4. To understand their experiences, children need access to many modes of representation—talking, writing, drawing and other media, movement and music, and dramatic play.

How do we know that the children are learning what they need to know? Interestingly, schools rarely ask parents what they want their children to learn; in most settings, curriculum objectives are a given. In contrast, in an emergent curriculum approach, all the stakeholders are consulted—district and state mandates, parents, and children (who often have definite goals for themselves [Ayers 1993]).

Teachers, parents, and the larger community all have an investment in the success of schooling. The challenge for teachers is to piece together all these interests (sometimes competing) into a coherent plan. The final portions of this book move beyond the classroom and its families and neighborhood to examine issues of assessment and advocacy.

Developing an emergent curriculum is much more complicated than teaching a canned curriculum. However, with some experience, any competent teacher who is organized and genuinely cares for people can effectively use the two strategies—stage setting and community building—described in the previous and present sections, in which the teacher relies both on environmental structure and on others (peers, parents, and community members) as resources for teaching.

Teachers becoming experts

Many early childhood educators intuitively develop their competence; they have empathy for children and easily tune in to their needs and interests. They link children to the interesting things in the world, go with the flow, and create rich learning environments without relying on theoretical analysis of their practice. Professional development strengthens and furthers the natural abilities of these teachers and supports and prepares other teachers in developing these skills. It offers them opportunity to connect their practice with the theories of experts.

Some teachers genuinely internalize and build upon the theories they are taught, becoming articulate professionals in their own right. It's this next level of teacher awareness—conscious expertise—that we discuss in the next section and in Part 4. Many teachers won't get to this level in their teaching. They are content in their classrooms and may lack motivation to achieve the mature professionalism and leadership style that are necessary to negotiate the school system and public expectations.

Teachers who do take such initiative tend to seek support through peer dialogue, graduate education, and professional activism. They become leaders. Some leave the classroom. They teach adults instead; they administer programs, consult, write, or advocate. That's what some of us have done.

Kathleen, originally a preschool teacher, spent a number of years as director of a preschool before moving into public school teaching 10 years ago. Kay began in the classroom in daily contact with children and has stayed for more than 20 years. Both Kay and Kathleen also teach adults, write, and advocate. They are avid learners.

In Kathleen's search for in-depth understanding of children's development of literacy, she trained as a Reading Recovery teacher. She discovered that her combination day (reading tutorials with English-speaking children in the morning, kindergarten with Mien-speaking children in the afternoon) stimulated her thinking about how young children learn.

Kathleen says her work in Reading Recovery "has informed my classroom teaching in very profound ways." She thinks the program's emphasis on working from what a child knows and always making the learning easy by teaching in manageable increments have made her a much more effective kindergarten teacher. Reading Recovery is emergent curriculum in a minute form. In the best teaching, the child guides the lesson. Although the lesson format is highly prescribed, moment-by-moment teaching decisions are based on what the child can do and is most likely to be able to do in the next moment.

Self-constructed expertise is not required of teachers. The intense reflective dialogue in which disequilibrium and construction of one's own theory take place is rare in both preservice and inservice teacher education. Although, as is true in other professions, participation in continuing education of some sort is a condition of teachers' employment, it often takes the same form as that common in many classrooms for children: direct instruction and workbook-type activities.

Teachers are given recipes—textbooks, workbooks, craft activities—to transmit to children. They are given assessment tools as well. For beginning teachers still at the stage of "What do I do on Monday?" (Holt 1970), prescriptive training offers a reassuring tool kit as they begin the arduous process of juggling many balls at the same time in the classroom. A simple "What worked? What didn't work?" end-of-the-day reflection is a good start toward emergent curriculum and reflective teaching.

Teachers who are further along in their development have what Lilian Katz (1995) describes as "enough perspective to begin to ask deeper and more abstract questions, such as 'What are my historical and philosophical roots? What is the nature of growth and learning?'" (see "Stages of Teacher Development," p. 11). They may not encounter encouragement, however, to pursue these questions. There is little opportunity for collegial dialogue in U.S. schools, but great opportunity to do prescribed curriculum, to administer prescribed tests, and to avoid making trouble.

Self-motivated teacher-learners risk getting into trouble. They choose being accountable not just to the system and its representatives but also to their own vision of education and to giving back to the community what has been given them by family, schools, and other institutions and individuals. Like the teacher/writers in this book, teachers making these choices may have concluded that they have an obligation to pay attention to every child—a challenge that others are unlikely to understand.

Teachers are expected to standardize children, to prepare them for the next grade and the next test. Teaching in public school, they are accountable, of course, to the taxpayers for the time they spend in classrooms with other people's children.

The basic question, "How do we know the children are learning?" shapes a variety of prescribed approaches to accountability. Some approaches may diverge from a teacher's understanding of his or her role and responsibility. Teachers who are visionaries and knowledgeable through experience develop strategies for remaining true to their vision while still acknowledging the expectations of other stakeholders. Next we examine some of these strategies.

—BJ

How Do We Know
If They're Learning?

School has always been about the three R's, and it still is. Especially in the primary grades, basic literacy and numeracy are what matter to everyone. The question, "Are the children learning in school?" is all about academics—reading, writing, and arithmetic. Kindergarten—the "children's garden"—used to be exempt from this pressure, but it isn't anymore.

Each of us, the teacher/writers in this book, has worked within this social-political context, although we experienced different pressures in our different settings. In my magnet school, teachers have had decision-making power about the process of reporting outcomes to parents, even as we sometimes had to fend off the latest district policy. Kathleen lacked official leeway but was secure and assertive in taking a stand and identifying the congruence between children's activity, district checklists, and state standards.

In a high-pressure suburban school and less experienced in developmental approaches to assessment, Carolyn wrestled with the tensions generated by assessment criteria, as do many teachers. "How do you respond to children's interests without losing sight of the objectives?" she asked in our dialogues together. "In our half day I squeezed out 40 minutes for choice and

spent the rest of the day scrambling to teach to objectives."

Teachers *are* responsible for assessing the growth of children and communicating their assessments to parents and other people. But typically, in American education, these assessments are quantified into grades and test scores, implying a single standard against which all children are measured. (By its very definition, 50% of all children will not measure up.) Standardized testing interrupts teaching—interrupts the routine of the whole school during one or more days of high anxiety. It tests teachers as well as children; it's an external inspection of teachers' work.

"Are children learning?" usually translates as "Are their test scores high enough?" Standardized testing is a twentieth-century invention. The American public has completely bought into it in spite of all that is known about its limitations (Kamii 1990; Kohn 2000, 2001; Wesson 2001). So many important learnings go unmeasured in testing.

Children aren't all alike, and teaching and testing them as if they were is counterproductive. There are "multiple intelligences" (Gardner 1983)—various ways of thinking and learning—and different children are differently oriented to the world. Families aren't all alike, and one of the important sources of an emergent curriculum is *values* held in the school and community, family, and culture.

Every child starts kindergarten at a different place. Some children, through no fault or lack of effort, find themselves on a very uneven playing field. Others have been read to frequently, have traveled, have gone on excursions, and have had good preschool experiences. With teachers and classrooms that focus on the growth and development of every child, all children have the opportunity to be competent in school. "Research from a variety of theoretical perspectives suggests that a defining feature of a supportive environment is a responsible and responsive adult" (Bowman, Donovan, & Burns 2000).

Integrating skills teaching

"It is important to be accountable to others' expectations and to *evaluate* programs in that framework" (Jones & Nimmo 1994, 127). In my experience in teaching literacy, *of course* phonics is integrated within a developmentally appropriate, whole language, and literature-based approach. Phonetic clues are among the many clues used by a proficient reader, and they need to be learned. But you don't have to schedule phonics as a separate lesson; you just have to be sure you know what the expectations are for the grade level and that you teach each as a need for it arises, covering them all by the end of the year.

Kathleen comments similarly, "*Of course* I teach to objectives. I teach to the school's objectives within the broader context of my own goals for the children." She agrees that there are basic skills to be learned in kindergarten/primary and has no quarrel with that. After many years of experience, she is clear on what the learning expectations are, how to meet them, and how each child will fare in reaching them.

Beginning teachers haven't that long view just yet, and Kathleen feels that state standards can be useful in providing this. "The trick," she says, "is to understand the best path to each goal, how a child might reach it, why she hasn't if she hasn't, and what to do to get her as close to that goal as possible. This requires reflective assessment. Accountability is basic in all we do."

In our group dialogues Marsha reminded us that while *we* may have a clear understanding of integrated skill teaching, not everyone does. "What if the principal walks into your classroom to evaluate you, and it is choice (toy) time?" Marsha asked. "Wouldn't she be likely to say what my friend's principal said to her once: 'I'll come back when you're teaching'?"

When children are learning through playing, it doesn't look like teaching is going on. I have developed several strategies for dealing with administrators, colleagues, or parents who question the value of play. The first strategy is preemptive: over each center in our classroom I hang a description of the learning occurring there (see "Signs for Learning Centers," opposite page). I post the signs in Spanish and English, with the heading written large and pictures added of children working, for example, with blocks. This serves to communicate the activity to children as well as to adults. I feature the same signs as headings in my weekly parent newsletter, Special Edition. Story inserts add what is happening right now in each particular center. I also give a copy of the newsletter to the principal to keep him informed of children's learnings.

Another preemptive strategy is using displays just outside the classroom. I never thought I would enjoy having bulletin boards. But when my classroom moved back into our building after the year of the tomato-colored house, lots of bulletin boards were installed in the school hallways. I have three and use one to communicate with

Signs for Learning Centers

Reading Place

The reading place is a relaxing center that encourages the child to

- handle books with comfort and independence
- read picture books
- enjoy browsing through books
- extend her understanding of various media (photographs, illustrations, words) for expressing thoughts and feelings
- develop personal reading interests
- observe other children reading
- use books as reference materials
- use picture clues to predict fantasy or reality in a story
- explore the relationship of stories and print

EL CENTRO DE LECTURA

El Centro de Lectura es un lugar cómodo (lleno de almohadas) que da al niño la oportunidad de...
- usar los libros con facilidad y independencia.
- "leer" varias clases de libros con dibujos.
- leer libros por placer.
- extender la comprensión de varios tipos de ayuda visuales (Fotografías, dibujos, pintados, etc.) que expresan pensamientos y sentimientos.
- desarrollar interés personal en leer.
- explorar libros de muchas culturas.
- observar a los otros niños que están leyendo.
- leer a otros y ser leído por otros.
- usar los detalles de dibujos para predecir fantasía o realidad en una historia.

Sand table

Sand provides the child the opportunity to

- explore the properties of wet and dry sand
- experience sensory pleasure in sand
- enjoy creating buildings of all types
- work cooperatively
- enjoy solitary play
- dig to one's heart's content
- create roadways, castles, tunnels, volcanoes, and so on
- work with the scientific concept of evaporation and other science ideas
- enjoy the feeling of being "dirty"

LA ARENA

La Arena da al niño la oportunidad de...
- explorar las propiedades de la arena mojada y seca.
- explorar mientras trabajando en la mesa de arena o la caja de arena.
- hallar placer sensorial en la textura.
- disfrutar creando varias structuras usando moldes o forma libre.
- trabajar cooperativamente.
- gozar trabando solo/a.
- excavar a todo gusto.
- crear carreteras, castillos, túneles, volcanes, etc.
- trabajar con conceptos científicos como evaporación, despárrame, etc.
- entender que los niños y niñas pueden suciarse y disfrutar de juego desordenado.

parents. The other two I change frequently as documentation boards filled with my stories and photos of the children's work, children's words about it, and their work itself. Now the children are measuring themselves with blocks. Last year they hauled rocks for our garden, and we documented the number of wagon loads hauled and how many rocks all together (first estimated, then counted). You could call these "working bulletin boards," since the children also used them to relive each experience and talk about it some more.

The third strategy I use to communicate what learning is going on happens on the spot when someone asks, "Why are they playing?" The challenge is not to choke but to say calmly, "I know that until you take some time to watch, it only looks like playing. But I really want you to stand near the play hospital and note the oral language and vocabulary development that's happening."

My fourth strategy is to call attention to the children's drawings and other documentation of their play—for example, all their drawings of houses that year we spent in a new neighborhood. And the fifth strategy is to share my observational notes and checklists of the growth and development I've seen in children during their play.

Assessment through observation

A rich, responsible emergent curriculum is dependent on the teacher's skills in observing, documenting, and reflecting on the behaviors of children. To teach effectively, I need to spend more time observing and listening than I do showing and telling. Kathleen's analysis of her day impresses me (see "A Teacher's Day in Kindergarten," p. 85); she really does consciously balance it in that way.

To assess children's learning I must know enough about every child to construct a

narrative assessment, not just a collection of scores on checklists. I need to know the answers to such questions as

> Who is this child, physically, culturally, emotionally?
>
> What are her interpersonal skills and interests?
>
> What in the world interests this child—challenges his thinking?
>
> What does this child already understand about representational systems?
>
> What is she ready to learn next?

Knowing all of this is how I make teaching decisions for individual children and for the group. What are children confused about? What is the right challenge for them? In what ways do they feel capable? Who will be helpful peers for them in this activity?

Many teachers would say they're way too busy, every minute, to get to know each child (see "Getting to Know Each Child," opposite page). I think they have their priorities wrong; NAEYC's position is that observation is vital to the teaching process (Bredekamp & Copple 1997). I especially appreciate what Kathleen said about such teachers in one of our teacher/writers' conversations:

> They're too busy because they believe they have to control every aspect of the room. My first suggestion to these teachers is to list everything in their rooms that they think children can do independently and note how many children at a time can do each thing and for how long. In this process teachers begin to see that there is time for them to observe, assess, and work with individuals or small groups. But it is still a leap of faith to trust that 5- and 6-year-olds will make wise, capable, and independent choices.

In a primary school that created a Profile of Developmental Outcomes to replace the more conventional report card, the result was that the profile not only changed the report card, it also changed the ways in which teachers looked at children and taught. Assessment measures have a powerful influence on teaching. Teachers actively participated in the process of developing this new assessment tool and had frequent opportunities to critique it. Here's a sample of some discussion at one meeting, as summarized by a visitor observer:

> In some of the kindergarten classrooms, teachers made clear, there was no opportunity for children to practice writing spontaneously or "to work competently on notably complex, creative, imaginative, self-initiated tasks" (one of our definitions). All activities were teacher-directed, and short time blocks did not allow for complex projects. Teachers' time was spent in leading groups, large and small, and overseeing children's moves from one activity to the next. They weren't free to observe children.
> . . . [T]wo of the teachers, after extended discussion, decided that perhaps on Fridays they might replace their usual tight schedule with a long choice time, which would free children to be spontaneous and teachers to observe them in action. (Meade-Roberts, Jones, & Hillard 1993, 82)

Expectations and objectives: Classifying children's learning

To teach in a way that's responsive to children, confident in integrating skill learning into the emergent curriculum, the teacher has to know a lot about child development, especially about how children learn the three R's. In this sense, doing my homework—learning in depth about children's development in both reading and math, especially math—has made a world of difference. I can speak with some authority, as someone who knows the research and knows children as well.

I loved blocks for engaging children's hands, minds, and imaginations, even before I loved math. When academic pressures on kindergarten teachers began to increase, I found myself having to justify in academic terms all the time we spent with blocks. That's part of my responsibility as a teacher—being accountable for what I do.

Getting to Know Each Child

To help children learn to write in school, Donald Graves says that teachers must often help them discover the topics they want to write about. To do this, he believes they must "know the children." Graves proposes this exercise for teachers:

1. Make three columns on a sheet of paper.

2. In the first column list from memory all the children in your class.

3. In the middle column opposite each child's name, write something each child knows, something unique to that child—an experience, a collection, an interest.

4. In the third column, check whether you have specifically confirmed—acknowledged the particulars of—what you wrote in the middle column about each child, through conversations [a form of *conferring*] with each child. [See "Conferring," p. 102.]

It is important that the teacher, Graves says, "carry the unique territories of information about the children in memory. . . . Those children for whom it is most difficult to come up with a territory or information are those who need it most. They are often the children who find it difficult to choose topics, to locate a territory of their own. They perceive themselves as nonknowers, persons without turf, with no place to stand."

Source: Adapted, by permission, from *Writing: Teachers and Children at Work* by Donald H. Graves. Copyright © 1983 by Donald H. Graves. Published by Heinemann, a division of Reed Elsevier Inc., Portsmouth, NH.

As teacher/writers of this book we've had a lot of discussion about the challenge of accountability. Following are some of our thoughts:

MW: Isn't the real challenge not teaching to objectives but rather getting good at assessing whether they're being achieved and letting other people know? I found myself getting better at that as our Romeo and Juliet play project went on, propelled partly by anxiety I suppose. I became quite proficient at naming our activities in academic terms (estimation, vocabulary-building, investigation, critical thinking, and all the rest).

KE: Yes, I think you've got it. *Classification* is an important objective for teachers' learning!

We had a mandated English Language Development time, one hour per day, and the administration's idea was something highly structured, systematic, and explicit. I went ballistic over this one, since I felt that my English-language development program was the net cast over every part of the day. I told the official from the bilingual office he was welcome to spend a week in my classroom if he needed convincing.

I told the principal she could transfer me to an English-only school if she didn't believe me, but I was not going to spend precious time each day in a structured English lesson. Fortunately I had my assessments, writing samples, and dictated stories as documentation of stages of English-language development for each of the English-language learners. I knew, to the exact date, when each child had mastered a skill.

I keep continuous notes on children's progress, classifying outcomes by specific district objectives, by what I recognize as that which a child needs to know and do to succeed in first grade, and by what I recognize for myself as developmentally appropriate and as appropriate for the individual child.

KR: I do too. Teachers at the magnet school where I teach have spent a great deal of time over the years developing a narrative to use instead of a report card (see "Learning Outcomes for Children," opposite page). The school has categorical goals for children, which we translated into six areas of focus for the narrative. All of us use the format slightly differently, but its intent is as a guide for narrative writing. I take the basic categories and then develop a set of questions I want to answer about each child.

BJ: These are such complex objectives!

KR: They imply high-level observation skills by teachers. In contrast, most kindergarten checklists seem to focus on isolated skills and bits of knowledge. Children are asked to name shapes and colors, count, recognize letters, tell their names and addresses.

CS: Yes, what you describe sounds like the checklist I had to use.

BJ: Items such as those in a typical checklist for kindergarten are all based on practice or memory, not on the construction of understanding and habits of learning.

MW: That's how reading and math are often taught too—through drill on letter and number memorization.

KE: It is really rare that a child doesn't absorb colors, letter names, and so on during kindergarten (but I do worry about the one or two who don't). These are basic recognitions almost anyone who's attending can master. I am more concerned about children's ability to see patterns and connections in their learning and bring these to a new experience. I'm particularly interested in *organization:* How

---

MW—Marsha Williams, **KE**—Kathleen Evans, **KR**—Kay Stritzel Rencken, **BJ**—Elizabeth Jones, **CS**—Carolyn Stringer

Learning Outcomes for Children—
Borton Primary Magnet School

Goals for learners: intrapersonal, creativity, social, interpersonal, linguistic, logical-mathematical, spatial/bodily kinesthetic. (Teachers use this outline as a guide for narrative writing.)

I know myself and what makes me special.

The learner has an accurate self-concept. The learner can identify and demonstrate skills and talents.

Intrapersonal
—expression of joy
—persistence
—expression of feelings
—temperament
—self-confidence

I am responsible for what I do.
The learner can work alone or in groups, knows how to ask for help, and accepts consequences for actions.

—initiates
—handles transitions
—takes risks
—adjusts to school or new situations
—is flexible

I recognize beauty and use my imagination to create.
The learner has a sense of aesthetics and expresses creativity in personal style and in writing, problem solving, play, movement, and the arts.

Creativity (art/music)   *Play*
—choosing   —sociodramatic activi-
—reproducing   ties: housekeeping,
—composing   puppets, blocks
—experimenting   —expression of feelings
                                in play

I show respect and care for others.
The learner is polite and aware of others' feelings, accepts differences, and works toward cooperation with others.

Interpersonal
—group activities (small/large)
—relationships (peers/adults)

—fair play
—friends
—roles
—stages of social play: solitary, parallel, cooperative

I am always learning.

The learner demonstrates and reflects growth in reading, writing, mathematics, second-language learning, and content area studies.

Linguistics   *Logical/ mathematical*

—word play   —patterns
—expression of ideas: books, —classification
  reading, pattern books   —counting
—conversations   —puzzles
—choosing   —pattern blocks
—problem solving

I can use my body and tools to help me work, play, and stay healthy.

The learner exercises, uses playground equipment, and masters classroom tools and technology.

Spatial   *Bodily-kinesthetic*
—development of large and small muscles:
  climbing   writing
  using rings
—ability to move through space:
  jumping rope   ball handling
  riding bikes/scooters   dancing

Equipment
—computers
—centers

does the child organize ideas in paintings, stories, construction, and so forth?

CS: How do you keep a record of that?

KE: I collect their drawings and stories. And I find that materials like pattern blocks, which invite organization of form, are a big help both in teaching and in assessing.

I see some really disorganized thinking when children first encounter pattern blocks. Here's an example of a child's first try: △ ⬡ "I'm done." Nothing was connected. There was no sense of structure or form. This beginning also closely resembled that child's drawing, painting, and driting.

Form begins to appear after a child's further encounters. This speaks of an inner plan, a mental schema of what to do with pattern blocks. It's important to me that I see that development take place.

KR: Oh yes! It doesn't occur to some children that the blocks can do anything but be messed around with or tossed. But through the year children gradually get to form, maybe even to pattern. There's a predictable skills sequence in which children move from open-ended work with real blocks to reproducing the patterns created, using pattern stickers and then cutouts, tracing patterns on paper, drawing from the pattern, and re-creating the pattern on the computer. The last is the most abstract, farthest removed from the blocks themselves.

Do you keep a portfolio record of children's patterns, Kathleen? I do.

KE: Yes. They are laminated in class books—long books for pattern-block trains, bigger books to handle larger designs. We bind traced patterns into coloring books.

Sometimes I assign a task with the blocks to see what the children can do. When we were investigating plants, I asked them to make a tree with the pattern blocks. The variety amazed me.

KR: I had each of my children create a design with the pattern-block stickers. We identified each one by title and author and put them all into a book. Children could look in the book to make the same pattern again. For one activity I asked them to re-create someone else's pattern. "I made Monique's pattern today," is the comment I would hear. Now a second book of photos from many years of pattern-block designs sits on the shelf with the pattern blocks.

KE: I encouraged children's attention to one another's patterns by laminating their sticker representations and using them as task cards. Some children simply matched the blocks on top of the cards. But most of them moved to tracing patterns and eventually to copying designs. Those are important representational skills.

KR: In all of this activity, skill learnings are embedded. Teachers' anxiety about emergent curriculum seems to be about the question, "Are they getting enough skills?"

The wider the range of possibilities we offer children, the more intense will be their motivations and the richer their experiences. We must widen the range of topics and goals, the types of situations we offer and their degree of structure, the kinds and combinations of resources and materials, and the possible interactions with things, peers, and adults. Moreover, widening the range of possibilities for children also has consequences for others. It renders teachers to be more attentive and aware . . . more responsive to children's feedback.
—Loris Malaguzzi

KE: Yes, but teachers need a clear understanding of what those skills are, and they need to take the time to document each child's mastery. Unfortunately, back-to-basics math does little to inform beginning teachers about the hierarchy of children's mathematical thinking.

Blocks: A basic teaching tool

The pattern blocks we have just been discussing are a table activity, easily manageable in any classroom. The standard floor blocks (Pratt 1948; Stritzel 1989) are my first love, however, and a lot of our curriculum emerges in the block center. I find it distressing to see many kindergartens without the space or time for block building.

The block center helps the child to

• enjoy the manipulation of blocks

• enjoy the sensory and kinesthetic pleasure of the blocks

• improve small- and large-muscle coordination

• learn to share ideas and work together in a group

• develop concepts such as big, little, more than, less than, equal to, shape, size, and so forth

• express creativity

• have the opportunity for nonverbal expression and emotional release

• understand that boys and girls can build with blocks

• develop physical concepts of balance, symmetry, and gravity

• work alone or in small groups on projects

• map out a real or imaginary world

As I observe children building with blocks during their choosing time, I may notice that a child is having difficulty with stacking or making the enclosures work. I write down this observation and continue to watch that child over the next few days. It often happens that he will notice how other children stack or enclose blocks and will imitate them. But if he remains stuck or frustrated, then I work with him during our committee time, which is when I set challenges for children. I don't interrupt play, but I offer assistance with this skill—just as I would with reading or math if a child is having difficulty.

I document the children's block work, beginning by taking photos. Block building develops in stages (see "Stages in Block Building," p. 132), but nothing exists in standard checklists to measure children's progress with blocks. First I devised my own checklist; then I realized that the children were doing more than a checklist could show, and I began having them tell or write a story about their constructions. I placed each of these accounts on a page next to my photo of the building and/or process of building. These went into one of our class block books, which children read and reread. About two years ago I began having children draw their buildings as well, and each drawing went into the book with the photo and the story.

Different modes of representation—building with blocks, drawing what has been built, telling a story about it—provide fascinating illustrations of the different areas of a child's brain at work. Often there is a notable difference in a child's ability to represent verbally compared to visually. Some children who build wonderfully cannot tell the story of what they did but can draw their constructions very well. Here's yet another opportunity to recognize multiple intelligences and to scaffold new challenges for each child.

This documentation proves to be very helpful in conferencing with parents about their children's progress in block building (which reflects many mathematical concepts), storytelling, writing (if they wrote themselves rather than dictating), and in representational drawing. I sometimes post these sets of work on the bulletin board outside our room to demonstrate the work going on within.

To really know what blocks can do, the teacher has to have played with them, observed children with them, and read about and talked about them too. These are all important parts of developmentally appropriate teacher education. To construct their own understanding, students of teaching must have experience with materials, experience with children, and continuing dialogue about the theory that helps us classify our experience (Jones 1986; Carter & Curtis 1994; Curtis & Carter 1996).

Being a responsible communicator

Others with a stake in the learning of the children we teach—parents, administrators, and community members—rarely see the children in action in our classrooms. It is useful for us teachers to remember this; we owe them *representations* of children's significant understandings.

Representation and documentation

Fortunately, human beings represent their experience all the time, using oral and written language, drawings and constructions, song and dance. And the three R's, children's learning challenge in school, are forms of representation.

Stages in Block Building

Stage 1. Blocks are carried around, not used for construction.

Stage 2. Building begins. Children make mostly rows, either horizontal (on the floor) or vertical (stacking). There is much repetition in this early building pattern.

Stage 3. Bridging—two blocks with a space between them, connected by a third block—is used.

Stage 4. Enclosures—blocks placed in such a way that they enclose a space—are made. Bridging and enclosures are among the earliest technical building problems that children have to solve. They occur soon after a child begins to use blocks regularly.

Stage 5. When facility with blocks is acquired, decorative patterns appear. Much symmetry can be observed. Buildings generally are not yet named.

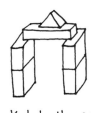

Stage 6. Naming of structures for dramatic play begins. Before this stage, children also may have named their structures, but the names were not necessarily related to the function of the building.

Katy's House

Stage 7. Block buildings often reproduce or symbolize actual structures children know, and there is a strong impulse toward dramatic play around the block structures. (Hirsch 1996, 142–48)

In the years from 3 to 5, as Elizabeth Jones and Gretchen Reynolds write, "The child first becomes a competent representer of experience rather than simply a doer of it. Human society and human thought are built on the achievement of *representation*, which makes possible both looking back and looking ahead, rather than simply living in the moment, and communication removed in both place and time, rather than simply face-to-face" (1992, 4). Learning to initiate and carry through representational activities, especially play of many sorts and language, is *the* developmental task of this stage of the life cycle.

If representation is what young children are busy practicing in school, *documentation* is what their teachers need to be practicing. A look around the walls and shelves and tables of any early childhood classroom gives an idea of the work that is valued here (Jones & Villarino 1994). What work by children, in what media, is displayed? What work by the teacher (as scribe, photographer, book binder, exhibit manager) do we see (Carter & Curtis 1996; Helm, Beneke, & Steinheimer 1998)? What's the balance between commercial representations (posters, textbooks, worksheets) and documentation of the real life of this unique classroom? How much of the children's work is a standardization of adult-chosen patterns rather than a reflection of the variety of children's individual interests and perceptions?

What I've really learned from the Reggio Emilia approach is how important documentation is. The teachers initiate a documentation process in order to understand how children are thinking and what aspects of any experience have caught children's attention and roused their curiosity. The adults acknowledge children as competent thinkers and as artists in many languages (Edwards, Gandini, & Forman 1998). Children are provided all sorts of materials and guided in the use of them; they discuss their work and see it beautifully displayed. Not surprisingly, American teachers are amazed by the quality of these Italian children's work.

In a dialogue with my fellow teacher/ writers of this book, we explored more of our questions about this approach:

BJ: I've wondered how Reggio Emilia staff find time to create so many displays. It must help to have an artist-in-residence! I noticed a comment in an article about American teachers trying to "do Reggio," saying that "the extensive time required to prepare [displays] continued to frustrate the staff throughout the year" (Staley 1998, 24). That's predictable, I think.

KR: Actually, I've worried whether, in the creation of Reggio-style displays, adults may tend to become show-offs, taking over a task that is rightfully the children's. You've heard me express my ambivalence about that as it surfaced in the houses project in my class. As children's interest in houses went on, they simply tacked up their own drawings one on top of the other as a growing record of their changing insights over time. That felt right to me. I explained in the story I wrote, "We were documenting for ourselves and what worked for us. This was not an aesthetically organized display; it was a functional display, largely controlled by the children, and it was always in process."

CS: But don't we owe it to children to display their work beautifully? That helps them see it and themselves through new eyes.

KE: I agree. I have an aesthetic for my classroom that goes for what I produce and what I post: photographs that sequence a project, children's own reflections at each stage of the experience, even the skills introduced and mastered. These documentations are up for all to see and made very clear for parents, many of whom have had little schooling. Parents look carefully because they know they'll find a photo of their child.

For my colleagues and the school administration, I pitch the learning aspect. This has been a very effective strategy for getting teachers to buy into developmentally appropriate practice.

KR: Providing displays that impress adults is important public relations, I grant you that. But documentation is also a basic *teaching* tool. It challenges children to reflect both on their experiences and on their representations of those experiences. This became so clear to me while my children were drawing all those houses. They kept comparing the photos of the houses with their drawings.

Photos and drawings are two kinds of representation (which the children were *reading*), and talking about them is another representation. We'd go back for another walk to the real houses, and the children made more comparisons—in words—while we were walking. Then they were back to drawing as soon as we hit the classroom. As they compared, they had a lot to say about the drawings getting better and noticed interesting features of each other's drawings. There's assessment for you!

KE: I had a similar experience as I took the children on walks past their own houses. Their block play and their drawings and paintings became more complex as we looked at and discussed different kinds of houses. When I commented on these changes, they did more. They looked at the photos of themselves in front of their houses and tried to re-create them at the easel. Their conversations included more and more words and ideas about houses, more than I could ever have planned or predicted.

BJ: So both of you went through this sequence, with houses as your focus. You went walking to look at real houses, and you talked with the children as you walked. You followed up with representational activities of all sorts—discussion, drawing, block building, counting, story dictation—based on the children's shared discoveries. A house is more than a 5-year-old's conventional drawing of a box with windows, chimney, and pointed roof. What do our neighborhoods really look like? What are a neighborhood's shapes, its colors, and its stories?

KE: That's how debriefing goes. In its many forms, whether in the whole group or in casual conversations, debriefing invites children to think in greater depth about their representations.

KR: Debriefing is the oral form of documentation. We construct a record of our mutual learning. Records are kept by taping our spoken words or writing them down, by drawing and painting and building, by taking photographs of representations like block buildings that we can't save because blocks aren't an expendable material (Kuschner 1989), and by creating displays or books or videos that preserve the story of our learning process.

BJ: It's all this documentation that makes portfolio assessment and narrative reporting possible. Test results, the schools' most familiar symbolic communication, give a very limited picture of any child's competence and are certainly no measure of how much a child has grown and developed. Displays, portfolios, and conversations help round out the picture, while assuring parents that their child is known and appreciated in this place called *school* and their concerns for his/her growth are being taken seriously.

Expectations for assessment

Representation and documentation are an essential part of teaching as well as an evaluation of children's learning. We all agree on this as this book's teacher/writers. To do both well is a constant challenge but one we welcome because it's part of our theory of teaching and learning. Some of us, however, face other expectations that conflict with our theory. High on the list of typical expectations are standardized assessments, including testing and grading, which are intended not to teach children or acknowledge them as multifaceted learners but to rank them.

As a magnet school, Borton Primary has been able to emphasize alternative forms of assessment. We do narrative evaluations designed by our own teaching staff. I enjoy writing them; it focuses my attention on each child. Some teachers think they're too much work though.

Borton's kindergartens were exempt from from district testing until three years ago when someone came up with the Kindergarten Learning Assessment, a local attempt at a standardized test that is neither local nor standardized. It is lengthy. We resisted this testing the first year, did a little of it the second, and the third year decided as a team to select portions in a very streamlined way to satisfy the powers-that-be.

A district-wide portfolio system is in place, with different requirements at each grade level. For a kindergartner's cumulative file there must be

• a self-portrait and name-writing sample from the beginning of the school year and at the end,
• the score sheet from the Learning Assessment,
• evidence of work (the choice of work is left up to the teacher), and
• a narrative assessment and/or report card.

Comparing our notes as teacher/writers, we learned about the pressures on each other.

CS: We had report cards for which I had to complete a skills checklist on each child. I did them myself, pulling out children individually during choice time. I found this stressful, interruptive of important activities, all to do something I saw as unimportant. I could have delegated these skills assessments to parent volunteers, but I chose to do them myself because I know the children best and I care about their feelings. But I wondered why I should give time and energy to a task I truly did not value—a test that isolates the child and the skill from a meaningful context. The next year I realized that I could keep the checklists accessible and check them whenever I noticed a child was demonstrating any of the skills on the list. That gave me more accurate data than a one-shot test, I was happy to discover.

KE: To get Title I funding at our school we have been required to complete a kindergarten checklist at the beginning of the year when hardly any child can do well on it. It really is a test of what a child needs to know upon entering first grade, so I wonder—Why bother at the beginning of kindergarten? Wouldn't it be better at the start for a teacher to have a clear idea about how closely each child might be able to participate in what she has planned,

---

All people—and I mean scholars, researchers, and teachers, who in any place have set themselves to study children seriously—have ended up by discovering not so much the limits and weaknesses of children but rather their surprising and extraordinary strengths and capabilities linked with an inexhaustible need for expression and realization.

—Loris Malaguzzi

check on how it's going midyear, then plan for the remainder of the year? I am philosophically opposed to any assessment that makes a young child feel incompetent, and I will quietly resist as far as I can while keeping my job.

On the other hand, I did take district objectives seriously since I wanted the children to succeed in first grade. Our required checklist included children's ability to identify letters of the alphabet, and while that isn't a good use of time at the beginning of the year, it's something I kept track of as we went along. By midyear I had a record of every child's known letters, confusions, and omissions, which I analyzed for what each child seemed to be attending to and neglecting. My assistant, Mrs. Lee, took my plan on teaching children a strategy for looking at letters, and during literacy time she worked individually with the half dozen children out of 27 who needed this level of help. Using kinesthetic activities—sandpaper, sand tray, playdough, pipe cleaners, glitter and glue, rubber letters, water and chalk—she systematically taught letters, while reinforcing other letters the child knew. The lesson lasted three or four minutes.

MW: So you were not systematically teaching all the letters to the whole class, only to the children who hadn't picked them up during your other literacy activities?

KR: That's so much more efficient. Why should children who know letters be expected to sit still for Letter of the Week? Standardized teaching and assessment ignore all we know about the complexity of learning—that it has to be motivated, it has to be meaningful to the learner, learners have to construct knowledge for themselves. None of this happens en masse. It happens one-to-one. A teacher teaches each child and therefore needs to get to know each child as a person. Children learn from each other, so they need to talk and work together.

KE: I do feel ongoing assessment is important. But I wanted it to reflect the individual style and competences of each child. It worried me that some of my school's goals were too simple, while others were not attainable by most of my children. For example, kindergarten children intuitively know more about math than grade-level standards allow, but recognizing 30 sight words may be too much for a child new to literacy.

School goals seldom mention things I really value, such as making a plan, including others in your plan, sticking with your plan to fruition, and then taking something from that activity and applying it to a new plan or to what someone else has done. I've never seen as a goal, Recognizes the Works of an Author, but one of my children, Chio Choy, could easily pick out any book by "that Eric Carle guy" just by looking at a picture. And another child, David, could tell me that *Arrow to the Sun: A Pueblo Indian Tale* (McDermott 1977) was a lot like a Jesus story; also Kinith noticed elements of Buddhism in *Raven: A Trickster Tale from the Pacific Northwest* (McDermott 1993), although comparative religion is hardly a kindergarten learning goal!

Sadly, if one were forced to look at national averages (based on English language proficiency), all my children were well below the average. And the reasons for this were officially dismissed. I owed parents a more detailed picture of their child than any set of standards covers. I owed it to the children to notice and honor all the amazing, wise, and capable things they did each day.

Rinaldi's thinking reinforces mine:

> The cornerstone of our experience . . . is the image of the children as rich, strong, and powerful. The emphasis is placed on seeing

the children as unique subjects with rights rather than simply needs. They have potential, plasticity, the desire to grow, curiosity, the ability to be amazed, and the desire to relate to other people and to communicate. Their need and right to communicate and interact with others emerges at birth and is [an] essential element for survival and identification with the species. This probably explains why children are so eager to express themselves within the context of a plurality of symbolic languages. . . . (1993, 102–03)

BJ: Do you think of assessing as teaching?

KR: It's certainly part of what I call teaching. But it's hard to change others' images of the *busy teacher* moving from activity to activity to an image of *quiet teacher* standing (or, heaven forbid, sitting) and observing children. I can make some observations while I'm in the participant mode, then record them later. But there are a million minutes before I can get them recorded, and they might be lost. When I'm in spectator mode, I can make observations and jot them down right away.

BJ: I've seen and admired the portfolios Kathleen keeps for every child. Testing, as we've been saying, will never show all children as competent; that's not what it's for. Portfolio assessment, in contrast, relies on documentation of individual interests and choices as well as developmental milestones. And so every child is represented as a learner.

Communication (public relations)

In each of the strategies we teachers adopted at Borton Primary for being accountable, we discovered benefits for children as well as for the adults who want evidence that children are learning. In all our classes children had opportunities for self-assessment, kindergarten style. Children in three of our classes also had planned opportunities for closure of thematic activities or projects. Since I'm the one who didn't provide for this, it has been interesting to me to listen to the assessments of my teacher/writer colleagues.

KE: Increasingly I've become aware that documentation needs to reflect group interests and achievements as well as those of the individual. For our relationships with parents and the larger community, it's important to have public events celebrating accomplishments and providing closure.

Thinking about closure as being important has been a major change in how I plan curriculum. In my story I spoke of just letting a theme die a natural death. Now I think it's important to have a culminating event and product. Often it is a party to unveil a class book or a mural, to perform informally some of the songs and poems we have learned, or to share with parents, another class, or the principal the artifacts we have produced.

MW: Events like these also let the children know there are times when we celebrate our learning and hard work. It's a little like graduation.

BJ: To me it seems that documentation involving the *public* representation of experience serves several important functions, not the least of which is public relations. Marsha has thoughtfully analyzed the cognitive development of her kindergartners that was integrated into the play production; it is also clear that the Romeo and Juliet play became a memorable community event, demonstrating to parents and grandparents, administrators and teaching colleagues that hers was a classroom where things happen.

MW: It was an event that adults and children could tell stories about.

BJ: Reggio Emilia's public relations, I keep realizing, is built on their extraordinary storytelling—in exhibits, videos, and publications as well as invitations to other teachers to visit on field trips to Italy—about the wonderful things that happen in the community's early childhood programs. But before all the international excitement happened, within the community of Reggio Emilia the centers had become places of family celebration. Projects undertaken by small groups of children and teachers were documented for the rest of the class, school, and community, providing closure and recognition while reinforcing what children had learned. In extending this celebration beyond their local community, Reggio professionals have not only challenged their own thinking and energies but also have become famous. Now everyone's telling their stories.

KR: Fame, justly earned, is a boost to self-esteem and continuing learning, whether you're 5 years old or 45. Elegant representations of children's learning are cause for celebration in any community, aren't they? Especially when the children have been genuine participants in project creation, not simply performers memorizing their lines and moves.

BJ: Your improvised play, Marsha, was an accomplishment that involved and impressed the local grownups.

MW: I saw the older children impressed too with what my kids thought was just matter-of-fact!

KR: I have avoided doing play performances with children. When I started reading about yours, Marsha, I wasn't at all sure about the idea. Fives are so young to invest all that preparation time in a public performance.

MW: I agree. I didn't expect it would ever come to that. I thought we were just playing at making a play, not preparing for a real one. That's how I could stay relaxed about it. The children were relaxed because it was an improvisation, and they were good at improvisation. The real leadership and energy came from a small group of children, and they saw it through with my support.

KE: *Leadership* is seldom a box on kindergarten checklists, but I'll bet in several years it will still be a memorable part of kindergarten for many of your kids.

BJ: In telling your story, Marsha, you convinced me that the whole project maintained the spontaneity important to learning in early childhood. You didn't seem to lose your sense of humor along the way; that carried over to the children.

MW: Isn't there something to be said for enabling children to collaborate with adults in work toward a common goal?

CS: Thank you for saying that, Marsha. That was my intention all along in the sandbox project.

BJ: And it's important to acknowledge, Carolyn, that your adult community was certainly impressed. Your principal got involved in documentation, didn't she?

CS: Yes. After we invited her to work with the Landscapers team to help choose the location for the sandbox, she arranged to videotape the meeting of the design committee with Mike the engineer. She was working on a project to encourage business partnerships with public schools and wanted footage on collaboration in action. The children took Mike to the site, showed him exactly what they wanted, and answered his questions. They were impressive.

BJ: Public relations is a real issue in many schools. You've made that clear, Carolyn, in explaining the pressure you felt to perform.

CS: Yes. My school had weekly visitors from other districts, parading through the halls and classrooms, taking pictures of a model school.

What's our theory?

How do we as teachers view what we have learned, what we believe? These are the points I would make:

1. Authentic assessment of young children occurs while they are actively learning— building, talking, climbing, driting, and all the rest. One does learn some useful things about butterflies by impaling them on a pin—but only about how they are put together, not about their flight. We learn only a little about children by telling them to sit still and follow unfamiliar directions. We learn more by systematically watching them in spontaneous action, imposing the discipline on our grownup selves rather than on them.

2. Classification is an important objective for teachers' learning. A teacher who holds the constructivist view that skills are best learned in meaningful context is not thus freed from the demand for accountability. Not only must she observe, she must also be able to classify what she sees in terms of imposed standards as well as her own.

3. To demonstrate accountability, the teacher has to know a lot. She must know both how children learn and what learning potential is inherent in the materials of the classroom.

4. The teacher must become skillful and persistent in communicating what she knows to convince the other stakeholders in schools that this radical approach is also a responsible approach.

PERSPECTIVE

Schools are not designed to give priority to the growth of teachers (Sarason 1972). Those teachers who insist on growing despite the obstacles discover survival strategies to make possible a satisfying career. Our teacher/writers in this book have found strategies that worked for them, including creating a school of like-minded folks and staying there, transferring to other more congenial sites, and even just lying low so that nobody pays attention to what you're really doing.

Can innovative, emergent teachers survive?

Kay began teaching at Borton Primary Magnet School in Tucson, Arizona, when it was created in 1979 as a clearly defined response to mandated school integration. The school's vision—supporting integration through an enriched constructivist program—matches her values and theory on education. She has helped shape the school as well as her classroom. With her many years there and strong relationships, she will stay, even though she had some apprehension about renegotiating a previously dependable relationship, with the hiring of a new principal.

Marsha has made only one move, transferring from the school where her story takes place (and where she was frustrated by lack of administrative support) to another, more innovative school within the district where more colleagues are using an active-learning approach. She has also become a collaborative participant in districtwide early childhood program development for which teacher representatives receive release time.

Carolyn, after one more year of teaching following the year of her story, left the classroom. She explains, "I was exhausted. I'm one of those people who must always take a breather from things because they do them with too much intensity. So I quit teaching for a while—to build a house, which seemed more manageable. Teaching is still in my blood. I'm still a teacher, but I'm looking for a different way."

Kathleen, in her seven years at Garfield, found it useful to lie low. In this urban school of more than one thousand children, she had four principals and even more assistant principals. In such circumstances, she explains, "Expectations are miraculously and sadly reduced. If the noise level is maintained within the walls of the classroom and the children behave well in the cafeteria and assemblies, no one from above concerns themselves much with what else goes on. I could remain relatively unnoticed by administrators and colleagues, which is in itself a sad comment on a school's lack of genuine commitment to the learning of inner-city children."

Finally Kathleen moved within the district to become reading specialist and teacher at a nearby school of comparable size with similar demographics and community. She was impressed by its stable administrative team, which had been at the school for many years and conveyed a reassuring sense of ownership of the school. And the principal had a clear and convincing plan to develop effective teaching of literacy.

Later, however, the school district mandated a prescriptive, closely monitored curriculum for teaching reading, at odds with the principal's plan and with Kathleen's values and practice. During a year of intense frustration, she joined a concerned group of teacher and parent activists to create a new small school (a recently state-approved option) within the district. In becoming its educational leader this year, the prospect both excites her and raises ethical concerns for her. She explains: "I know that the Mien children I taught will be going on to classrooms that provide no follow-up to what I offered them. They will encounter short-sighted teachers and standardized tests, and most of the children won't make it. There are exceptional teachers in every district and in every school, but they are not the norm. And then some of them get together with parents and start small schools and charter schools and magnet schools—schools-of-choice, of whatever philosophy, a demonstrably effective alternative for providing a better education for a limited num-ber of children. In the process, things become a little worse, as Seymour Sarason [1998] confirms, for the children left behind in the old setting."

Effective education is, above all, the outcome of relationships. It is no accident that the Reggio Emilia preschools in Italy, hon-ored internationally as an exemplary program, put relationship at the core of their work. It's as Susan Fraser (2000, 102) describes, "Everyone involved—children, families, and teachers—needs to feel that they play an integral part in what Carolyn Edwards calls 'the circle of we'." Yet in American schools such stability is lowest in those schools where, it can be argued, children at risk need it most. Our highly mobile urban society, in carrying out the task of education, relies not on particular persons but on bureaucratic roles and rules to ensure that the schools are staffed and the buses run. Understandably, there is pressure to standardize teaching as well—to make it teacher-proof. This solution risks making learning child-proof too.

Can emergent teachers survive? It isn't easy. Among our teacher/writers, Carolyn was the most isolated in the challenge she set for herself: finding "a new way of being teacher." Her primary support came from her participation in a Reggio Emilia network and the active journaling she carried on with her thesis committee chair. She had no congenial colleagues or opportunity for dialogue at her high-pressure suburban school. Emergent curriculum, which is dependent on active teacher involvement and creativity, needs stable teachers, excellent documentation, and supportive relationships if it is to thrive in any setting. Teachers need to build community with colleagues—for play, for theory building, and for survival.

—*BJ*

PART IV

Advocating for Change

In Community with Colleagues: Professionals Learning Together

All learners need peers to interact with. Children need to talk with each other, and so do teachers. In a community of peers comparing notes and sharing ideas, the disequilibrium created by the differences among us generates problems. It is in the problem solving that quality of understanding and of relationships is achieved. This is the democratic ideal. Democracy is harder to achieve, in schools and elsewhere, than is dictatorship, but democratic structures make better use of a community's human resources.

Teacher/writers Kay and Marsha both established relationships within their school communities. Kay has been on the teaching staff for many years. She has had a long relationship with her full-time classroom assistant—one of the extraordinary perks provided by her magnet school. Marsha had a half-time (three hours) assistant and reliable parent volunteers. Having previously taught preschool at this site, she knew many of the parents before their children came to kindergarten. They provided active support, even as the principal imposed new expectations on Marsha as a new kindergarten teacher.

Kathleen, as she has explained, participates in established collegial networks outside school. Within the school where she taught in her story, she was one of several progressive teachers who supported each other in a very difficult situation. She also found friends and colleagues in her two Mien assistants, who shared her commitment to the success of the children and to whom she offered as much training in observation, assessment, and teaching strategies as time permitted.

Carolyn, on the other hand, lacked supportive colleagueship. She explained her situation to us in one of our group conversations.

CS: What I needed, without knowing it at the time, was collegial dialogue to take a look at the children's questions, conversations, play, writing, theories, and so forth, and to research what they were about. This had to be on-site research. But I didn't truly recognize my own role as researcher, so I couldn't create a structure to support it.

I have the feeling that answers to questions are inside me all the time but need the right set of circumstances to surface. One need is for me to relax. Finding answers and solving problems work best when my mind is "at play." By this I mean literally playing with a mixture of ideas, unconcerned with outcome but enjoying the process of fantasy and internal brainstorming. I can do that with others if it's

---

CS—Carolyn Stringer, BJ—Elizabeth Jones, KE—Kathleen Evans, KR—Kay Stritzel Rencken, MW—Marsha Williams

safe. Then I enjoy formulating ideas and being challenged by the thinking of others. I can reflect on another's thinking and mix it up with my own, and we can both go to places in our thinking that we couldn't do alone.

BJ: Carolyn, were your conversations with Laurie—the other kindergarten teacher—helpful?

CS: We didn't have that many. I got some good ideas for activities from her, but we were very different. She ran a teacher-centered classroom and had no intention of exploring a stance that felt uncertain or out of control. When she and I were doing some casual planning of activities together, I became more aware of how her expertise at control undermined my growing conviction that when I expected a specific outcome things didn't go as well. It's so hard to let expectations go.

I was trying activities with Laurie from a Design Technology curriculum (Dunn & Larson 1990). Basically, it invited children to explore ways of attaching things together, starting with brads, paper clips, tape, string, and paper. Gradually, we posed more challenges as the children seemed ready, giving them problems to solve such as, "Can you attach two pieces together and make a moving part?" The children seemed really invested in the problems and exploration.

And then I wrote in my journal, "Today it happened. Nothing big, just another small case of my refusal to let go of my expectations. The problem to be solved today was to attach the rectangle to the circle, making it rotate around the circle without touching the rectangle with your hands. Most everyone got the idea of using the brad so the paper would rotate. Some kids blew the rectangle, some whipped it around, and some attached string to the

rectangle and pulled it around. All of this would have been much more delightful to me, and magical, if I hadn't talked to Laurie first. She did the exercise the day before. We have both been excited about how our kids are thinking, and what they seem to be learning. She told me in vivid detail how every one of the children responded and how things were followed up by *debriefing* (a term used by Selma Wassermann [2000])."

Equipped with my *expectations*, I refused to find delight in my own children's learning and failed to respond to their rhythm. Once again, I was in control and responding with the professional insecurity that the system fosters and that all of us get trapped by.

KE: I think the system fosters competition and mistrust among colleagues. That's one reason I prefer urban teaching in which there is a siege mentality and people who share a philosophy will collaborate, support, and sustain each other.

BJ: If teachers keep getting caught up in competition, how can children possibly not do the same? Carolyn, in our earlier dialogues, didn't you say this about Laurie: "She had lots of ideas. I didn't"?

CS: Yes, she was big on ideas. She wasn't an observer of children though. Our conversation about sand was the first real conversation I felt I had with Laurie, in terms of really looking at what children are trying to say.

KR: Her first suggestion—"Why not dump a load of sand on the playground?"—was genuinely playful and responsive to children's interest. Her second suggestion to build a sandbox was more controlled, controlling, and sensible, and that's the one you bought into.

CS: I was on the fringes of transformation, knowing what I didn't want, completely uncertain of how to go about doing whatever it was I wanted. It took another year before I realized that it is not just a luxury, this collegial dialogue. I didn't ever find that dialogue in my school. It is imperative, I believe, to the emergence of a rich and complex curriculum.

What's our theory?

Our understandings about ourselves as teachers and about teaching lead to the construction of theories we can know and believe in and that can guide our practice. Reflecting on our need for collegiality, we have learned the following:

1. Teaching is too hard to do alone. The school's response is to standardize, hand out textbooks and workbooks and teacher guides, and provide lectures by experts at required inservices. A teacher-proof curriculum is mentioned in some quarters as an ideal. But standardized curriculum, designed to be teacher-proof, to some degree is child-proof as well. It doesn't reach all the children. By their very nature children resist being standardized. Teachers should follow children's example.

When teachers are with other adults learning about teaching, they need to talk more than they need to listen to experts, just as children need to talk in order to learn. Teachers need to tell stories, hear and respond to questions about their practice, engage their minds in what Carolyn calls "research on children." To help group discussions become more than dysfunctional gripe sessions, it is helpful to have a de facto or appointed facilitator with the skills to keep probing, questioning, and thinking alive (Jones 1993).

Teachers need to research the curriculum, the environment, and the effect of their actions on that pervasive educational concept, *outcomes.* They need permission to experiment with what experts say and to critique, modify, and reject what doesn't work for them.

2. Teaching, like reading and writing and other complex skills, must be constructed by the doer. Piaget's and Vygotsky's constructivist theories apply as surely to teachers' learning about teaching as they do to young children's learning about practically everything. Knowledge is constructed through the process of acting, reflecting, interacting with peers, reflecting, and repeating this cycle again and again. Disequilibrium—discovering that one's hunches about how to do it don't work—is the necessary condition for the effort of changing one's thinking and doing.

Vygotsky adds to this basic theory the concepts of *scaffolding* and *zone of proximal development* (Berk & Winsler 1995). Proximal development represents any learner's next stage of competence—what she can't yet do by herself but can do in collaboration, with well-timed guidance. The scaffolder offers the scaffold that gives access to the knowledge that's building—under construction. All teachers need some scaffolding; new teachers need a lot of it. It cannot be standardized or provided en masse. It can happen one-on-one with a mentor, and it can happen in peer dialogue in groups small enough that everyone gets a chance to tell stories and ask questions. Its curriculum is (of course!) emergent (Jones 1993).

3. Without trusting relationships, dialogue doesn't get very far. A school, just like a classroom, must build trust among peers if teachers are to scaffold each other's growth. In a competitive system, trust is difficult to accomplish. In a high-turnover, large-scale system, it is probably impossible to accomplish except within voluntary subgroups. Thus teachers, like children, need choice time—opportunities to choose who to collaborate with and what goals to work on next.

4. In most schools teachers do not share a common philosophy. It is no accident that schools-of-choice—magnet schools, charter schools, nonpublic schools—frequently show up as more effective by many measures, *no matter what their particular philosophy is.* It is easier to work effectively with people like oneself in world view. Yet here, of course, is the dilemma facing all efforts at educational reform: In a heterogeneous society, how can one advocate for homogeneous schools? But without some significant unity of purpose at the level of details, as well as in generically stated visions, collaboration on genuine teaching questions is unproductive.

How much dissonance is healthy? When does it break down into dysfunction? Each of us has to struggle with these questions, and we have found no dependable answers. Reshifting our connections with colleagues as our tasks shift makes it possible for us as teachers to find and appreciate the likenesses among our differences. The practical question is, Are you my ally on the things that matter most to me?

The culture of competition seems to foster a climate where disagreements surface only as conflicts. In contrast, some professional groups with diverse philosophies do manage to develop a spirit of open critique in which questions can be asked and responded to without too much defensiveness.

5. All beginning teachers can learn to practice self-questioning and reflection. This is important because it is not always possible to be in a collegial situation. Reflection is a discipline just like other forms of introspection or meditation. When it is practiced with a clear recognition of one's possible biases, a teacher can master tendencies toward denial or overly harsh self-criticism.

Telling it like it is: Teaching kids to play the school game

Teaching children doesn't guarantee their learning. The civil rights movements of the last half-century have publicized schools' basic inequities, and educational researchers have continued to analyze them (Green 1968; Kozol 1985, 1991, 1995; Kohn 2000).

Although the nation's public schools by law serve all children, they do not promote all children's success. In fact, they were not designed to do so. In reality most schools weed out the less intelligent, less diligent, and less well-connected. Then, standardized testing rates everyone on a single standard that predicts success in the system as it is, maintaining society's status quo. Children of families with educational and material advantages take their places at the top of the ladder; few children from less advantaged backgrounds make it past the bottom rung.

Such is the system teacher/writer Kathleen won't buy into. In our group's dialogue, she stated her position:

> I have made an ethical choice to teach very bright, competent children who are at high risk of school failure. I have to be accountable to myself and to the children's families and to respect the children and the culture they come from. I have to be realistic as well about the pressures the kids I teach will face in first grade and beyond. So I have been challenged in two directions: (1) to learn all I can about how children learn the three R's and (2) to become strategic in "playing the school game" and teaching children and their parents to do the same.

Lisa Delpit (1995) writes about providing access to "the culture of power" as represented by schools. Just as 5-year-olds unfamiliar with books are helped by having words separated and named for them, any children lacking membership in the culture of power gain by having its rules identified and explained.

For our group of teacher/writers, as for teachers everywhere, these ideas keep generating questions. Kathleen is particularly passionate about the importance of telling of it like it is.

KE: Urban schools are written off by the culture of power. Even deeply committed urban educators have failed to look at what it will take to move the entire population of the school where I taught into having access to power. Somehow all involved have come to accept the status quo. Parents don't believe they're entitled to be treated with courtesy and respect. Children come to accept stultifying boredom and unsafe, unclean conditions. Teachers accept the belief that children are less bright and parents less caring, that only a few children will make it, and so on up the ladder. But if your eyes are open, it doesn't take long to realize that urban children are bright, hopeful, and resilient beyond all expectations.

The school didn't ask me to teach my kids and their families about access to the culture of power. But I'm someone with power who, if I choose to, can offer them a bridge—both of caring and expertise. I did choose to. This was my objective, not the school's. This was an ethical decision based on my belief in social justice and on what my experience with inner-city children has proven to me.

CS: How are your teaching goals different from what schools expect of all the children: good behavior and attention to the conventions of the English language? Well learned, don't these skills give access to the culture of power?

BJ: Good behavior and language are both culture specific. Kids whose homes have the same behavioral and language patterns as the school's have a head start in school. Children from other backgrounds

Demystifying the Culture of Power

Issues of power are enacted in classrooms. Power bases include the power of the teacher over the students, of publishers of textbooks and developers of curriculum in determining the view of the world presented, of the state in enforcing compulsory schooling, and of individuals or a group in determining another's intelligence or normalcy.

There are codes/rules for participating in power. The culture of power includes linguistic forms, communication strategies, and presentation of self—ways of talking, writing, dressing, and interacting.

Rules reflect the rule and culture of those having power. Success in institutions—schools, workplaces, and so on—is predicated upon acquiring the culture of those in power. Children from middle-class homes tend to do better in school than those from non-middle-class homes. Children from other kinds of families operate well within their own viable cultures but not in cultures having the codes or rules of power.

Learning the rules makes acquiring power easier. Members of any culture transmit information implicitly to co-members, but across cultures communication frequently breaks down. Explicit presentation of the rules makes learning immeasurably easier.

The powerless are the most aware of power's existence. Power holders are frequently unaware of or unwilling to acknowledge having power. Students must be taught the codes needed to participate fully in the mainstream of American life. In learning the culture of power, children must also learn the arbitrariness of those codes and the power relationships they represent.

are likely to stay permanently behind in school unless someone clues them in on how the system works to their disadvantage.

KE: If we're to equip children for survival in alienating places, they need both pride in who they are and what they *did* learn from birth in *their* homes and neighborhoods and awareness of the rules of the game. The rules of the game need to be explicit, as do the reasons for playing it. I believe we need to talk about the inherent unfairness of the game in a way that children can comprehend.

BJ: What that includes is being taught that power *is* a game. In a heterogeneous society there are choices among acceptable behaviors. Different people have different expectations. As a visitor to classrooms for 4-year-olds, I have been impressed in encountering Spanish-speaking children who have already figured out the game. They look at me carefully to decide which language to speak to this stranger—Spanish or English.

KR: That's a good survival skill—switching language or other codes depending on the territory. The people, including teachers, who control access to things kids may want—education, jobs, power—have specific expectations. Kids need this reality named for them.

BJ: In most schools both behavior and curriculum are givens; they aren't open for discussion.

MW: I can understand how this demystifying might work with older kids. It's cool; they'd like that. But I don't know about 5-year-olds, with their rigidity about right and wrong.

KR: It's certainly possible to be up front, even with fives, when you think someone else's expectations are arbitrary. We've all mentioned examples of such expectations: skills checklists, walking in line, conventional spelling. Grownups in a diverse society don't have to present a united front to children. Children need to learn that there are contradictions to be dealt with in behavior as well as in language and to practice making informed decisions. I want them to think critically about social justice issues as well as about mathematics.

KE: Lisa Delpit (1995) emphasizes a firm grounding in one's own language and culture, *not* the melting-pot assimilation that schools have typically promoted. I wanted the children I taught to be able to code-switch and to know that's what they're doing—to speak both Mien and English, to be able to bridge their heritage and the modern society in which, willy-nilly, they now live. This implies *consciousness*. Representational skills including speaking, reading, and writing are among the best tools there are for living one's life consciously, with awareness of alternatives and the ability to choose among them. I hope my classroom offered that challenge in microcosm.

As Paulo Freire (1970) insists, education is not a neutral process. Either it domesticates or it liberates.

From theory to visionary action: Advocating for educational and social change

Those of us looking for social justice see schools as one of the places where we can make a difference. We can create a thinking democracy for the children in our classes. We can encourage them to question the status quo. We can encourage them and their parents to advocate against unfairness.

We can teach them consciously about the culture of power and ways to play the school game, model ways to be effectively bicultural by recognizing and building on children's strengths, and choose the population to which we will devote our energies.

But are we likely to last as school-system employees if we have illusions that we can change the underlying purpose of schooling? Teaching is "a conserving activity" says Postman (1979). Inequality—the way things are—is built into our politics and the practical realities of schooling. Schools in the mass society function not as democratic learning communities but as settings for the control of children, with knowledge being imposed on children to turn out workers and consumers (Green 1968; Birdsall 1998). School funding inequities almost ensure that relatively few poor kids will succeed. Even where funding is directed toward equity of opportunity, it may not really be intended to succeed in its goals (Kozol 1991).

The politics of accountability

With the present testing design and practices prevalent in most school districts, relatively few poor kids will succeed (Kozol 2000; Wesson 2001). In fact, the best predictor of a school's test scores is the socioeconomic level of the families it serves (Wesson 2001). With test content based on what people with success and power already know, their children tend to perform well and go on to attain success and power themselves. And less advantaged families' children, typically labeled low achievers by the tests, grow up to fill the low-status jobs that have to be done.

Critical thinking is not encouraged in most classrooms except, perhaps, in private and suburban schools enrolling the children of the privileged, who are the beneficiaries of the status quo and can be counted on not to think too critically about its inequities.

Dewey's progressive education, in the years of its influence in public schools before *progressive* became an epithet, was implemented primarily for children of the prosperous. Today, many affluent parents send their children to private schools or move to suburbs high on the realtors' lists, where exclusive schools are tax supported (Kozol 1991).

The public schools are, after all, large institutions accountable to a diverse political constituency. And they have to let in all children, no matter what their background or when they show up. It is difficult for a school system, or even for an individual school, ever to get past the survival stage, no matter how impressive the words in the official educational vision. Management of a mass enterprise with open admission makes it necessary to define classrooms as *slots* into which X number of small and large bodies can be fitted, to meet bus and cafeteria schedules, to cover the published curriculum, and to rely on standardized tests to prove the effectiveness of teaching.

Politically and managerially, public schools have little to gain and much to lose by encouraging or even permitting emergent curriculum. Such a curriculum encourages innovative thinking and intellectual autonomy in both teachers and children. Insistence on covering predetermined curriculum has been an effective anxiety-generating strategy to keep teachers in their place, even though many wise teachers would in their hearts agree with David Hawkins's comment to Eleanor Duckworth (1987, 7) that our task is not to cover curriculum but to *uncover* it.

When schools and teachers focus on "teaching to the test," they are participating in a scam. Under pressure themselves to reassure the public and those higher up in the education bureaucracy that all is well, they prepare children to perform on the test so it will look as if they are learning what they need to know. But such learning is typically superficial and short-lived. Teaching for real learning is harder.

Advocates at odds with the system

In the educational context described above, teachers creating democratic classrooms are likely to find themselves at odds with most others in the system. It is important for teachers to anticipate a dynamic tension and to develop strategies for surviving. To be consistent with our vision, it is useful to remember that we are morally obligated to have empathy for those we serve and those we work with even when we don't agree with their values and perceptions (Elbow 1986).

Every committed group of parents and teachers that starts a school-of-choice of whatever stripe is doing the most effective thing that can be done to provide a better education for those children. And, as an undesired consequence, things are left a little worse for the children who remain in the old setting. This is indeed an ethical dilemma for advocates.

Other teachers will elect to stay in the system, even though they find themselves at odds with it. They will need allies. They need to be savvy about the politics of their work, both for their own survival in the system and for effective action on behalf of children. They need to inform and mobilize parents about the continuing injustice wrought upon their children when test scores and canned curricula are all that is offered in school reform packages. And since cynicism is not a useful attitude for working with children, teachers need to continue articulating collaborative visions of the possible.

Envisioning the changing school

"The factory school," says Les Birdsall, "was designed to meet the education needs of the old industrial society, in which most jobs were unskilled and semiskilled and less than 10% of high school graduates went to college. . . . The factory school is characterized by self-contained, same-age classes;

teacher-directed lessons; a 40-week, text-book-driven learning pace; a one-size-fits-all, time-limited instructional approach; and final grades" (1998, M6).

We have many questions to ask ourselves on what children need in today's post industrial world. Birdsall provides some answers: "They should be able to find, categorize, and analyze data; establish and use evaluation criteria; design and manage projects; be effective team players; and skillfully use computers for a variety of purposes. Mastery of these skills produces higher-achieving students" (1998, M6).

With the 20th century having just ended, an era that became more articulate about a democratic vision of social justice based on unity in diversity, John Dewey's vision of democracy in education still offers us a caring model of schooling designed to empower every child in order to enrich society (Noddings 1992).

In Birdsall's vision, "A multiaged group of children would be assigned, for an extended number of years, to a team of a dozen or more teachers who would be jointly responsible for their success, academic achievement, emotional health and character development." He sees the new century's school as "a partnership with each child. . . . As each child grows and develops, acquiring new skills and capabilities, he or she can become responsible for managing his or her own project-based education and working, independently, with other children" (1998, M6).

The real curriculum is *what happens* in a classroom, and it is only through observation and documentation of the process that we are able to understand what children have learned and what they want to know more about. The chaos and complexity theories of modern science, which describe the spontaneous creation of order out of the unknown, offer more illuminating metaphors for teaching and learning than the engineer-

Early Childhood Education in a Postmodern World

In the modern world of the last few centuries, science has held out the hope of making everything knowable through rational, objective observation. Recent postmodernist thinkers, however, have radically questioned this ideal, suggesting there is no such thing as objectivity.

Pence writes, "Postmodernism is largely about the loss of certainty, control, and predictability. It is about the presence of many voices and many views and the need to engage with those other views and open oneself to exploring a world of profound diversity. In a postmodern world, process, engagement, dialogue, and co-construction take precedence over routines, best practice, exclusivity, and the safe haven of predetermined outcomes" (2000, xi).

Theories from physical and social sciences that support this view are variously called chaos theory, complexity theory, enactivist theory.

Chaos theory emphasizes nonlinearity, unpredictability, and interdependence. VanderVen emphasizes the implications of this view for emergent, play-based curriculum: "Children [and adults] who play are best able to understand the essential complex, chaotic nature of the world. Non-play, on the other hand, can be conver-

gent, invariant, sequenced, and static. Play embodies all of the aspects of chaos—children learn to understand and deal with the reality of the world. They learn to understand change" (1995, 4).

Complexity theory rejects the modernist tendencies to use machine-based metaphors to analyze human happenings. Davis and Sumara explain it: "Machines, however complicated, are always reducible to the sum of their respective parts, whereas complex systems—such as human beings or human communities—in contrast, are more dynamic, more unpredictable, more alive" (1997, 117).

Enactivist theory, described by Davis and Sumara, has its implications for play and the arts in education: "Teaching and learning . . . occur in the relations between the individual and the collective, between accepted truth and emerging sense, and between actualities and possibilities . . . . What is imagined, what is fantasized, what is guessed at, what is intuited are not marginalized to the fringes of valued thought and resulting actions, but are understood as vitally contributing to the conscious experience of everyday life" (1997, 120).

ing model supremely useful for practical construction with inanimate objects. For unlike the products of engineering, the children we teach need, above all, to see themselves as learners and to take seriously the project of learning, using it to create self-knowledge throughout the rest of their lives.

In an early childhood program freeing itself, as Alan Pence (2000) describes, from

"the safe haven of predetermined outcomes," it is necessary for us, as Loris Malaguzzi indicates, "to think of school as a sort of construction in motion, continuously adjusting itself" (1993, 56). Malaguzzi suggests that "teachers must possess a habit of questioning their certainties" and that "to learn together and relearn with the children is our line of work" (1993, 63, 82).

Sociodramatic play, Vygotsky insisted, is rule governed—not undisciplined—behavior (Berk & Winsler 1995). Children's talk— "You be the baby, OK?"—is a familiar example of the sort of mutual agreement necessary to sustain interesting play. Acceptance of and debate about emergent rules enable the players to collaborate in constructing understanding of the realities and possibilities in the world they inhabit.

It is not a world fully under human control. "There be dragons," we might say, as well as babies and loving parents. What is imagined is as important as what is present. Human knowledge is constructed on visions of the possible and the impossible.

Empowering children and teachers

As responsible grownups, teachers must, of course, keep the possible in mind. The classroom context—time, space, and materials—demands some engineering: the stuff must be present, the limits must be clear. But beyond beginnings, in an emergent classroom the planning is shared *with the learners*. If we are going to give a play, what will we need? If we go for a walk, what do you want to find out? The answers are not known until after the questions are asked. Thus curriculum is improvised all along the way, although the structure and cycle of the project are always the same.

Accountability necessarily takes the form of documentation rather than of lesson plans. Lesson plans are placeholders to get things responsibly started. Followed to the letter, preplanned lessons may well create chaos in the heads of children if not in their overt behavior, since predesigns ignore what children already know and care about and thus interrupt the sequence of their learning.

In 1972 anthropologist Margaret Mead gave a keynote address at NAEYC's Annual Conference in Atlanta, and she said,

Unless we respect the differences among the children, cultivate them, and give equal weighting to a great many more kinds of gifts than we do at present, we produce a deadening uniformity that doesn't have enough content in it to really make discussion and communication possible. [The] egalitarian effort to give all our children the same things is very laudable, but we ought to take a better look at the things that we are giving them.

I think that the most dangerous thing that is happening to children in this country is boredom. This is more dangerous than any of the other things that are happening (and there are plenty of other dangerous things). But the transcendent boredom—to be shut up in a room, away from anything that moves or breathes or grows, in a controlled temperature, hour after hour after hour—means that we are taking away from them any kind of chance of responsiveness. (1973, 329)

Emergent curriculum efforts in public education, even in kindergarten, are not for the faint of heart. To survive in most public schools, teachers whose intent is to empower children as learners must become master jugglers and translators, be able to do many things at the same time, and communicate in more than one language. That's what emergent curriculum is designed to do: empower every child and every teacher.

The lively kindergarten— Emergent curriculum in action

Genuine learning is emergent in process, dramatic and unpredictable. It has many moments of routine, but these are punctuated by moments of disequilibrium, by surprises. Some of these surprises, such as this observer's descriptive discovery, should become curriculum.

The Santa Ana winds were blowing in Los Angeles, hot and exciting. Litter swirled around the playground, and the trees were bending over. The children were excited, and the teacher, firmly shutting the window blinds, was annoyed and muttered, "This wind! I can't get them to pay attention."

The children were eager to pay attention— but to the wind, not to reading. Wind, however, was not on the day's lesson plan.

All that energy can be resisted by teachers, with varying success, or they can co-opt it even into reading lessons. What do busy adults do when a hurricane or a tornado threatens? They don't just ignore it; wind is too big to ignore. They tie things down. Maybe they evacuate. Some of them interview other people, photograph what the wind has done, and write newspaper stories. They investigate and total the damages.

The drama of natural forces is not only an unwelcome interruption of routine; it also becomes an excitingly memorable event, part of a community's shared history. Our memories from our years in school are rarely the lessons we were taught; they are much more likely to be the stories of provocative events and important relationships (Egan 1989). Productive human living balances routine with drama. And natural drama happens when it happens, not on any human schedule. Some curriculum, in a responsive classroom, is serendipitous—"We are studying this because it *happened.*"

Similarly, the eruptions of feelings that happen unexpectedly in the best of classrooms can be deplored, ignored, or selectively transformed into curriculum. Feelings that are ignored generally reemerge in some mutation that disrupts learning. Living together in restricted space, day-to-day, is even more challenging than the three R's.

Territorial disputes have generated wars, divorces, and abuse of all sorts. Competent human beings need social as well as academic skills, and the classroom, where children spend their days together, is an important setting in which to learn about effective *conflict maintenance* (Jones & Nimmo 1999). Interpersonal conflicts create fully as much drama as the warring of the winds, and fully as much can be learned from the study of them—*when they happen,* not when a canned Human Relations curriculum has been scheduled.

On a walking field trip, two 10-year-old girls began a hair-pulling fight in the middle of the crosswalk at a major intersection. The light changed, and cars were honking. Their friends and teacher intervened to get them out of the street. Everyone walked soberly back to school and, without prompting, moved the chairs into their accustomed problem-solving circle.

Math was canceled? Of course! This drama had *happened*; it needed to be addressed now, by the whole class. "How can all of us keep it from happening again?" Behavior control isn't just the teacher's problem or the principal's. It's a skill to be learned by everyone, and so it's curriculum.

Emergent curriculum harnesses the interest of children and teachers in the events of the physical and social world. It is unpredictable as well as planned. It cultivates the disposition to respond to the unexpected with interest and logical thinking rather than with fear and foolishness. The world in which our children are growing up is full of the unexpected. To confront it effectively, they need to practice intellectual and moral autonomy (Piaget 1973; Kamii 1982) rather than conformity without questioning why. Their teachers, doing the same to keep up with the children, are likely to find teaching an intellectual and moral challenge worthy of their professional commitment.

References and Resources

Apple, M.W. 1986. *Teachers and texts: A political economy of class and gender relations in education.* New York: Routledge & Kegan Paul.

Armington, D. 1997. *The living classroom: Writing, reading, and beyond.* Washington, DC: NAEYC.

Ashton-Warner, S. 1963. *Teacher.* New York: Simon & Schuster.

Ayers, W. 1993. *To teach: The journey of a teacher.* New York: Teachers College Press.

Ballenger, C. 1999. *Teaching other people's children: Literacy and learning in a bilingual classroom:* New York: Teachers College Press.

Bateson, M.C. 1994. *Peripheral visions: Learning along the way.* New York: HarperCollins.

Beck, I. 1992. *Five little ducks.* New York: Bill Martin, Trumpet Club.

Berk, L., & A. Winsler. 1995. *Scaffolding children's learning: Vygotsky and early childhood education.* Washington, DC: NAEYC.

Birdsall, L. 1998. The "factory school" should be retired. *Los Angeles Times,* 27 September, M1, M6.

Bowman, B., M.S. Donovan, & M.S. Burns, eds. 2000. *Eager to Learn: Educating our preschoolers.* Executive summary. Washington, DC: National Academy Press.

Bredekamp, S., & C. Copple, eds. 1997. *Developmentally appropriate practice in early childhood programs.* Rev. ed. Washington, DC: NAEYC.

Bredekamp, S., & T. Rosegrant, eds. 1992. *Reaching potentials: Appropriate curriculum and assessment for young children, volume 1.* Washington, DC: NAEYC.

Bredekamp, S., & T. Rosegrant, eds. 1995. *Reaching potentials: Transforming early childhood curriculum and assessment, volume 2.* Washington, DC: NAEYC.

Brown, C. 1978. An interview with Herbert Kohl. In *Literacy in 30 hours: Paulo Freire's process in North East Brazil,* 35–49. Chicago: Alternative Schools Network.

Carroll, L. [1862] 1979. *Through the looking glass.* Reprint. New York: Grosset & Dunlap.

Carter, M., & D. Curtis. 1994. *Training teachers: A harvest of theory and practice.* St. Paul, MN: Redleaf.

Carter, M., & D. Curtis. 1996. *Spreading the news: Sharing the stories of early childhood education.* St. Paul, MN: Redleaf.

Clay, M. 1975. *What did I write?* Auckland, New Zealand: Heinemann.

Clay, M. 1991. *Becoming literate: The construction of inner control.* Portsmouth, NH: Heinemann.

Clay, M. 1993. Learning to look at print. In *Reading Recovery: A guidebook for teachers in training,* 23–27. Portsmouth, NH: Heinemann.

Cowley, J. 1986. *Yuck soup.* Bothell, WA: Sunshine, Wright Group

Cuffaro, H.K. 1995. *Experimenting with the world: John Dewey and the early childhood classroom.* New York: Teachers College Press.

Cunningham, P.M., & R.L. Allington. 1994. *Classrooms that work: They can all read and write.* New York: HarperCollins.

Curtis, D., & M. Carter. 1996. *Reflecting children's lives: A handbook for planning child-centered curriculum.* St. Paul, MN: Redleaf.

Dancing with the pen: The learner as a writer. 1992. Wellington, New Zealand: Ministry of Education, Learning Media.

Darder, A. 1991. *Culture and power in the classroom: A critical foundation for bicultural education.* New York: Bergin & Garvey.

Davidson, J. 1996. *Emergent literacy and dramatic play in early education.* Albany, NY: Delmar.

Davis, B., & D.J. Sumara. 1997. Cognition, complexity, and teacher education. *Harvard Educational Review* 67 (1): 105–25.

Delpit, L. 1995. The silenced dialogue: Power and pedagogy in educating other people's children. In *Other people's children: Cultural conflict in the classroom,* 21–47. New York: New Press.

Dewey, J. [1916] 1966. *Democracy and education.* Reprint. New York: Free Press.

Dewey, J. [1938] 1997. *Experience and education.* Reprint. New York: Macmillan.

Dewey, J. 1964. Reflective thinking, an aim (from *How we think: A restatement of the relation of reflective thinking to the educative process* [1933]). In *John Dewey on education: Selected writings,* ed. R. Archambault. Chicago: University of Chicago Press.

Donmoyer, R. 1981. The politics of play: Ideological and organizational constraints on the inclusion of play experiences in the school curriculum. *Journal of Research and Development in Education* 14 (3): 11–18.

Duckworth, E. 1987. *"The having of wonderful ideas" and other essays on teaching and learning.* New York: Teachers College Press.

Dunn, S., & R. Larson. 1990. *Design technology: Children's engineering.* New York: Falmer.

Dyson, A.H. 1989. *Multiple worlds of child writers: Friends learning to write.* New York: Teachers College Press.

Dyson, A.H. 1993. *Social worlds of children: Learning to write in an urban primary school.* New York: Teachers College Press.

Edwards, C., L. Gandini, & G. Forman, eds. 1993. *The hundred languages of children: The Reggio Emilia approach to early childhood education.* Norwood, NJ: Ablex.

Edwards, C., L. Gandini & G. Forman, eds. 1998. *The hundred languages of children: The Reggio Emilia approach—Advanced reflections.* 2d ed. Greenwich, CT: Ablex.

Egan, K. 1989. *Teaching as storytelling: An alternative approach to teaching and curriculum in elementary school.* Chicago: University of Chicago Press.

Elbow, P. 1986. *Embracing contraries: Explorations in teaching and learning.* New York: Oxford University Press.

Erikson, E. 1950. *Childhood and society.* New York: Norton.

Evans, K. 1999. Play in a classroom of Iu Mien children. *Child Care Information Exchange* 125: 49–51.

Ferreiro, E., & A. Teberosky. 1982. *Literacy before schooling.* Portsmouth, NH: Heinemann.

Flores, B., & E. Garcia. 1984. A collaborative learning and teaching experience using journal writing. *NABE* [National Association for Bilingual Education] *Journal* 8 (2): 67–83.

Forman, G. 1989. Helping children ask good questions. In *The wonder of it: Exploring how the world works,* ed. B. Neugebauer, 21–24. Redmond, WA: Exchange Press.

Fox, M. 1992. *Hattie and the fox.* Illustrated by P. Mullins. New York: Macmillan.

Franklin, M., & B. Biber. 1977. Psychological perspectives and early childhood education: Some relations between theory and practice. In *Current topics in early childhood education, vol. 1,* ed. L. Katz. Norwood, NJ: Ablex.

Fraser, S. 2000. *Authentic childhood: Experiencing Reggio Emilia in the classroom.* Scarborough, ONT, Canada: Nelson.

Freire, P. 1970. *Pedagogy of the oppressed.* New York: Seabury.

Gag, W. 1977. *Millions of cats.* New York: Putnam.

Gandini, L. 1994. Celebrating children day by day: A conversation with Amelia Gambetti. *Child Care Information Exchange* 100: 52–55.

Gandini, I. 1998. Educational and caring spaces. In *The hundred languages of children: The Reggio Emillia approach—Advanced reflections.,* 2d ed., eds. C. Edwards, L. Gandini, & G. Forman, 161–78. Greenwich, CT: Ablex.

Gardner, H. 1983. *Frames of mind: The theory of multiple intelligences.* New York: Basic.

Genishi, C., ed. 1992. *Ways of assessing children and curriculum: Stories of early childhood practice.* New York: Teachers College Press.

Gleick, J. 1988. *Chaos: Making a new science.* New York: Viking/Penguin.

Goffin, S., & D. Stegelin. 1992. *Changing kindergartens: Four success stories.* Washington, DC: NAEYC.

Goodman, K.S., E.B. Smith, R. Meredith, Y. Goodman. 1987. *Language and thinking in school: A whole language curriculum.* New York: Richard C. Owen.

Graves, D. 1983. *Writing: Teachers and children at work.* Portsmouth, NH: Heinemann.

Green, T.H. 1968. *Work, leisure, and the American schools.* New York: Random House.

Greenberg, P. 1998. Some thoughts about phonics, feelings, Don Quixote, diversity, and democracy: Teaching young children to read, write, and spell. *Young Children* 53 (4): 72–83.

Greenberg, P. 1998. Warmly and calmly teaching young children to read, write, and spell: Thoughts about the first four of twelve well-known principles. *Young Children* 53 (5): 68–82.

Greenberg, P. 1998. Thinking about goals for grownups and young children while we teach writing, reading, and spelling (and a few thoughts about the "J" word). *Young Children* 53 (6): 31–42.

Griffin, E. 1982. *Island of childhood: Education in the special world of the nursery school.* New York: Teachers College Press.

Guanella, F. 1934. Block building activities of young children. *Archives of Psychology* 174: 1–92.

Harste, J., V. Woodward, & C. Burke. 1984. *Language stories and literacy lessons.* Portsmouth, NH: Heinemann.

Hawkins, D. 1974a. I, thou, and it. In *The informed vision: Essays on learning and human nature,* 48–62. New York: Agathon.

Hawkins, D. 1974b. Messing about in science. In *The informed vision: Essays on learning and human nature,* 63–75. New York: Agathon.

Heath, S.B. 1983. *Ways with words: Language, life, and work in communities and classrooms.* Cambridge: Cambridge University Press.

Helm, J.H., S. Beneke, & K. Steinheimer. 1998. *Windows on learning: Documenting young children's work.* New York: Teachers College Press.

Herndon, J. 1971. *How to survive in your native land.* New York: Simon & Schuster.

Hirsch, E.S., ed. 1996. *The block book.* 3d ed. Washington, DC: NAEYC.

Holt, J. 1970. *What do I do on Monday?* New York: Dutton.

Hubbard, R.S. 1998. Creating a classroom where children can think. *Young Children* 53 (5): 26–31.

Jervis, K. 1996. *Eyes on the child: Three portfolios.* New York: Teachers College Press.

Jones, E. 1986. *Teaching adults: An active learning approach.* Washington, DC: NAEYC.

Jones, E., ed. 1993. *Growing teachers: Partnerships in staff development.* Washington, DC: NAEYC.

Jones, E., & J. Meade-Roberts. 1991. Assessment through observation: A profile of developmental outcomes. *Pacific Oaks Occasional Paper.* Pasadena, CA: Pacific Oaks College.

Jones, E., & J. Nimmo. 1994. *Emergent curriculum.* Washington, DC: NAEYC.

Jones, E., & J. Nimmo. 1999. Collaboration, conflict, and change: Thoughts on education as provocation. *Young Children* 54 (1): 5–10.

Jones, E., & E. Prescott. 1984. *Dimensions of teaching-learning environments: A handbook for teachers in elementary schools and day care centers.* Pasadena, CA: Pacific Oaks College.

Jones, E., & G. Reynolds. 1992. *The play's the thing: Teachers' roles in children's play.* New York: Teachers College Press.

Jones, E., & G. Reynolds. 1997. *Master players: Learning from children at play.* New York: Teachers College Press.

Jones, E., & G. Villarino. 1994. What goes up on the classroom walls—and why? *Young Children* 49 (2): 38–40.

Kamii, C. 1982. Autonomy as the aim of education: Implications of Piaget's theory. Appendix to *Number in preschool and kindergarten.* Washington, DC: NAEYC.

Kamii, C. 1985. Leading primary education toward excellence: Beyond worksheets and drill. *Young Children* 40 (6): 3–9.

Kamii, C., ed. 1990. *Achievement testing in the early grades: The games grown-ups play.* Washington, DC: NAEYC.

Kamii, C. 2000. *Young children reinvent arithmetic: Implications of Piaget's theory.* New York: Teachers College Press.

Katz, L. 1980. Mothering and teaching: Some significant distinctions. In *Current topics in early childhood education, vol. 3,* ed. L. Katz, 47–63. Norwood, NJ: Ablex.

Katz, L. 1995. The developmental stages of teachers [1977]. In *Talks with teachers of young children: A collection,* 205-08. Norwood, NJ: Ablex.

Katz, L., & S. Chard. 1989. *Engaging children's minds: The project approach.* Norwood, NJ: Ablex.

Kohl, H. 1994. *"I won't learn from you" and other thoughts on creative maladjustment.* New York: New Press.

Kohn, A. 2000. *The case against standardized testing: Raising the scores, ruining the schools.* Portsmouth, NH: Heinemann.

Kohn, A. 2001. Fighting the tests: Turning frustration into action. *Young Children* 56 (2): 19–24.

Kozol, J. 1985. *Illiterate America.* Garden City, NY: Anchor/Doubleday.

Kozol, J. 1991. *Savage inequalities: Children in America's schools.* New York: Crown.

Kozol, J. 1995. *Amazing grace: The lives of children and the conscience of a nation.* New York: Crown.

Kozol, J. 2000. Foreword to *Will standards save public education?* By D. Meier. Boston: Beacon.

Krashen, S. 1993. *The power of reading.* Englewood, CO: Libraries Unlimited/Children's Books.

Kritchevsky, S., & E. Prescott. 1977. *Planning environments for young children: Physical space.* 2d ed. Washington, DC: NAEYC.

Kuschner, D. 1989. "Put your name on your painting but . . . the blocks go back on the shelves." *Young Children* 45 (1): 45–56.

Labinowicz, E. 1980. *The Piaget primer: Thinking, learning, teaching.* Menlo Park, CA: Addison-Wesley.

Lareau, A. 1989. *Home advantage: Social class and parental intervention in elementary education.* London/New York: Falmer.

Lather, P. 1991. *Getting smart: Feminist research and pedagogy within the postmodern.* London: Routledge.

Loughlin, C.E., & M.D. Martin. 1987. *Supporting literacy: Developing effective learning environments.* New York: Teachers College Press.

Loughlin, C.E., & J.H. Suina. 1982. *The learning environment: An instructional strategy.* New York: Teachers College Press.

Macaulay, D. 1982. *Castle.* Boston: Houghton Mifflin.

Malaguzzi, L. 1993. History, ideas, and basic philosophy: An interview with Lella Gandini. Translated by L. Gandini. In *The hundred languages of children: The Reggio Emilia approach to early childhood education,* eds. C. Edwards, L. Gandini, & G. Forman, 41–89. Norwood, NJ: Ablex.

McDermott, G. 1977. *Arrow to the sun: A Pueblo Indian tale.* New York: Puffin.

McDermott, G. 1993. *Raven: A trickster tale from the Pacific Northwest.* New York: Harcourt Brace.

Mead, M. 1970. *Culture and commitment: A study of the generation gap.* Garden City, NY: Natural History Press/Doubleday.

Mead, M. 1973. Can the socialization of children lead to greater acceptance of diversity? *Young Children* 28 (6): 322–29.

Meade-Roberts, J., E. Jones, & J. Hillard. 1993. Change making in a primary school: Soledad, California. In *Growing teachers: Partnerships in staff development,* ed. E. Jones, 76–88. Washington, DC: NAEYC.

Miles, B. 1976. *Favorite tales from Shakespeare.* London: Hamlyn.

Mooney, M.E. 1990. *Reading to, with, and by children.* Katonah, NY: Richard C. Owen.

Moore, K. 1998. Extending experience: John Dewey—Intercommunication and conversation in the early childhood classroom. Master's thesis, Pacific Oaks College, Pasadena, California.

Myrdal, G. [1944] 1996. *An American dilemma: The Negro problem and modern democracy.* New Brunswick, NJ: Transaction.

Noddings, N. 1992. *The challenge to care in schools: An alternative approach to education.* New York: Teachers College Press.

Orwell, G. 1945. *Animal farm: A fairy story.* New York: Longman.

Paley, V.G. 1984. *Boys and girls: Superheroes in the doll corner.* Chicago: University of Chicago Press.

Paley, V. 1986. On listening to what the children say. *Harvard Educational Review* 56 (2): 122–31.

Paley, V.G. 1997. *The girl with the brown crayon.* Cambridge, MA: Harvard University Press.

Palmer, P. 1998. *The courage to teach.* San Francisco: Jossey-Bass.

Parkes, B., & J. Smith. 1986. *The enormous watermelon.* Melbourne, Australia: Methuen.

Pence, A. 2000. ECE's passage from a modern to a postmodern world: Reggio Emilia as pioneer. Foreword to *Authentic childhood: Experiencing Reggio Emilia in the classroom,* by S. Fraser. Scarborough, ONT, Canada: Nelson.

Pelo, A., & F. Davidson. 2000. *That's not fair! A teacher's guide to activism with young children.* St. Paul, MN: Redleaf.

Peterson, R., & V. Felton-Collins. 1986. *The Piaget handbook for teachers and parents.* New York: Teachers College Press.

Piaget, J. 1954. *The construction of reality in the child.* New York: Basic.

Piaget, J. 1973. *To understand is to invent.* New York: Grossman.

Piper, W. [1930] 1998. *The little engine that could.* Reprint. Illustrated by Richard Bernal. New York: Dutton.

Postman, N. 1979. *Teaching as a conserving activity.* New York: Delacorte.

Pratt, C. 1948. *I learn from children.* New York: Simon & Schuster.

Provenzo, E.F., & A. Brett. 1983. *The complete block book.* Syracuse, NY: Syracuse University Press.

Raffi. 1990. *Five little ducks.* Illustrated by J. Aruego & A. Dewey. New York: Crown.

Rankin, B. 1993. Curriculum development in Reggio Emilia: A long-term curriculum project about dinosaurs. In *The hundred languages of children: The Reggio Emilia approach to early childhood education,* eds. C. Edwards, L. Gandini, & G. Forman, 189–211. Norwood, NJ: Ablex.

Read, L. 1992. Different abilities: A continually emerging curriculum. *Pacific Oaks Occasional Paper.* Pasadena, CA: Pacific Oaks College.

Reading in junior classes. 1985. Wellington, New Zealand: Ministry of Education, Learning Media.

Reagon, B.J. 1983. Coalition politics: Turning the century. In *Home girls: A black feminist anthology,* ed. B. Smith, 356–68. New York: Kitchen Table, Women of Color Press.

Reynolds, G. 1988. "When I was little I used to play a lot . . . " In *Reading, writing and talking with four, five and six year olds,* ed. E. Jones, 85–90. Pasadena, CA: Pacific Oaks College.

Reynolds, G., & E. Jones. 1997. *Master players: Learning from children at play.* New York: Teachers College Press.

Rinaldi, C. 1993. The emergent curriculum and social constructivism: An interview with Lella Gandini. In *The hundred languages of children: The Reggio Emilia approach to early childhood education,* eds. C. Edwards, L. Gandini, & G. Forman, 101–11. Norwood, NJ: Ablex.

Ringgold, F. 1991. *Tar beach.* New York: Crown.

Rosen, M. 1989. *We're going on a bear hunt.* Illustrated by H. Oxenbury. New York: McElderry.

Routman, R. 1991. *Invitations: Changing as teachers and learners K–12.* Portsmouth, NH: Heinemann.

Sarason, S.B. 1972. *The creation of settings and the future societies.* San Francisco: Jossey-Bass.

Sarason, S.B. 1996. *Revisiting "The culture of the school and the problem of change."* New York: Teachers College Press.

Sarason, S.B. 1998. *Charter schools: Another flawed educational reform?* New York: Teachers College Press.

Shonkoff, J.P., & D.A. Phillips, eds. 2000. *From neurons to neighborhoods: The science of early childhood development.* Washington, DC: National Academy Press.

Silko, L.M. 1997. *Ceremony.* New York: Viking Penguin.

Staley, L. 1998. Beginning to implement the Reggio philosophy. *Young Children* 53 (5): 20–25.

Stritzel, K. 1989. Block building and gender. *Pacific Oaks Occasional Paper.* Pasadena, CA: Pacific Oaks College.

Stritzel, K. 1994. What children learn here. In *Emergent curriculum,* by E. Jones & J. Nimmo, 104. Washington, DC: NAEYC.

Tertell, E.A., S.M. Klein, & J.L. Jewett, eds. 1998. *When teachers reflect: Journeys toward effective, inclusive practice.* Washington, DC: NAEYC.

Torgerson, L. 1994. Building community: Starting with stories. *Pacific Oaks Occasional paper.* Pasadena, CA: Pacific Oaks College.

Torgerson, L. 1996. Starting with stories: Building a sense of community. *Child Care Information Exchange* 109: 55–58.

Van Hoorn, J., P. Nourot, B. Scales, & K. Alward. 1993. *Play at the center of the curriculum.* Columbus: Merrill.

VanderVen, K. 1995. The relationship between chaos theory and play. In *Play, Policy, and Practice Connections* 2 (Autumn): 4.

Vipont, E. 1969. *The elephant and the bad baby.* Illustrated by R. Briggs. New York: Coward-McCann.

Vygotsky, L.S. 1962. *Thought and language.* Cambridge, MA: M.I.T. Press.

Vygotsky, L. 1978. *Mind in society: The development of higher psychological processes.* Cambridge, MA: Harvard University Press.

Walsh, E.S. 1991. *Mouse count.* New York: Harcourt Brace.

Wassermann, S. [1990] 2000. *Serious players in the primary classroom.* New York: Teachers College Press.

Wesson, K.A. 2001. The "Volvo effect"—Questioning standardized tests. *Young Children* 56 (2): 16–18.

Wien, C.A. 1995. *Developmentally appropriate practice in "real life": Stories of teacher practical knowledge.* New York: Teachers College Press.

Wien, C.A., & S. Kirby-Smith. 1998. Untiming the curriculum: A case study of removing clocks from the program. *Young Children* 53 (5): 8–13.

Williams, V.B. 1982. *A chair for my mother.* New York: Scholastic.

Wilson, C. 2000. *Telling a different story: Teaching and literacy in an urban preschool.* New York: Teachers College Press.

Wood, A.1987. *Heckedy peg.* Illustrated by D. Wood. New York: Harcourt Brace.

Information about NAEYC

NAEYC is . . .

an organization of nearly 100,000 members, founded in 1926, that is committed to fostering the development and learning of children from birth through age 8. Membership is open to all who share a commitment to promote excellence in early childhood education and to act on behalf of the needs and rights of all children.

NAEYC provides . . .

- *Young Children,* the peer-reviewed journal for early childhood educators
- **Books, posters, brochures, and videos** to expand your knowledge and commitment and support your work with young children and families
- **A network of nearly 450 local, state, and regional Affiliates**
- **Research-based position statements and professional standards** on issues such as inclusion, diversity, literacy, assessment, developmentally appropriate practice, and teacher preparation
- **Professional development resources and programs,** including the annual National Institute for Early Childhood Professional Development, improving the quality and consistency of early childhood professional preparation and leadership
- **Public policy information** through NAEYC resources and the Children's Champions Action Center, for conducting effective advocacy in government and in the media
- **An Annual Conference,** the largest education conference in North America, that brings people together from across the United States and other countries to share their expertise and advocate on behalf of children and families
- **A national, voluntary, professionally sponsored accreditation system** for high-quality early education through the National Academy of Early Childhood Programs
- *Early Childhood Research Quarterly,* the field's leading scholarly publication; special rate for NAEYC members
- **Young Children International,** encouraging information exchange and networking among NAEYC's international colleagues
- **Week of the Young Child** celebrations planned annually by NAEYC Affiliate Groups in communities across the country to call public attention to the critical significance of the child's early years
- **Insurance plans** for members and programs

For information about membership, publications, or other NAEYC services, visit NAEYC online at www.naeyc.org.

**National Association for the Education
of Young Children
1509 16th Street, NW
Washington, DC 20036-1426
202-232-8777 or 800-424-2460**